Advanced C

Herbert Schildt

Osborne **McGraw-Hill**
Berkeley, California

Osborne **McGraw-Hill**
2600 Tenth Street
Berkeley, California 94710
U.S.A.

For information on translations and book distributors outside of the U.S.A., please write to
Osborne **McGraw-Hill** at the above address.
  MS-DOS is a registered trademark of Microsoft Corporation.
  IBM is a registered trademark of International Business Machines, Inc.
  CP/M is a registered trademark of Digital Research.
  UNIX is a trademark of Bell Laboratories.

Advanced C

1234567890 DODO 898765

ISBN 0-07-881208-9

Jon Erickson, Acquisitions Editor
Lorraine Aochi, Technical Editor
Tim Field, Technical Reviewer
Kevin Shafer, Senior Editor
Lynn Heimbucher, Editorial Assistant
Kay Luthin, Copy Editor
Yashi Okita, Cover Design

C O N T E N T S

To my children—
Sasha, Josselyn, Jonathan, and Rachel

INTRODUCTION

I have been fortunate to be able to write the kind of programming book that I have always wanted. Years ago, when I started to program, I tried to find a book that had algorithms for such tasks as sorts, linked lists, simulations, and expression parsers in a straightforward presentation. I wanted a book that would give me insight into programming, but I also wanted a book that I could take off the shelf to find what I needed when I needed it. Unfortunately, I never found the exact book I was looking for—so I decided to write it.

This book explores a wide range of subjects and contains many useful algorithms, functions, and approaches written in the C language. C is the de facto systems programming language, as well as one of the most popular general-purpose professional programming languages available. A wide variety of C compilers is available for virtually all computers, and many are quite inexpensive. I used the Aztec C86 compiler for the IBM PC; however, with only a few exceptions, any version 7, UNIX-compatible C compiler will compile and run all the code in this book.

Chapter 1 begins with a brief history of C and a short review of the language. The sorting of both arrays and disk files is explained in Chapter 2. Chapter 3 deals with stacks, queues, linked lists, and binary trees. (You may think that's a lot to cover in one chapter; however, the subjects go together nicely and form a solid unit.) Dynamic allocation methods are discussed in Chapter 4. Chapter 5 presents an overview of operating-system interfacing and assembly language linkage. Chapter 6 covers statistics and includes a complete statistics program. Codes, ciphers, and data compression are the topics of Chapter 7, which also includes a short history of cryptography. Chapter 8 details several random number generators and then discusses how to use them in two simulations. The first simulation is a check-out line in a store; the second is a random-walk portfolio management program.

Chapter 9 is my personal favorite because it contains the complete code for a recursive descent parser. Years ago, I would have given just about anything to have had that code! If you need to evaluate expressions, Chapter 9 is for you. Chapters 10 and 11 discuss conversions from other languages, efficiency, porting, and debugging.

H.S.

If you would like to obtain an IBM PC-compatible diskette that contains all of the programs and algorithms in this book, please complete the order form and mail it with payment enclosed. If you are in a hurry, you can call (217) 586-4021 and place your order by telephone.

Please send me _____ copies, at $29.95 each, of the programs in this book. Foreign orders: Please add $5.00 for shipping and handling.

Name _____

Address _____

City _____ State _____ ZIP _____

Telephone _____

Method of payment: check _____ Visa _____ MC _____

Credit card number: _____

Expiration date: _____

Signature: _____

Send to:
   Herbert Schildt
   RR 1, Box 130
   Mahomet, IL 61853

A Review of C

C H A P T E R 1

This book uses a problem-solving approach to illustrate advanced concepts in the C programming language: it examines common programming tasks and develops solutions with an emphasis on style and structure. Through this approach, various advanced C topics and nuances are covered, as well as the general programming theory behind each solution. You should have a working knowledge of C; however, your experience need not be extensive. A review of the C language is presented later in this chapter.

Two notational conventions are used throughout this book. First, all variable names and C keywords are printed in boldface. Second, all C functions are boldface and are followed immediately by a set of parentheses. These conventions will eliminate confusion between variable names and function names. For example, a variable called "test" is printed as **test**, whereas a function by the same name is printed as **test( )**.

All examples and programs in this book were compiled and run using both the Aztec C compiler and the SuperSoft C compiler for the IBM PC. Generally, any version 7 UNIX-compatible compiler, such as the Lattice or Microsoft compilers, will compile and run the code in this book. There are several compilers available for most computers, and you should have little trouble finding one that suits your needs. Remember, however, that all compilers differ slightly—especially in their libraries—so be sure to read the user manual of the compiler that you are using.

The Origins of C

C was invented and first implemented by Dennis Ritchie on a DEC PDP-11 using the UNIX operating system. C is the result of a development process that started with an older language called BCPL, which is still in use primarily in Europe. BCPL, developed by Martin Richards, influenced a language called B, which was invented by Ken Thompson and led to the development of C.

Although C has seven built-in data types, it is not a strongly typed language in comparison to Pascal or Ada. C allows almost all type conversions, and character and integer types can be intermixed freely in most expressions. No run-time error checking—such as array boundary checking or argument-type compatibility checking—is done. This is the responsibility of the programmer.

C is special in that it allows the direct manipulation of bits, bytes, words, and pointers. This makes it well suited for system-level programming, where these operations are common. Another advantage of C is that it has only 28 *keywords*, which are the commands that make up the C language. For comparison, consider IBM PC BASIC: it has 159 keywords.

Although initially developed to run under the UNIX operating system, C has become so popular that compilers are available for virtually all computers and operating systems. This means that C code is very portable between computers and operating systems, making it possible to write code once and use it anywhere.

C as a Structured Language

C is commonly considered to be a structured language with some similarities to Algol and Pascal. Although the term *block-structured language* does not strictly apply to C in an academic sense, C is informally part of that language group. The distinguishing feature of a block-structured language is the *compartmentalization of code and data*. This means the language can section off and hide from the rest of the program all information and instructions necessary to perform a specific task. Generally, compartmentalization is achieved by subroutines with *local variables*, which are temporary. In this way, it is possible to write subroutines so that the events occurring within them cause no side effects in other parts of the program. Excessive use of *global variables* (variables known throughout the entire program) may allow bugs to creep into a program by allowing unwanted side effects. In C, all subroutines are discrete functions.

Functions are the building blocks of C in which all program activity occurs. They allow specific tasks in a program to be defined and coded separately. After debugging a function that uses only local variables, you can rely on the function to work properly in various situations without creating side effects in other parts of the program. All variables declared in a particular function will be known only to that function.

In C, using blocks of code also creates program structure. A *block of code* is a logically connected group of program statements that can be treated as a unit. It is created by placing lines of code between opening and closing curly braces, as shown here:

```
if(x<10) {
        printf("too low, try again");
        reset_counter(-1);
}
```

In this example the two statements after the **if** between curly braces are both executed if **x** is less than 10. These two statements together with the braces represent a block of code. They are linked together: one of the statements cannot execute without the other also executing. In C, every statement can be either a single statement or a block of statements. The use of code blocks creates readable programs with logic that is easy to follow.

C is a programmer's language. Unlike most high-level computer languages, C imposes few restrictions on what you can do with it. By using C a programmer can avoid using assembly code in all but the most demanding situations. In fact, one motive for the invention of C was to provide an alternative to assembly language programming.

Assembly language uses a symbolic representation of the actual binary code that the computer directly executes. Each assembly language operation maps into a single task for the computer to perform. Although assembly language gives programmers the potential for accomplishing tasks with maximum flexibility and efficiency, it is notoriously difficult to work with when developing and debugging a program. Furthermore, since assembly language is unstructured by nature, the final program tends to be "spaghetti code," a tangle of jumps, calls, and indexes. This makes assembly language programs difficult to read, enhance, and maintain.

Initially, C was used for systems programming. A *systems program* is part of a large class of programs that form a portion of the operating system of the computer or its support utilities. For example, the following are commonly called systems programs:

- Operating systems
- Interpreters
- Editors
- Assemblers
- Compilers
- Database managers

As C grew in popularity, many programmers began to use C to program all tasks because of its portability and efficiency. Since there are C compilers for virtually all computers, it is easy to take code written for one machine and then compile and run it with few or no changes on another machine. This portability saves both time and money. C compilers also tend to produce tight, fast object code—smaller and faster than most BASIC compilers, for example.

Perhaps the real reason that C is used in all types of programming tasks is because programmers like it. C has the speed of assembler and the extensibility of FORTH, while having few of the restrictions of Pascal. A C programmer can create and maintain a unique library of functions that have been tailored to his or her own personality. Because C allows—and indeed encourages—separate compilation, large projects are easily managed.

Many programs in this book use a function called **getnum( )**. C has no built-in method to enter decimal numbers from the keyboard and, contrary to popular belief, the standard library function **scanf( )** is generally unsuitable for human use. Therefore, the special function **getnum( )** is used whenever a decimal number needs to be read from the keyboard. The source code for **getnum( )** is shown here:

```
getnum()    /* read a decimal number from the
            keyboard */
{
        char s[80];

        gets(s);
        return(atoi(s));

}
```

The **atoi( )** function is the standard library function used to convert a string of digits into an integer. If your compiler is supplied with a function similar to **getnum( )**, feel free to substitute it.

A Brief Review

Before you begin to explore various programming problems and solutions, read the rest of this chapter to review the C language. If you are an experienced C programmer, skip to Chapter 2.

Refer to Appendix A for a statement summary of most of the keywords in C, a review of the preprocessor directives, and a description of some of the standard library functions used in this book.

The following 28 keywords, combined with the formal C syntax, form the C programming language:

auto	double	if	static
break	else	int	struct
case	entry	long	switch
char	extern	register	typedef
continue	float	return	union
default	for	short	unsigned
do	goto	sizeof	while

C keywords are always in lowercase letters. In C, uppercase or lowercase makes a difference; that is, **else** is a keyword, but ELSE is not.

Variables—Types and Declarations

C has seven built-in data types, as shown here:

Data Type	C Keyword Equivalent
character	**char**
short integer	**short int**
integer	**int**
unsigned integer	**unsigned int**
long integer	**long int**
floating point	**float**
double floating point	**double**

Some implementations of C also support **unsigned long int** and **unsigned short int**.

Variable names are strings of letters from one to several characters long; the maximum length depends on your compiler. For clarity, the underscore may also be used as part of the variable name (for example, **first_time**). Don't forget that in C, uppercase and lowercase are different—**test** and **TEST** will be two different variables.

All variables must be declared prior to use. The general form of the declaration is

type **variable_name;**

For example, to declare **x** to be a floating point, **y** to be an integer, and **ch** to be a character, you would type

```
float x;
int y;
char ch;
```

In addition to the built-in types, you can create combinations of built-in types by using **struct** and **union**. You can also create new names for variable types by using **typedef**.

A *structure* is a collection of variables grouped and referenced under one name. The general form of a structure declaration is

> **struct struct—name** {
>   *element 1;*
>   *element 2;*
>   .
>   .
>   .
> } **struct—variable;**

As an example, the following structure has two elements: **name**, a character array, and **balance**, a floating-point number.

```
struct client {
        char name[80];
        float balance;
};
```

To reference individual structure elements, the dot operator is used if the structure is global or declared in the function referencing it. The arrow operator is used in all other cases.

When two or more variables share the same memory, a **union** is defined. The general form for a **union** is

> **union union—name** {
>   *element 1;*
>   *element 2;*
>   .
>   .
>   .
> } **union—variable;**

The elements of a **union** overlay each other. For example, the following declares a **union t**, which in memory looks like Figure 1-1.

```
union tom {
        char ch;
        int x;
} t;
```

The individual variables that comprise the **union** are referenced using the

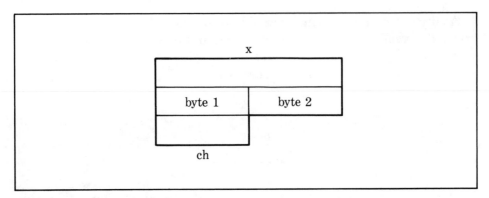

Figure 1-1. The **union t** in memory

dot operator if the **union** is global or is declared in the same function as the reference. The arrow operator is used in all other cases.

The three type modifiers in C—**extern, register,** and **static**—can be used to alter the way C treats the variables that follow them. If the **extern** modifier is placed before a variable name, the compiler will know that the variable has been declared elsewhere. The **extern** modifier is commonly used when there are two or more files sharing the same global variables.

The **register** modifier can be used only on local integer or character variables. It causes the compiler to try to keep the value in a register of the CPU instead of placing it in memory. This can make all references to that variable extremely fast. Throughout this book, **register** variables are used for loop control. For example, the following function uses a **register** variable for loop control:

```
f1( )
{
    register int t;
    for(t=0;t<10000;++t) {
        .
        .
        .
    }
}
```

The **static** modifier instructs the C compiler to keep a local variable in existence during the lifetime of the program, instead of creating and destroying it. Remember that the values of local variables are discarded when a function finishes and returns. Using **static** maintains the value of a variable between function calls.

Arrays   You may declare arrays on any of the data types discussed earlier. For example, to declare an integer array **x** of 100 elements, you would write

```
int x[100];
```

This creates an array that is 100 elements long; the first element is 0 and the last is 99. For example, this loop loads the numbers 0 through 99 into array **x**:

```
for(t=0;t<100; t++) x[t]=t;
```

Multidimensional arrays are declared by placing the additional dimensions inside another pair of brackets. For example, to declare a 10-by-20-integer array, you would write

```
int x[10][20];
```

Operators

C has a rich set of operators that can be divided into classes: *arithmetic, relational and logical, bitwise, pointer, assignment,* and *miscellaneous.*

Arithmetic Operators   C has seven arithmetic operators:

Arithmetic Operator	Action
−	subtraction, unary minus
+	addition
*	multiplication
/	division
%	modulo division
−−	decrement
++	increment

The precedence of these operators is

$$\text{highest} \quad ++ \quad -- \quad -(\text{unary minus})$$
$$* \; / \; \%$$
$$\text{lowest} \quad + \; -$$

Operators on the same precedence level are evaluated from left to right.

Relational and Logical Operators   Relational and logical operators are used to produce TRUE/FALSE results and are often used together. In C, any nonzero number evaluates TRUE. However, a C relational or logical operator produces the number 1 for TRUE and 0 for FALSE. Here are the relational and logical operators:

Relational Operator	Meaning
>	greater than
>=	greater than or equal
<	less than
<=	less than or equal
==	equal
!=	not equal

Logical Operator	Meaning
&&	AND
¦¦	OR
!	NOT

The precedence of these operators is

$$\begin{array}{ll} \text{highest !} \\ > \; >= \; < \; <= \\ == \; != \\ \&\& \\ \text{lowest ¦¦} \end{array}$$

For example, this expression evaluates as TRUE:

```
(100<200) && 10
```

Bitwise Operators   Unlike most other programming languages, C provides bitwise operators that manipulate the actual bits inside a variable. The bitwise operators, listed here, can only be used on integers or characters.

Bitwise Operator	Meaning
&	AND
¦	OR
^	XOR
~	one's complement
>>	right shift
<<	left shift

The truth tables for AND, OR, and XOR are as follows:

```
& 0 1
0 0 0
1 0 1
```

```
| 0 1
0 0 1
1 1 1
```

```
^ 0 1
0 0 1
1 1 0
```

These rules are applied to each bit in a byte when the bitwise AND, OR, and XOR operations are performed; for example,

```
  0 1 0 0    1 1 0 1
& 0 0 1 1    1 0 1 1
  -------    -------
  0 0 0 0    1 0 0 1
```

```
  0 1 0 0    1 1 0 1
| 0 0 1 1    1 0 1 1
  -------    -------
  0 1 1 1    1 1 1 1
```

```
  0 1 0 0    1 1 0 1
^ 0 0 1 1    1 0 1 1
  -------    -------
  0 1 1 1    0 1 1 0
```

In a program, you use the &, |, and ^ like any other operator, as shown here:

```
main()
{
        char x,y,z;

        x=1; y=2; z=4;

        x=x & y;  /* x now equals zero */

        y=x | z;  /* y now equals 4 */

}
```

The one's complement operator (~) inverts all the bits in a byte. For example, if the character variable **ch** has the bit pattern

$$0\ 0\ 1\ 1\quad 1\ 0\ 0\ 1$$

then

```
ch=~ch;
```

places the bit pattern

$$1\ 1\ 0\ 0\quad 0\ 1\ 1\ 0$$

into **ch**.

The right shift and left shift operators move all bits in a byte or a word right or left by some specified number of bits. As bits are shifted, zeros are brought in. The number on the right side of the shift operator specifies the number of positions to shift. The general forms of the shift operators are

$$variable >> number\ of\ bit\ positions$$
$$variable << number\ of\ bit\ positions$$

For example, given the bit pattern

$$0\ 0\ 1\ 1\quad 1\ 1\ 0\ 1$$

a single shift right yields

$$0\ 0\ 0\ 1\quad 1\ 1\ 1\ 0$$

while a single shift left produces

$$0\ 1\ 1\ 1\quad 1\ 0\ 1\ 0$$

A shift right is effectively a division by 2, and a shift left is a multiplication by 2. For example, follow this fragment as it first multiplies and then divides the value in **x**.

```
int x;
x=10;
x=x<<1;
x=x>>1;
```

Because of the way negative numbers are represented inside the machine, you must be careful when you try to use a shift for multiplication or division. Moving a 1 into the most significant bit position causes the computer to think that the number is a negative number.

Remember: the bitwise operators are used to modify the value of a variable—they differ from the logical and relational operators, which produce a TRUE or FALSE result.

The precedence of the bitwise operators is as follows:

$$
\begin{array}{ll}
\text{highest} & \sim \\
& >> \; << \\
& \& \\
& \wedge \\
\text{lowest} & |
\end{array}
$$

Pointer Operators   Pointer operators are important in C: not only do they allow strings, arrays, and structures to be passed to functions, but they also allow C functions to modify their calling arguments. The two pointer operators are & and *. (Unfortunately, these operators use the same symbols as the multiply and bitwise AND, which are completely unrelated to them.)

The **&** operator returns the address of the variable it precedes. For example, if the integer **x** is located at memory address 2000, then

```
y=&x;
```

places the value 2000 into **y**. The **&** can be read as "the address of." For example, the previous statement could be read as "Place the address of **x** into **y**."

The * operator takes the value of the variable it precedes and uses that value as the address of the information in memory. For example,

```
y=&x;
```

```
*y=100;
```

places the value 100 into **x**. The * can be read as "at address." In this example, it could be read as "Place the value 100 at address y." The * operator can also be used on the right-hand side of an assignment. For example,

```
y=&x;

*y=100;

z=*y/10;
```

places the value of 10 into **z**.

These operators are called pointer operators because they are designed to work on *pointer variables*. A pointer variable holds the address of another variable; in essence, it "points" to that variable, as shown in Figure 1-2.

Assignment Operators   In C, the assignment operator is the single equal sign. However, C allows a convenient "shorthand" for assignments of the general type

$$variable1 = variable1\ operator\ expression;$$

Here are two examples:

$$x=x+10;$$
$$y=y/z;$$

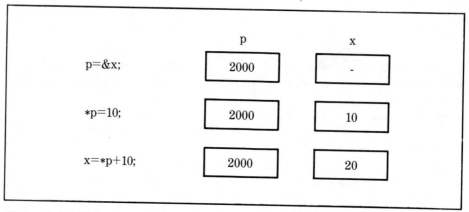

Figure 1-2.   Pointer operations for character pointer **p** and integer **x**, with **x** at memory location 2000

Assignments of this type can be shortened to the general form

$$variable1 \; operator = expression;$$

In the case of the two examples, they can be shortened to

```
x+=10;
y/=z;
```

This shorthand notation is used often in C programs written by experienced C programmers, so you should become familiar with it.

The ? Operator   The ? operator is a ternary operator that is used to replace **if** statements of the general type

$$\textbf{if } expression1 \textbf{ then } \textbf{x} = expression2$$
$$\textbf{else } \textbf{x} = expression2$$

The general form of the ? operator is

$$variable = expression1 \; \textbf{?} \; expression2 : expression3;$$

If *expression1* is TRUE, then the value of *expression2* is assigned to the *variable*; otherwise, *variable* is assigned the value of *expression3*. For example,

```
x=(y<10) ? 20 : 40;
```

assigns to **x** either the value of 20 if **y** is less than 10 or the value of 40 if **y** is not.

The ? operator exists because a C compiler may be able to produce very efficient code for this type of statement—much faster than the equivalent **if/else** statement.

Miscellaneous Operators   The . (dot) operator and the → (arrow) operator are used to reference individual elements of structures and unions. The dot operator is used when the structure or union is global or when the referencing code is in the same function as the structure or union declaration. The arrow operator is used when a structure or union is passed to a function or when only a pointer to a structure or a union is available. For example, given the global structure

```
struct tom {
        char ch;
        float w;
} clyde;
```

you would write

```
clyde.w=123.23;
```

to assign the value 123.23 to element **w** of structure **clyde**.

The , (comma) operator is usually used in the **for** statement. It causes a sequence of operations to be performed. When it is used on the right side of an assignment statement, the value of the entire expression is the value of the last expression of the comma-separated list. For example, after the execution of

```
y=10;
```

```
x=(y=y-5,25/y);
```

x has the value 5 because **y**'s original value of 10 is reduced by 5, and then that value is divided into 25, yielding a result of 5.

Although **sizeof** is also considered a keyword, it is a compile-time operator used to determine the size of a data type in bytes, including user-defined structures and unions. For example,

```
int x;
```

```
printf("%d", sizeof(x));
```

prints the number 2 for many microcomputers.

Parentheses are considered operators that increase the precedence of the operations inside them. Square brackets perform array indexing.

A *cast* is a special operator that forces the conversion of one data type into another. The general form is

(type) variable

For example, in order for the integer **count** to be used in a call to **sqrt( )**, which is the square root routine in C's standard library and requires a floating-point parameter, a cast forces **count** to be treated as type **float**:

```
float y;
int count;

count = 10;

y=sqrt((float)count);
```

Table 1-1 lists the precedence of all C operators. Note that all operators—except the unary operators and ?—associate from left to right. The unary operators (∗, &, and −) and the ? operator associate from right to left.

Functions

A C program is a collection of one or more user-defined functions. One of the functions must be **main( )** because execution begins at this function. Historically, **main( )** is usually the first function in a program; however, it could go anywhere.

Table 1-1. The Precedence of C Operators

Highest	( ) [ ] → .
	! ~ ++ −− − (type) ∗ & sizeof
	∗ / %
	+ −
	<< >>
	< <= > >:
	== !=
	&
	^
	¦
	&&
	¦¦
	?:
	= += −= ∗= /= %= >>= <<= &= ^= ¦=
Lowest	,

The general form of a C function is

> **function__name**(*parameter list*)
> *parameter declaration*
> {
>   *body of function*
> }

If the function has no parameters, no parameter declaration is needed. All functions terminate and return to the calling procedure automatically when the last brace is encountered. You may force return prior to that by using the **return** statement.

All functions return a value. If a **return** statement is partof the function, then the value of the function is the value in the **return** statement. If no **return** is present, the function returns zero. For example,

```
f1()
{
        int x;

        x=100;
        return(x/10);
}
```

returns the value 10, whereas

```
f2()
{
        int x;

        x=100;
        x=x/10;
}
```

returns the value zero because no explicit **return** statement was encountered.

Because all functions have values, they may be used in any arithmetic statement. For example, beginning C programmers tend to write code like this:

```
x=sqrt(y);

z=sin(x);
```

A more experienced programmer would write the following.

```
z=sin(sqrt(y));
```

Remember that in order for the program to determine the value of a function, it must be executed. This means that the following code reads keystrokes from the keyboard until a **u** is typed:

```
while((ch=getchar())!='u') ;
```

This code works because **getchar( )** must be executed to determine its value, which is the character typed at the keyboard.

The Relationship Between Functions and Variable Classes   C

has two general classes of variables: *global* and *local*. A global variable is available for use by all functions in the program, while a local variable is known and used only by the function in which it was declared. In some C literature, global variables are referred to as *external variables* and local variables are called *dynamic* or *automatic variables*. However, this book uses the terms *global* and *local* because they are the generally accepted terms.

A global variable must be declared outside of all functions, including the **main( )** function. Global variables are usually placed at the top of the file before **main( )**, because this makes the program easier to read and because a variable must be declared before it is used. A local variable is declared inside a function after the function's opening brace. For example, the following program declares a global variable, **x** , and two local variables, **x** and **y**.

```
int x;

main()
{
        int y;

        y=get_value();

        x=100;

        printf("%d  %d",x,x*y);

}
f1()
{
        int x;
```

```
        x=getnum();

        return x;

}
```

This program multiplies the number entered from the keyboard by 100. Note that the local variable **x** in **f1( )** has no relationship to the global variable **x**, because local variables that have the same name as global variables always take precedence over the global ones.

Global variables exist during the entire program. Local variables are created when the function is entered and are destroyed when the function is exited. This means that a local variable does not keep its value between function calls. You can use the **static** modifier, however, to preserve values between calls. (You will see examples of **static** later in this book.)

The formal parameters to a function are also local variables, and except for receiving the value of the calling arguments, they behave and can be used like any other local variable.

The main( ) Function As previously mentioned, all C programs must have a **main( )** function. When execution begins, **main( )** is the first function called. You must not have more than one function called **main( )**. When **main( )** terminates, the program is over, and control passes back to the operating system.

The only parameters that **main( )** is allowed to have are **argc** and **argv**. The variable **argc** holds the number of command-line arguments, and the variable **argv** holds a character pointer to them. *Command-line arguments* are the information that you type in after the program name when a program is executed. For example, when you compile a C program, you type

CC MYPROG.C

where **MYPROG.C** is the name of the program you wish to compile. Since most C compilers are themselves programs written in C, **MYPROG.C** is passed to the compiler using the **argc-argv** mechanism.

The value of **argc** is always at least 1, because C considers the program name to be the first argument. If a C program uses **argc** and **argv**, **argv** must be declared as an array of character pointers and **argc** as an integer. This is shown in the following short program, which prints your name on the screen.

```
main(argc,argv)
int argc;
char *argv[];
{
    if(argc<2)
        printf("enter your name on the command line.\n");
    else
        printf("hello %s\n",argv[1]);

}
```

Notice that **argv** is declared as a character pointer array of unknown size. The C compiler automatically determines the size of the array that is necessary to contain all of the command-line arguments.

Command-line arguments can give your programs a professional look and feel, as well as allowing the programs to be placed into a batch file for automatic usage.

Now that you have read this review, you are ready to explore C programming problems and their solutions. Remember, Appendix A contains a summary of most of the C keywords, the preprocessor directives, and some of the standard library functions used in this book.

Sorting and Searching

C H A P T E R   2

In the world of computer science, perhaps no other tasks are more fundamental or as extensively analyzed as those of sorting and searching. These routines are used in virtually all database programs, as well as in compilers, interpreters, and operating systems. This chapter introduces you to the basics of sorting and searching. Since sorting data generally makes searching the data easier and faster, sorting is discussed first.

Sorting

Sorting is the process of arranging a set of similar pieces of information into an increasing or decreasing order; specifically, given a sorted list i of n elements,

$$i_1 <= i_2 <= \ldots <= i_n$$

There are two categories of sorting algorithms: the sorting of arrays, both in memory and in random-access disk files; and the sorting of sequential disk or tape files. This chapter will focus on the first category because it is of most interest to the microcomputer user. However, the general method of sorting sequential files will also be introduced.

The main difference between sorting arrays and sorting sequential files is that each element of the array is always available. This means that any element may be compared or exchanged with any other element at any time. In a sequential file, however, only one element is available at any one time. Because of this difference, sorting techniques differ greatly between the two.

Generally, when information is sorted, a small portion of that information is used as the *sort key* on which comparisons are based. When an exchange must be made, the entire data structure is transferred. In a mailing list, for example, the ZIP code field might be used as the key, but the entire name and address accompanies the ZIP code when the exchange is made. For the sake of simplicity, examples of the various sorting methods presented here will focus on sorting character arrays. Later, you will learn how to adapt any of these methods to any type of data structure.

Classes of Sorting Algorithms

There are three general methods that can be used to sort arrays:

- By exchange
- By selection
- By insertion.

Imagine a deck of cards. To sort the cards by *exchange,* you would spread the cards, face up, on a table and then proceed to exchange out-of-order cards until the deck is ordered.

To sort by *selection,* you would spread the cards on the table, select the lowest-value card, and take it out of the deck. Then, from the remaining cards on the table, you would select the lowest card and place it behind the one already in your hand. This process would continue until all of the cards were in your hand. Because you always selected the lowest card from those remaining on the table, when the process was complete, the cards in your hand would be sorted.

To sort by *insertion*, you would hold the cards in your hand, taking one at a time. As you took cards from the deck, you would place them into a new deck on the table, always inserting them in the correct position. The deck would be sorted when you had no cards in your hand.

Judging Sorting Algorithms

There are many algorithms for each of the three sorting methods. Each algorithm has its merits, but the general criteria for judging a sorting algorithm are based on the answers to the following questions:

- How fast can the algorithm sort information in an average case?

- How fast are its best and worst cases?

- Does the algorithm exhibit *natural* or *unnatural* behavior?

- Does it rearrange elements with equal keys?

How fast a particular algorithm sorts is of great concern. The speed with which an array can be sorted is directly related to the number of comparisons and the number of exchanges required, with exchanges taking more time. Later in this chapter you will see that some sorts require an exponential amount of time per element to sort, and some require logarithmic time.

The best- and worst-case run times are important if you expect to encounter best- and worst-case situations frequently. Often a sort will have a good average case but a terrible worst case, or vice versa.

A sort is said to exhibit *natural* behavior if it works least when the list is already in order, harder as the list becomes less ordered, and hardest when a list is in inverse order. How hard a sort works is based on the number of comparisons and moves that must be executed.

To understand the importance of rearranging elements with equal keys, imagine a database that is sorted on a main key and a subkey — for example, a mailing list with the ZIP code as the main key and the last name within the same ZIP code as the subkey. When a new address is added to the list and the list is sorted again, you do not want the subkeys to be rearranged. To guarantee this, a sort must not exchange main keys of equal value.

In the following sections, representative sorts from each class of sorting algorithms are analyzed to judge their efficiency.

The Bubble Sort The best-known (and most infamous) sort is the *Bubble sort*. Its popularity is derived from its catchy name and its simplicity. However, it is one of the worst sorts ever conceived.

The Bubble sort uses the exchange method of sorting. It makes repeated comparisons and, if necessary, exchanges of adjacent elements. Its name comes from the method's similarity to bubbles in a tank of water, where each bubble seeks its own level. In this simplest form of the Bubble sort

```
bubble(item,count)   /* bubble sort */
char *item;
int count;
{
        register int a,b;
        register char t;

        for(a=1;a<count;++a)
                for(b=count-1;b>=a;--b) {
                        if(item[b-1] > item[b]) {
                                /* exchange elements */
                                t=item[b-1];
                                item[b-1]=item[b];
                                item[b]=t;
                        }
                }
}
```

item is a pointer to the character array to be sorted and **count** is the number of elements in the array.

The Bubble sort is driven by two loops. Since there are **count** elements in the array, the outer loop causes the array to be scanned **count−1** times. This ensures that, in the worst case, every element is in its proper position when the function terminates. The inner loop performs the actual comparisons and exchanges.

This version of the Bubble sort can be used to sort a character array into ascending order. For example, this program sorts a string typed in from the keyboard:

```
main()   /* sort a string from the keyboard */
{
        char s[80];
        int count;

        printf("enter a string:");
```

```
    gets(s);

    count=strlen(s);

    bubble(s,count);

    printf("the sorted string is: %s",s);

}
```

To illustrate the way that the Bubble sort works, here are the passes used to sort the array **dcab**:

initial	d c a b
pass 1	a d c b
pass 2	a b d c
pass 3	a b c d

When analyzing any sort, you must determine how many comparisons and exchanges will be performed for the best, average, and worst cases. With the Bubble sort, the number of comparisons is always the same because the two **for** loops will still repeat the specified number of times, whether the list is initially ordered or not. This means that the Bubble sort will always perform $1/2(n^2-n)$ comparisons, where n is the number of elements to be sorted. The formula is derived from the fact that the outer loop of the Bubble sort executes $n-1$ times and the inner loop $n/2$ times. Multiplying these together gives the formula.

The number of exchanges is 0 for the best case—an already sorted list. The numbers are $3/4(n^2-n)$ for the average case and $3/2(n^2-n)$ for the worst case. It is beyond the scope of this book to explain the derivation of these cases, but you can see that as the list becomes less ordered, the number of elements that are out of order approaches the number of comparisons. (There are three exchanges in a Bubble sort for every element out of order.) The Bubble sort is called an *n-squared algorithm* because its execution time is a multiple of the square of the number of elements. A Bubble sort is very bad for a large number of elements because execution time is directly related to the number of comparisons and exchanges.

For example, if you ignore the time it takes to exchange any out-of-position element, you can see that if each comparison takes 0.001 seconds, then sorting 10 elements will take about 0.05 seconds, sorting 100 elements will take about 5 seconds, and sorting 1000 elements will take about 500 seconds. A 100,000 element sort, the size of a small phone book, would take about 5,000,000 seconds, or about 1,400 hours — about two months of continuous sorting! The graph in Figure 2-1 shows how execution time increases in relation to the size of the array.

You can make some improvements to the Bubble sort to speed it up — and help its image a bit. For example, the Bubble sort has one peculiarity: an out-of-order element at the large end, such as the **a** in the **dcab** array example, will go to its proper position in one pass, but a misplaced element in the small end, such as the **d**, will rise very slowly to its proper place. Instead of always reading the array in the same direction, subsequent passes could reverse direction. Greatly out-of-place elements will travel more quickly to their correct position. Shown here, this version of the Bubble sort is called the *Shaker sort* because of its shaking motion over the array:

```
shaker(item,count) /* Shaker sort, an improved bubble sort */
char *item;
int count;
{
        register int a,b,c,d;
        char t;

        c=1;
        b=count-1; d=count-1;

        do {
                for(a=d; a>=c; --a) {
                        if(item[a-1]>item[a]) {
                                t=item[a-1];
                                item[a-1]=item[a];
                                item[a]=t;
                                b=a;
                        }
                }
                c=b+1;
                for(a=c;a<d+1;++a) {
                        if(item[a-1]>item[a]) {
                                t=item[a-1];
                                item[a-1]=item[a];
                                item[a]=t;
                                b=a;
                        }
                }
                d=b-1;
        } while (c<=d);
}
```

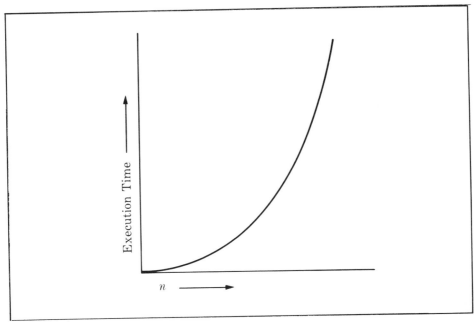

Figure 2-1.   The execution time of an n^2 sort in relation to array size

Although the Shaker sort does improve the Bubble sort, it still executes on the order of n^2 because the number of comparisons is unchanged and because the number of exchanges has only been reduced by a relatively small constant.

Sorting by Selection   A *Selection sort* selects the element with the lowest value and exchanges that with the first element. Then from the remaining $n-1$ elements, the element with the next-lowest value is found and exchanged with the second element, and so forth up to the last two elements. For example, if the selection method were used on the array **bdac**, each pass would look like this:

initial	b d a c
pass 1	a d b c
pass 2	a b d c
pass 3	a b c d

A simple form of the Selection sort is shown here:

```
select(item,count)    /* selection sort */
char *item;
int count;
{
        register int a,b,c;
        char t;

        for(a=0;a<count-1;++a) {
                c=a;
                t=item[a];
                for(b=a+1; b<count;++b) {
                        if(item[b]<t) {
                                c=b;
                                t=item[b];
                        }
                }
                item[c]=item[a];
                item[a]=t;
        }
}
```

Unfortunately, like the Bubble sort, the outer loop executes $n-1$ times and the inner loop $1/2(n)$ times. This means that the Selection sort requires $1/2(n^2-n)$ comparisons, which makes it too slow for a large number of items. The number of exchanges for the best case is $3(n-1)$ and for the worst case is $n^2/4+3(n-1)$.

For the best case (the list is ordered) only $n-1$ elements need to be moved, and each move requires three exchanges. The worst case approximates the number of comparisons. Although the average case is beyond the scope of this book to develop, it is $n(\ln n+y)$, where y is Euler's constant, about 0.577216. This means that although the number of comparisons for the Bubble sort and the Selection sort is the same, the number of exchanges in the average case is far less for the Selection sort.

Sorting by Insertion The Insertion sort is the last of the simple sorting algorithms. The Insertion sort initially sorts the first two members on the array. Next, the algorithm inserts the third member into its sorted position in relation to the first two members. Then the fourth element is inserted into the list of three elements. The process continues until all elements have been sorted. For example, in the array **dcab**, each pass of the Insertion sort would look like this.

initial	d c a b
pass 1	c d a b
pass 3	a c d b
pass 4	a b c d

A version of the Insertion sort is shown here:

```
insert(item,count) /* sorting by straight insertion */
char *item;
int count;
{
        register int a,b;
        char t;

        for(a=1; a<count; ++a) {
                t=item[a];
                b=a-1;
                while(b>=0 && t<item[b] ) {
                        item[b+1]=item[b];
                        b--;
                }
                item[b+1]=t;
        }
}
```

   Unlike the Bubble sort and the Selection sort, the number of comparisons that occur while the Insertion sort is used will depend upon how the list is initially ordered. If the list is in order, then the number of comparisons is $n-1$. If the list is out of order, then the number of comparisons is $1/2(n^2+n)-1$, while its average is $1/4(n^2+n-2)$.

   The number of exchanges for each case is as follows:

best	$2(n-1)$
average	$1/4(n^2+9n-10)$
worst	$1/2(n^2+3n-4)$

Therefore, the number for the worst case is as bad as those for the Bubble and Selection sorts, and the number for the average case is only slightly better.

   The Insertion sort does have two advantages, however. First, it behaves *naturally:* it works the least when the array is already sorted and the hardest when the array is sorted in inverse order. This makes the Insertion sort useful for lists that are almost in order. Second, it leaves the order of equal keys unchanged: if a list is sorted using two keys, it remains sorted for both keys after an Insertion sort.

Even though the number of comparisons may be fairly good for certain sets of data, the fact that the array must constantly be shifted means that the number of moves can be significant. However, the Insertion sort still behaves naturally, with the least exchanges occurring for an almost sorted list and the most exchanges for an inversely ordered array.

Improved Sorts

Each algorithm shown so far had the fatal flaw of executing in n^2 time. For large amounts of data, the sorts would be slow — in fact, at some point, too slow to use. Every computer programmer has heard, or told, the horror story of the "sort that took three days." Unfortunately, these stories are often true.

When a sort takes too long, it may be the fault of the underlying algorithm. However, a sad commentary is that the first response is often "let's write it in assembly code." Although assembler will almost always speed up a routine by a constant factor, if the underlying algorithm is bad, the sort will still be slow, no matter how optimal the coding. Remember, when the time of a routine is n^2, increasing the speed of either the coding or the computer will only cause a marginal improvement, because the rate at which the run time increases changes exponentially. (The graph in Figure 2-1 is shifted to the right slightly, but the curve is unchanged.) Keep in mind that if something is not fast enough in C, it won't be fast enough in assembler. The solution is to use a better sorting algorithm.

In this section, two excellent sorts will be developed. The first is the Shell sort and the second is the Quicksort, which is generally considered the best sorting routine. These sorts run so fast that if you blink, you will miss them.

The Shell Sort   The Shell sort is named after its inventor, D.L. Shell. However, the name seems to have stuck because its method of operation resembles sea shells piled upon one another.

The general method, derived from the Insertion sort, is based on diminishing increments. Figure 2-2 gives a diagram of a Shell sort on the array **fdacbe**. First, all elements that are three positions apart are sorted. Then all elements that are two positions apart are sorted. Finally, all those adjacent to each other are sorted.

It may not be obvious that this method yields good results, or even that it

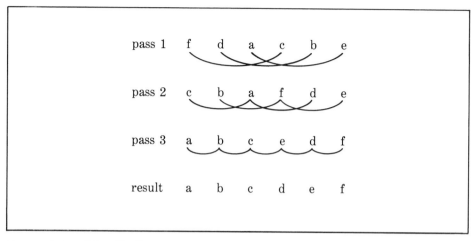

Figure 2-2. The Shell sort

will sort the array, but it does both. This algorithm is efficient because each sorting pass involves either relatively few elements or elements that are already in reasonable order; therefore each pass increases the order of the data.

The exact sequence for the increments can be changed. The only rule is that the last increment must be 1. For example, the sequence 9, 5, 3, 1 works well and is used in the Shell sort shown here. Avoid sequences that are powers of 2 because, for mathematically complex reasons, they reduce the efficiency of the sorting algorithm. (However, even if you used them, the sort would still work.)

```
shell(item,count)
char *item;
int count;
{
        register int i,j,k,s,w;
        char x, a[5];

        a[0]=9; a[1]=5; a[2]=3; a[3]=3; a[4]=1;

        for(w=0; w<5; w++) {
                k=a[w]; s=-k;
                for(i=k; i<count;++i) {
                        x=item[i];
                        j=i-k;
```

```
if(s==0){ s=-k;
          s++;
          item[s]=x;
}
while(x<item[j] && j>=0 && j<=count) {
          item[j+k]=item[j];
          j=j-k;
}
item[j+k]=x;
            }
        }
    }
```

You may have noticed that the inner **while** loop has three test conditions. The **x<item[j]** is a comparison necessary for the sorting process. The tests **j>=0** and **j<=count** are used to keep the sort from overrunning the boundary of the array **item**. These extra checks will degrade the performance of the Shell sort to some extent. Slightly different versions of the Shell sort employ special array elements, called *sentinels*, which are not actually part of the array to be sorted. Sentinels hold special termination values that indicate the least and greatest possible elements. In this way, the boundary checks are unnecessary. However, using sentinels requires a specific knowledge of the data, which limits the generality of the sort function.

The analysis of the Shell sort presents some difficult mathematical problems that are beyond the scope of this book. However, execution time is proportional to $n^{1.2}$ for sorting n elements. This is a significant improvement over the n^2 sorts of the previous section; see Figure 2-3, which graphs an n^2 curve and an $n^{1.2}$ curve together. However, before you decide to use the Shell sort, you should know that the Quicksort is even better.

The Quicksort   The Quicksort, invented and named by C. A. R. Hoare, is generally considered the best sorting algorithm currently available. It is based on the exchange method of sorting. This is surprising if you consider the terrible performance of the Bubble sort, which is also based on the exchange method.

The Quicksort is built on the idea of partitions. The general procedure selects a value called the *comparand* and then partitions the array into two parts, with all elements greater than or equal to the partition value on one side and those less than the partition value on the other. This process is repeated for each remaining part until the array is sorted. For example, given the array **fedacb** and the value **d** for the partition, the first pass of the

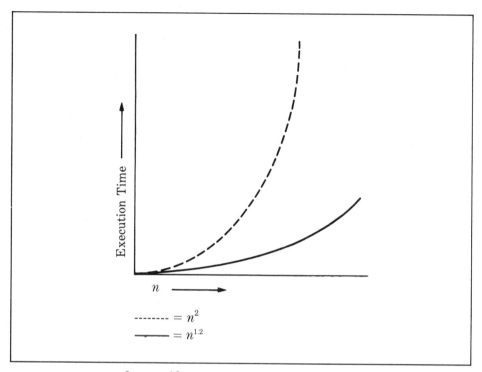

Figure 2-3. The n^2 and $n^{1.2}$ curves

Quicksort would rearrange the array like this:

initial	f e d a c b
pass 1	b c a d e f

This process is repeated for each part (**bca** and **def**). The process is essentially recursive; indeed, the cleanest implementations of Quicksort are recursive algorithms.

The selection of the middle comparand value can be accomplished in two ways. The value can be chosen either at random or by averaging a small set of values taken from the array. For optimal sorting it is best to select a value that is precisely in the middle of the range of values. However, this is not easy to do for most sets of data. Even in the worst case—the value chosen is at one extremity—Quicksort will still perform reasonably well.

The following version of Quicksort selects the middle element of the array. Although this may not always result in a good choice, it is a simple, quick technique, and still performs correctly.

```
quick(item,count)   /* quick sort set up */
char *item;
int count;
{

        qs(item,0,count-1);

}

qs(item,left,right)   /* quick sort */
char *item;
int left,right;
{

        register int i,j;
        char x,y;

        i=left; j=right;
        x=item[(left+right)/2];

        do {
                while(item[i]<x && i<right) i++;
                while(x<item[j] && j>left) j--;

                if(i<=j) {
                        y=item[i];
                        item[i]=item[j];
                        item[j]=y;
                        i++; j--;
                }
        } while(i<=j);

        if(left<j)  qs(item,left,j);
        if(i<right) qs(item,i,right);
}
```

Here, **quick( )** sets up a call to the main sorting function, called **qs( )**. While this maintains the same common interface for **item** and **count**, it is not essential, because **qs( )** could have been called directly by using three arguments.

The derivation of the number of comparisons and the number of exchanges that Quicksort performs requires mathematics beyond the scope of this book. However, you can assume that the number of comparisons is $n \log n$, and that the number of exchanges is approximately $n/6 \log n$. These are significantly better than any of the sorts discussed so far.

The equation

$$N = a^x$$

can be rewritten as

$$x = \log_a N$$

This means, for example, that if 100 elements were to be sorted, Quicksort would require an average of 100 * 2, or 200, comparisons because log 100 is 2. Compared with the Bubble sort's average of 990 comparisons, this number is quite good.

However, there is one nasty aspect of Quicksort that you should be aware of. If the comparand value for each partition happens to be the largest value, then Quicksort degenerates into "slowsort" with an n^2 run time. Generally, though, this does not happen.

You must take care in choosing a method to determine the value of the comparand. Often the value is determined by the actual data that you are sorting. In large mailing lists where sorting is often done by ZIP code, the selection is simple, because the ZIP codes are distributed fairly evenly and an algebraic function can determine a suitable comparand. However, in certain databases, the sort keys may be so close in value, with many having the same value, that a random selection is often the best method available. A common and fairly effective method is to sample three elements from a partition and take the middle value.

Sorting Other Data Structures

Until now, the sorts have only been applied to arrays of characters. This has made it easy to present each sorting routine. Obviously, arrays of any of the built-in data types can be sorted simply by changing the data types of the parameters and variables to the sort function. However, it is generally complex data types like strings or structures that need to be sorted. (Remember, most sorting involves a key and information linked to that key.) To adapt the algorithms to sort other data structures, you need to change either the comparison section or the exchange section, or both. The basic algorithm itself will remain unchanged.

Because Quicksort is one of the best general-purpose routines available at this time, it will be used in our examples. The same techniques, however, will apply to any of the sorts described earlier.

Sorting Strings   The easiest way to sort strings is to create an array of character pointers to those strings. This allows you to maintain easy indexing, and it keeps the basic Quicksort algorithm unchanged. The string version of Quicksort shown here accepts an array of **char** pointers that point to the strings to be sorted. The sort rearranges the pointers to the strings, not the actual strings in memory. This version sorts the strings in alphabetical order.

```
quick_string(item,count)   /* quick sort for strings setup */
char *item[];
int count;
{

        qs(item,0,count-1);

}

qs_string(item,left,right)   /* quick sort for strings */
char *item[];
int left,right;
{
        register int i,j;
        char *x,*y;

        i=left; j=right;
        x=item[(left+right)/2];

        do {
                while(strcmp(item[i],x)<0 && i<right) i++;
                while(strcmp(item[j],x)>0 && j>left) j--;

                if(i<=j) {
                        y=item[i];
                        item[i]=item[j];
                        item[j]=y;
                        i++; j--;
                }
        } while(i<=j);

        if(left<j)  qs(item,left,j);
        if(i<right) qs(item,i,right);
}
```

The comparison step has been changed to use the function **strcmp( )**, which returns a negative number if the first string is lexicographically less than the second, 0 if the strings are equal, or a positive number if the first string is lexicographically greater than the second. The exchange part of the routine has been left unchanged because only the pointers are being exchanged — not the actual strings. To exchange the actual strings, you would have to use the function **strcpy( )**.

The use of **strcmp( )** slows down the sort for two reasons. First, it involves a function call, which always takes time; second, the **strcmp( )** function itself performs several (and sometimes many) comparisons to determine the relationship of the two strings. If speed is absolutely critical, the code for **strcmp( )** can be duplicated in line within the **quick __string** routine. However, there is no way to avoid comparing the strings, since this is by definition what the task involves.

Sorting Structures   Most application programs that require a sort will need to have a group of data sorted. A mailing list is an excellent example because a name, street, city, state, and ZIP code are all linked. When this conglomerate unit of data is sorted, a sort key is used, but the entire structure is also exchanged. To understand this process, you first need to create a structure. For a mailing-list example, a convenient structure is

```
struct address {
        char name[40];
        char street[40];
        char city[20];
        char state[3];
        char zip[10];
};
```

The **state** is three characters long and the **zip** is ten characters long because a string array always needs to be one character longer than the maximum length of any string in order to store the null terminator.

Since it is reasonable to arrange a mailing list as an array of structures, assume for this example that the sort routine sorts an array of structures of type **address** by the ZIP code field as shown here:

```
quick_structure(item,count)    /* quick sort for structure */
                               /* setup */
struct address item[];
int count;
{
        qs(item,0,count-1);

}
```

```
qs_structure(item,left,right)   /* quick sort for structures */
struct address item[];
int left,right;
{
        register int i,j;
        char *x,*y;

        i=left; j=right;
        x=item[(left+right)/2].zip;

        do {
                while(strcmp(item[i].zip,x)<0 && i<right) i++;
                while(strcmp(item[j].zip,x)>0 && j>left) j--;

                if(i<=j) {
                        swap_all_fields(item,i,j);
                        i++; j--;
                }
        } while(i<=j);

        if(left<j)  qs(item,left,j);
        if(i<right) qs(item,i,right);
}
```

Notice that both the comparison code and the exchange code needed to be altered. Because so many fields needed to be exchanged, a separate function called **swap—all—fields( )**, shown later, was created.

Sorting Disk Files

There are two types of disk files: *sequential* and *random-access*. If a disk file is small enough, it may be read into memory so that the array-sorting routines presented earlier can sort it most efficiently. However, many disk files are too large to be sorted easily in memory and require special techniques.

Sorting Random-Access Disk Files   Used by most microcomputer database applications, random-access disk files have two major advantages over sequential disk files. First, they are easy to maintain: you can update information without having to copy the entire list over. Second, random-access disk files can be treated as a large array on disk, which greatly simplifies sorting. Applying this method means that you can use the basic Quicksort with modifications to seek different records on the disk, instead of having to index an array. Unlike sorting a sequential disk file, sorting a random file in place also means that a full disk does not need to have room for both the sorted and unsorted files.

Each sorting situation differs with the exact data structure that is sorted and the key that is used. However, the general concept of sorting random-access disk files can be understood by developing a sort program that sorts the mailing-list structure called **address** that was defined earlier. This sample program assumes that the number of elements is fixed at 100, but in a real application, a record count would have to be dynamically maintained. Once again, the sort key is the ZIP code field.

```c
#include "stdio.h"
#define NUM_ELEMENTS 100   /* this is an arbitrary number
                              that should be determined
                              dynamically for each list */

struct address {
        char name[30];
        char street[40];
        char city[20];
        char state[3];
        char zip[10];
}ainfo;

main()
{
        FILE *fp;
        int t;

        if((fp=fopen("mlist","r+"))==0) {
                printf("cannot open file for read/write\n");
                exit (0);
        }

        quick_disk(fp,NUM_ELEMENTS);

        fclose(fp);

        printf("List sorted.\n");

}

quick_disk(fp,count)   /* quick sort for random files */
                       /* setup */
FILE *fp;
long int count;
{

        qs_disk(fp,0L,(long) count-1);

}

qs_disk(fp,left,right)   /* quick sort for random files */
FILE *fp;
long int left,right;
{

        long int i,j;
        char x[100],*y,*get_zip();
```

```
            i=left; j=right;

            strcpy(x,get_zip(fp,(long)(i+j)/2)); /* get the middle zip */

            do {
                    while(strcmp(get_zip(fp,i),x)<0 && i<right) i++;
                    while(strcmp(get_zip(fp,j),x)>0 && j>left) j--;

                    if(i<=j) {
                            swap_all_fields(fp,i,j);
                            i++; j--;
                    }
            } while(i<=j);

            if(left<j)  qs_disk(fp,left,j);
            if(i<right) qs_disk(fp,i,right);
}

swap_all_fields(fp,i,j)
FILE *fp;
long int i,j;
{

        char a[sizeof(ainfo)],b[sizeof(ainfo)];
        register int t;

        /* first read in record i and j */
        fseek(fp,sizeof(ainfo)*i,0);
        for(t=0;t<sizeof(ainfo);++t) a[t]=getc(fp);

        fseek(fp,sizeof(ainfo)*j,0);
        for(t=0;t<sizeof(ainfo);++t) b[t]=getc(fp);

        /* then write them back in opposite slots */
        fseek(fp,sizeof(ainfo)*j,0);
        for(t=0;t<sizeof(ainfo);++t) putc(a[t],fp);

        fseek(fp,sizeof(ainfo)*i,0);
        for(t=0;t<sizeof(ainfo);++t) putc(b[t],fp);
}

char *get_zip(fp,rec)
FILE *fp;
long int rec;
{

        char *p;
        register int t;

        p=&ainfo;

        fseek(fp,rec*sizeof(ainfo),0);
        for(t=0;t<sizeof(ainfo);++t) *p++=getc(fp);

        return ainfo.zip;

}
```

Several support functions had to be written to sort the address records. In the comparison section of the sort, **get_zip( )** returns a pointer to the ZIP code of the comparand and the record being checked. The **swap_all_ fields( )** function performs the actual exchange of the data. Under most operating systems, the order of reads and writes has a great impact on the speed of this sort. The code, as it is written, forces a **seek** to record **i** and then to **j**. While the head of the disk drive is still positioned at **j**, the data of **i** is written. This means that it is not necessary for the head to move a great distance. Had the code been written with the data of **i** to be written first, then an extra **seek** would have been necessary.

Sorting Sequential Files Unlike random-access files, sequential files generally do not have fixed record lengths, and they may be organized on storage devices that do not allow easy random access. Therefore, sequential disk files are common because a specific application is best suited to variable record lengths or because the storage device is sequential in nature. For example, most text files are sequential.

Although sorting a disk file as if it were an array has several advantages, this method cannot be used with sequential files—there is no way to achieve quick access to any arbitrary element. For example, no quick way exists to reach arbitrary records of a sequential file that is located on tape. It therefore would be difficult to apply any of the previously presented array-sorting algorithms to sequential files.

There are two approaches to sorting sequential files. The first approach reads the information into memory and sorts with one of the standard array-sorting algorithms. Although this approach is fast, memory constraints limit the size of the file that can be sorted.

The second approach, called a *Merge sort*, divides the file to be sorted into two files of equal length. Using these files, the sort reads an element from each file, orders that pair, and writes the elements to a third disk file. This new file is then divided, and the ordered doubles are merged into ordered quadruples. The new file is split again, and the same procedure is followed until the list is sorted. For historical reasons, this Merge sort is called a *three-tape merge* because it requires three files (tape drives) to be active at one time.

To understand how the Merge sort works, consider the following sequence:

1 4 3 8 6 7 2 5

The first split produces

$$1\ 4\ 3\ 8$$
$$6\ 7\ 2\ 5$$

The first merge yields

$$1\ 6 - 4\ 7 - 2\ 3 - 5\ 8$$

This is split again and becomes

$$1\ 6 - 4\ 7$$
$$2\ 3 - 5\ 8$$

The next merge yields

$$1\ 2\ 3\ 6 - 4\ 5\ 7\ 8$$

The final split is

$$1\ 2\ 3\ 6$$
$$4\ 5\ 7\ 8$$

with the outcome

$$1\ 2\ 3\ 4\ 5\ 6\ 7\ 8$$

As you may have guessed, the three-tape merge requires that each file be accessed $\log_2 n$ times, where n is the number of total elements to sort.

Here is a simple version of the Merge sort. It assumes that the input file is a character stream, such as a text file, and that the file is an even power of two in length. You can easily alter this version to sort any type of data file.

```
#include "stdio.h"

#define LENGTH 16  /* arbitrary */

main(argc,argv)  /* merge sort for disk files */
int argc;
char *argv[];
{
        FILE *fp1,*fp2,*fp3;
```

```
if((fp1=fopen(argv[1],"rw"))==0) {
        printf("cannot open file 1%s\n",argv[1]);
        exit(0);
}

if((fp2=fopen("sort1","rw"))==0) {
        printf("cannot open file 2\n");
        exit(0);
}

if((fp3=fopen("sort2","rw"))==0) {
        printf("cannot open file 3\n");
        exit(0);
}

merge(fp1,fp2,fp3,LENGTH);

fclose(fp1); fclose(fp2); fclose(fp3);
}

merge(fp1,fp2,fp3,count)
FILE *fp1,*fp2,*fp3;
int count;
{
        register int t,n,j,k,q;
        char x,y;

        for(n=1;n<count;n=n*2) {

                /* split file */
                for(t=0;t<count/2;++t) putc(getc(fp1),fp2);
                for(;t<count;++t) putc(getc(fp1),fp3);

                rewind(fp1,fp2,fp3);

                for(q=0;q<count/2;q+=n) {
                    x=getc(fp2);
                    y=getc(fp3);
                    for(j=k=0;;) {
                        if(x<y) {
                                putc(x,fp1);
                                j++;
                                if(j<n) x=getc(fp2);
                                else break;
                        }
                        else {
                                putc(y,fp1);
                                k++;
                                if(k<n) y=getc(fp3);
                                else break;
                        }
```

```
                                    }
                                    if(j<n)   {
                                         putc(x,fp1);
                                         j++;
                                    }
                                    if(k<n)   {
                                         putc(y,fp1);
                                         k++;
                                    }
                                    for(;j<n;++j) putc(getc(fp2),fp1);
                                    for(;k<n;++k) putc(getc(fp3),fp1);
                               }
                               rewind(fp1,fp2,fp3);
                    }
          }


    rewind(fp1,fp2,fp3)
    FILE *fp1,*fp2,*fp3;
    {
              fseek(fp1,(long)0,0);
              fseek(fp2,(long)0,0);
              fseek(fp3,(long)0,0);
    }
```

All three files have been opened for read/write mode, and **rewind( )** was created to reset the files each time. The cast **long** is used with **fseek( )** because it generally requires a long integer for the file offset.

Searching

Databases of information exist so that, from time to time, a user can locate and use the data in a given record as long as that record's key is known. There is only one method of finding information in an unsorted file or array and for a sorted file or array.

Searching Methods

Finding information in an unsorted array requires a sequential search, starting at the first element and stopping either when a match is found or when the end of the array is reached. This method must be used on unsorted data but can also be applied to sorted data. If the data has been sorted, then a *binary search* can be used, which will increase the speed of any search.

The Sequential Search   The sequential search is easy to code. The following function searches a character array of known length until a match is found with the specified key:

```
sequential_search(item,count,key)
char *item;
int count;
char key;
{

        register int t;

        for(t=0;t<count;++t)
                if(key==item[t]) return t;

        return -1;   /* no match */

}
```

This function returns either the index number of the matching entry if there is one, or −1 if there is not.

A straight sequential search will, on the average, test $1/2n$ elements. In the best case, it will test only one element and, in the worst case, n elements. If the information is stored on disk, the search time can be very long. But if the data is unsorted, a sequential search is the only method available.

The Binary Search   If the data to be searched is in sorted order, then a superior method, called the *binary search*, can be used to find a match. The method uses the "divide and conquer" approach. It first tests the middle element; if the element is larger than the key, it then tests the middle element of the first half; otherwise, it tests the middle element of the second half. This process is repeated until either a match is found or there are no more elements to test.

For example, to find the number 4 in the array **1 2 3 4 5 6 7 8 9**, the binary search would first test the middle element, which is **5**. Since this element is greater than 4, the search would continue with the first half, or

1 2 3 4 5

In this example, the middle element is **3**. This is less than 4, so the first half is discarded, and the search continues with

4 5

This time, the match is found.

In the binary search, the number of comparisons in the worst case is $\log_2 n$. With average cases, the number is somewhat better; in the best case, the number is 1.

You can use the following binary search function for character arrays to search any arbitrary data structure by changing the comparison portion of the routine:

```
bsearch(item,count,key)    /* Binary search */
char *item;
int count;
char key;
{

        int low,high, mid;

        low=0; high=count-1;

        while(low<=high) {
                mid=(low+high)/2;
                if(key<item[mid]) high=mid-1;
                else if(key>item[mid]) low=mid+1;
                else return mid;   /* found */
        }

        return -1;
}
```

The next chapter explores different approaches to data storage and retrieval, which, in some cases, can make sorting and searching much easier tasks.

Queues, Stacks, Linked Lists, And Binary Trees

CHAPTER 3

Programs consist of *algorithms* and *data structures*. The good program is a blend of both. Choosing and implementing a data structure are as important as the routines that manipulate the data. The way that information is organized and accessed is usually determined by the nature of the programming problem. Therefore, as a programmer you must have in your "bag of tricks" the right storage and retrieval method for any situation.

The actual representation of data in the computer is built "from the ground up," starting with the basic data types like **char**, **int**, and **float**. At the next level are arrays, which are organized collections of the basic data types. Next are structures, which are conglomerate data types accessed under one name. Transcending these physical aspects of the data, the final level concentrates on the sequence in which the data will be *stored* and *accessed*. In essence, the physical data is linked to a "data machine" that controls the way your program accesses information. There are four of these machines:

- A queue
- A stack
- A linked list
- A binary tree.

Each method provides a solution to a class of problems; each is essentially a "device" that performs a specific storage and retrieval operation on the given information according to the request it receives. The methods share two operations, *store an item* and *retrieve an item,* in which the item is one informational unit. This chapter shows you how to develop these methods for use in your own programs.

Queues

A *queue* is a linear list of information that is accessed in *first in, first out* order (sometimes called FIFO). The first item placed on the queue is the first item retrieved, the second item placed on the queue is the second item retrieved, and so on. This order is the only means of storage and retrieval; a queue does not allow random access of any specific item.

Action	Contents of Queue
qstore(A)	A
qstore(B)	A B
qstore(C)	A B C
qretrieve( ) returns A	B C
qstore(D)	B C D
qretrieve( ) returns B	C D
qretrieve( ) returns C	D

Figure 3-1.   A queue in action

Queues are common in everyday life. For example, a line at a bank or a fast-food restaurant is a queue (except when rude patrons push their way to the front). To visualize how a queue works, consider two functions: **qstore( )** and **qretrieve( )**. The **qstore( )** places an item onto the end of the queue, and the **qretrieve( )** removes the first item from the queue and returns its value. Figure 3-1 shows the effect of a series of these operations.

Keep in mind that a retrieve operation removes an item from the queue and, if the item is not stored elsewhere, destroys it. Therefore, even though the program is still active, a queue may be empty at any particular time because all of its items have been retrieved.

Queues are used in many types of programming situations, such as simulations (discussed later in their own chapter), event scheduling (as in a PERT or Gant chart), and I/O buffering.

For example, consider a simple event-scheduler program that allows you to enter a number of events. As each event is performed, it is taken off the list, and the next event is displayed. You might use a program like this to organize such events as a day's appointments. To simplify the example, the program uses an array of pointers to the event strings. It limits each event description to 256 characters and the number of events to 100. First, here are the functions **qstore( )** and **qretrieve( )** that will be used in the scheduling program:

```
#define MAX_EVENT 100

char *p[MAX_EVENT];
int spos;
int rpos;

qstore(q)
char *q;
{
        if(spos==MAX_EVENT) {
                printf("List full\n");
                return;
        }
        p[spos]=q;
        spos++;
}

qretrieve()
{
        if(rpos==spos) {
                printf("No events to perform.\n");
                return 0;
        }
        rpos++;
        return p[rpos-1];
}
```

These functions require two global variables: **spos**, which holds the position or index of the next free storage location, and **rpos**, which holds the index of the next item to retrieve.

In this program, the function **qstore( )** places pointers to new events on the end of the list and checks whether the list is full. The function **qretrieve( )** takes events off the queue while there are events to perform. When a new event is scheduled, **spos** is incremented, and when an event is completed, **rpos** is incremented. In essence, **rpos** "chases" **spos** through the queue. Figure 3-2 shows the way this process appears in memory as the program executes. If **rpos** equals **spos**, there are no events left in the schedule. Keep in

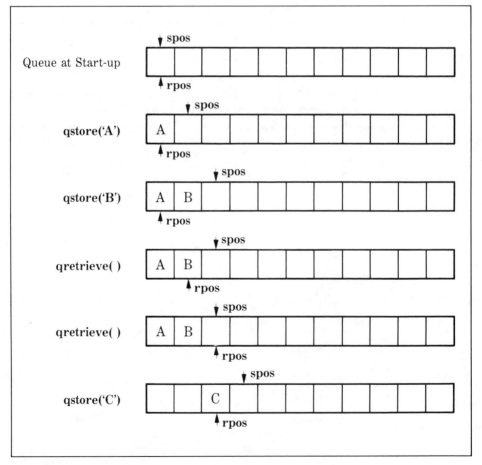

Figure 3-2.   The retrieve index chasing the store index

mind that even though the information stored in the queue is not actually destroyed by the **qretrieve( )** function, it can never be accessed again and is in effect destroyed.

Here is the entire program for a simple event scheduler. You may want to enhance this program for your own use.

```
#define MAX_EVENT 100

char *p[MAX_EVENT];
int spos;
int rpos;

main()   /* Mini-Scheduler */
{
        char s[80];
        register int t;

        for(t=0;t<MAX_EVENT;++t) p[t]=0; /* init array to nulls */
        spos=0; rpos=0;

        for(;;) {
                printf("Enter, Review, Perform, Quit: ");
                gets(s);
                *s=toupper(*s);

                switch(*s) {
                        case 'E':
                                enter();
                                break;
                        case 'R':
                                review();
                                break;
                        case 'P':
                                perform();
                                break;
                        case 'Q':
                                exit(0);
                }

        }

}

enter()
{
        char s[256], *p;

        do {
                printf("enter event %d:",spos+1);
                gets(s);
                if(*s==0) break;  /* no entry */
                p=malloc(strlen(s));
                if(p==0) {
                        printf("out of memory.\n");
                        return;
                }
                strcpy(p,s);
```

```
                        if(*s) qstore(p);
                }while(*s);
        }

        review()
        {

                register int t;

                for(t=rpos;t<spos;++t)
                        printf("%d. %s\n",t+1,p[t]);
        }

        perform()
        {
                char *p;

                if((p=qretrieve())==0) return;

                printf("%s\n",p);
        }

        qstore(q)
        char *q;
        {
                if(spos==MAX_EVENT) {
                        printf("List full\n");
                        return;
                }
                p[spos]=q;
                spos++;
        }

        qretrieve()
        {
                if(rpos==spos) {
                        printf("No events to perform.\n");
                        return 0;
                }
                rpos++;
                return p[rpos-1];
        }
```

The Circular Queue

In the previous section you may have thought of an improvement for the Mini-Scheduler program. Instead of having the program stop when it reaches the limit of the array used to store the queue, you could have both the store index **spos** and the retrieve index **rpos** loop back to the start of the array. This would allow any number of items to be placed on the queue, as long as items are also being taken off. Called a *circular queue*, this implementation of a queue uses its storage array as if it were a circle instead of a linear list.

To create a circular queue for the Mini-Scheduler program, the functions **qstore( )** and **qretrieve( )** need to be changed:

```
qstore(q)
char *q;
{
        if(spos+1==rpos) {
                printf("list full\n");
                return;
        }
        p[spos]=q;
        spos++;
        if(spos==MAX_EVENT) spos=0; /* loop back */
}

qretrieve()
{
        if(rpos==MAX_EVENT) rpos=0; /* loop back */
        if(rpos==spos) {
                printf("No events to perform.\n");
                return 0;
        }
        rpos++;
        return p[rpos-1];
}
```

In essence, the queue is only full when both the store index and the retrieve index are equal; otherwise, the queue still has room for another event. However, this means that when the program starts, the retrieve index **rpos** must not be set to 0, but rather to **MAX_EVENT** so that the first call to **qstore( )** does not produce the **queue full** message. It is important to note that the queue will hold only **MAX_EVENT** −1 elements because **rpos** and **spos** must always be at least one element apart; otherwise, it would be impossible to know whether the queue was full or empty. Figure 3-3 is a conceptual representation of the array used for the circular version of the Mini-Scheduler program. The most common use of a circular queue may be in operating systems that buffer the information read from and written to disk files or the console. Another common use is in real-time application programs in which, for example, the program performs another task while the user continues to input from the keyboard. Many word processors do this when they reformat a paragraph or justify a line. There is a brief period in which what is being typed is not displayed until the other process the program is working on is completed; the application program must continue to

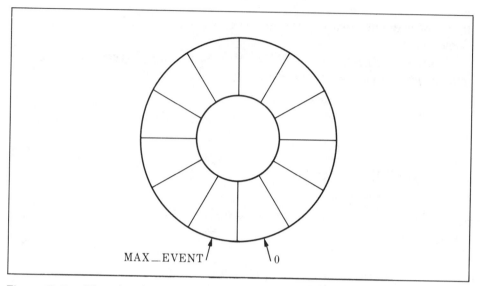

MAX_EVENT /   \ 0

Figure 3-3. The circular array for the Mini-Scheduler program

check for keyboard entry during the other process's execution. If a key has been typed, it is placed quickly in the queue and the process continues. After the process is complete, the characters are retrieved from the queue and handled in the normal manner.

To see how this is done, you can study the simple program presented next, which contains two processes. The first process prints the numbers 1 to 32,000 on the screen. The second process places characters into a circular queue as they are typed, without echoing them on the screen until a semi-colon is struck. The characters you type will not be displayed, because the first process is given priority over the screen at this time. After the semi-colon has been struck, the characters in the queue are retrieved and printed. Keep in mind that each operating system and C compiler differs in the way that it checks keyboard status. There is no standard library function to do this.

The short program given here works with the IBM PC and uses the Aztec C **bdos( )** function. This special function allows a program to use routines made available by the computer's operating system—in this case, PC-DOS. One such operating-system call determines and returns the keyboard status, as well as any character that has been pressed on the keyboard. The program uses the call to read characters without echoing them to the screen. Refer to your C compiler manual to find out what these functions are called by your compiler.

```
#define MAX 80

char buf[MAX+1];
int pos=0;

main() /* circular queue example - keyboard buffer */
{
        register char ch;
        int dx,dy,t;

        buf[80]=0;

        for(t=0;t<32000 && ch!=';';++t) {
                if(kbhit()) {
                        ch=bdos(7,dx,dy);
                        qstore(ch);
                }
                printf("%d ",t);
        }

        while((ch=qretrieve())!=0) putchar(ch); /* display buf */

}

qstore(ch)
register char ch;
{
        if(pos==MAX) pos=0;  /* go back to start */
        buf[pos]=ch;
        pos++;
}

qretrieve()
{
        static int dq_pos=MAX;

        dq_pos++;
        if(dq_pos>MAX) dq_pos=0; /* loop back to start */

        if(dq_pos==pos) {
                dq_pos--;
                return 0;
        }
        return buf[dq_pos];
}

kbhit()
{
        register int dx,dy;
        return(bdos(11,dx,dy));
}
```

The **kbhit( )** uses a function call to the operating system, which returns
TRUE when a key has been pressed, FALSE if not. The **bdos(7,dx,dy)** call
in **main( )** reads a key from the keyboard without echoing it to the screen. As

stated earlier, these calls work for the IBM PC only. (In Chapter 5, you will learn how to use these and other operating-system calls in depth.)

Stacks

A *stack* is the opposite of a queue because it uses *last-in, first-out* accessing (sometimes called LIFO). Imagine a stack of plates. The bottom plate in the stack is the last to be used, and the top plate (the last plate placed on the stack) is the first to be used. Stacks are used a great deal in system software, including compilers and interpreters. Most C compilers use a stack when passing arguments to functions.

For historical reasons, the two primary stack operations—*store* and *retrieve*—are usually called *push* and *pop*, respectively. Therefore, to implement a stack, you need two functions: **push( )**, which places a value on the stack, and **pop( )**, which retrieves the top value from the stack. You also need a region of memory to use as the stack: you could either use an array, or you could allocate a region of memory by using C's dynamic memory allocation functions. Like the queue, the retrieval function takes a value off the list and, if the value is not stored elsewhere, destroys it. Here are the general forms of **push( )** and **pop( )** that use an integer array:

```
int stack[MAX];
int tos=0;   /* top of stack */

push(i)  /* place element on the stack */
int i;
{
        if(tos>=MAX) {
                printf("stack full\n");
                return;
        }
        stack[tos]=i;
        tos++;
}


pop()    /* retrieve top element from the stack */
{
        tos--;
        if(tos<0) {
                printf("stack underflow\n");
                return 0;
        }
        return stack[tos];
}
```

Action	Contents of Stack
push(A)	A
push(B)	B A
push(C)	C B A
pop( ) retrieves C	B A
push(F)	F B A
pop( ) retrieves F	B A
pop( ) retrieves B	A
pop( ) retrieves A	*empty*

Figure 3-4. A stack in action

The variable **tos** is the index of the next open stack location. When implementing these functions, *always* remember to prevent overflow and underflow. In these routines, if **tos** equals 0, the stack is empty; if **tos** is greater than the last storage location, the stack is full. Figure 3-4 shows how a stack works.

An excellent example of stack usage is a four-function calculator. Most calculators today accept a standard form of expression called *infix notation*, which takes the general form *operand-operator-operand*. For example, to add 100 to 200, you would enter **100**, press +, enter **200**, and press the equal-sign key. However, some calculators use an expression evaluation called *postfix notation*, in which both operands are entered before the operator is entered. For example, to add 100 to 200 using postfix, you would first enter **100**, then enter **200**, and then press the + key. As operands are entered, they are placed on a stack; when an operator is entered, two operands are removed from the stack and the result is pushed back on the stack. The advantage of the postfix form is that complex expressions can be evaluated easily by the calculator without much code.

Before developing a full four-function calculator for postfix expressions, you need to modify the **push( )** and **pop( )** functions. C's dynamic memory allocation routines can provide memory for the stack. These functions, as used in the calculator example later, are shown here.

```
int *p; /* will point region of free memory */
int *tos; /* points to top of stack */
int *bos; /* points to bottom of stack */

push(i)  /* place element on the stack */
int i;
{

       if(p>bos) {
               printf("stack full\n");
               return;
       }
       *p=i;
       p++;
}


pop()    /* retrieve top element from the stack */
{
       p--;
       if(p<tos) {
               printf("stack underflow\n");
               return 0;
       }
       return *p;
}
```

Before you can use these functions, you must use **malloc( )**—sometimes called **alloc( )** by certain compilers—to allocate a region of free memory; you must also assign the address of the beginning of that region to **tos** and assign the address of the end to **bos**.

The entire calculator program is shown here:

```
int *p; /* will point region of free memory */
int *tos; /* points to top of stack */
int *bos; /* points to bottom of stack */

main()
{
       int a,b;
       char s[80];

       p=malloc(100);  /* get stack memory */
       tos=p;
       bos=p+(100/sizeof(int))-sizeof(int);

       printf("Four Function Calculator\n");

       do {
               printf(": ");
```

```
                gets(s);
                switch(*s) {
                        case '+':
                                a=pop();
                                b=pop();
                                printf("%d\n",a+b);
                                push(a+b);
                                break;
                        case '-':
                                a=pop();
                                b=pop();
                                printf("%d\n",b-a);
                                push(b-a);
                                break;
                        case '*':
                                a=pop();
                                b=pop();
                                printf("%d\n",b*a);
                                push(b*a);
                                break;
                        case '/':
                                a=pop();
                                b=pop();
                                if(a==0) {
                                    printf("divide by 0\n");
                                    break;
                                }
                                printf("%d\n",b/a);
                                push(b/a);
                                break;
                        default:
                                push(atoi(s));
                }
        } while(*s!='q');
}

push(i)   /* place element on the stack */
int i;
{

        if(p>bos) {
                printf("stack full\n");
                return;
        }
        *p=i;
        p++;
}

pop()     /* retrieve top element from the stack */
{
        p--;
        if(p<tos) {
                printf("stack underflow\n");
                return 0;
        }
        return *p;
}
```

Linked Lists

Queues and stacks share common traits. First, both have strict rules for referencing the data stored in them. Second, the retrieval operations are by nature *consumptive*; that is, accessing an item in a stack or queue requires its removal and, unless it is stored elsewhere, its destruction. Both stacks and queues also require, at least in concept, a contiguous region of memory in order to operate.

Unlike a stack or a queue, a *linked list* may access its storage in a random fashion, because each piece of information carries with it a *link* to the next data item in the chain. A linked list requires a complex data structure, whereas a stack or queue can operate on both simple and complex data items. (A link is sometimes called a *pointer* but, since C uses the word *pointer* to describe an altogether different element, this book uses the word *link*.) A linked-list retrieval operation does not remove and destroy an item from the list; a specific *deletion* operation must be added to do this.

Linked lists are used for two purposes. The first is to create arrays of unknown size in memory. If you know the amount of storage in advance, you can use a simple array; but if you do not know the actual size of a list, then you must use a linked list. The second use of a linked list is for the disk-file storage of databases. The linked list allows you to insert and delete items quickly and easily without rearranging the entire disk file. For these reasons, linked lists are used extensively in database-management software.

Linked lists can be either singly linked or doubly linked. A *singly linked list* contains a link to the next data item. A *doubly linked list* contains links to both the next element and the previous element in the list. The type that you use depends upon your application.

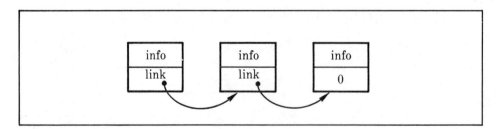

Figure 3-5. Singly linked list in memory

Singly Linked Lists

A singly linked list requires that each item of information contain a link to the next element in the list. Each data item generally consists of a structure that contains information fields and a link pointer. The concept of a singly linked list is shown in Figure 3-5.

There are two ways to build a singly linked list. The first simply adds each new item to the beginning or the end of the list. The other adds items into specific places in the list (for example, by ascending sorted order). The manner in which you build the list determines the way the *store function* will be coded, as shown in the simple case of creating a linked list by adding items on the end.

First you need to define a data structure to hold the information and the links. Because mailing lists are common, this example uses one. The data structure for each element in the mailing list is the same as in Chapter 2, except that a link has been added.

```
struct address {
        char name[40];
        char street[40];
        char city[20];
        char state[3];
        char zip[10];
        struct address *next;
} info;
```

The function **slstore( )** builds a singly linked list by placing each new element on the end. A pointer to a structure of type **address** must be passed to **slstore( )** as shown here:

```
slstore(i)
struct address *i;
{
        static struct address *last=0; /* start with null link */

        if(last==0) last=i; /* first item in list */
        else last->next=i;
        i->next=0;
        last=i;
}
```

Notice the use of the **static** variable **last**: because initialization of a **static** occurs once at the start of the program, a **static** can be used to start the list-building process. If your C compiler does not support either **static** or initializers, then you must make **last** into a global variable and explicitly initialize it in **main( )**.

Although you can sort the list created with **slstore( )** as a separate operation, it is easier to sort while building the list by inserting each new item in the proper sequence of the chain. Also, if the list is already sorted, then it is advantageous to keep it sorted by inserting new items in their proper location. To do this, the list is sequentially scanned until the proper location is found, the new address is inserted at that point, and the links are rearranged as necessary.

Three possible situations can occur when you insert an item in a singly linked list. First, the item can become the new first item; second, it can be

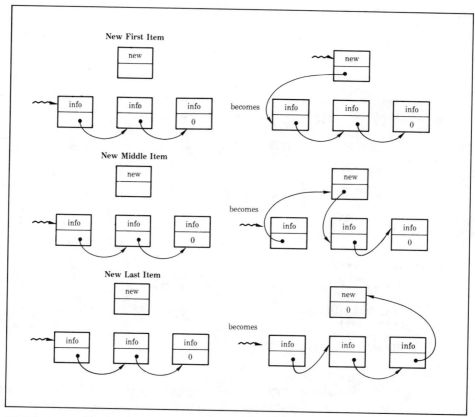

Figure 3-6.   Inserting an item into a singly linked list

inserted between two other items; third, it can become the last element. Figure 3-6 shows how the links are changed for each case.

If you change the first item in the list, you must update the entry point to the list elsewhere in your program. To avoid this you can use a *sentinel* as the first item. A sentinel is a special value that will always, under all circumstances, be first in the list. Using this method, you can keep the list's entry point from changing. However, this method has the disadvantage of using an extra storage location to hold the sentinel.

The function **sls—store( )**, shown here, inserts addresses into the mailing list in ascending order based on the **name** field. It returns a pointer to the first element in the list and also requires that the pointer to the start of the list be passed to it. When the first element is inserted, both **top** and **i** are the same.

```
struct address *sls_store(i,top)  /* store in sorted order */
struct address *i;       /* new element to store */
struct address *top;     /* start of list */
{
        static struct address *last=0; /* start with null link */
        struct address *old,*start;

        start=top;

        if(last==0) {  /* first element in list */
                i->next=0;
                last=i;
                return i;
        }

        old=0;
        while(top) {
                if(strcmp(top->name,i->name)<0) {
                        old=top;
                        top=top->next;
                }
                else {
                        if(old) {  /* goes in middle */
                                old->next=i;
                                i->next=top;
                                return start;
                        }
                        i->next=top; /* new first element */
                        return  i;
                }
        }
        last->next=i; /* put on end */
        i->next=0;
        last=i;
        return start;
}
```

In a linked list it is uncommon to find a specific function dedicated to the *retrieve process*, which returns item after item in list order. This code is usually so short that it is simply placed inside another routine, such as a search, delete, or display function. For example, this routine displays all of the names in a mailing list:

```
display(top)
struct address *top;
{
        while(top) {
                printf(top->name);
                top=top->next;
        }
}
```

Here, **top** is a pointer to the first structure in the list, and **top** must be initialized to 0 elsewhere in the program. Retrieving items from the list is as simple as following a chain. A search routine based on the **name** field could be written like this:

```
struct address *search(top,n)
struct address *top;
char *n;
{
        while(top) {
                if(!strcmp(n,top->name)) return top;
                top=top->next;
        }
        return 0;  /* no match */
}
```

Because **search( )** returns a pointer to the list item that matches the search name, **search( )** must be declared as returning a structure pointer of type **address**. If there is no match, a null is returned.

The process of deleting an item from a singly linked list is straightforward. As with insertion, there are three cases: deleting the first item, deleting a middle item, and deleting the last item. Figure 3-7 shows each case.

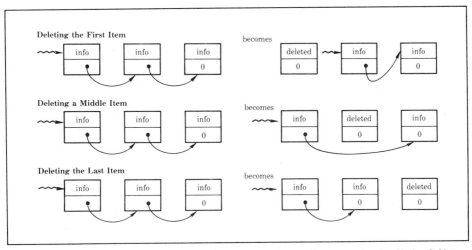

Figure 3-7. The three cases of deleting an item from a singly linked list

This function deletes a given item from a list of structures of type **address**:

```
struct address *sldelete(p,i,top)
struct address *p; /* previous item */
struct address *i; /* item to delete */
struct address *top;  /* start of list */
{
        if(p) p->next=i->next;
        else  top=i->next;

        return top;
}
```

Pointers to the deleted item, to the item before it in the chain, and to the start of the list must be sent to **sldelete( )**. If the first item is to be removed, then the previous pointer must be 0. The function must return a pointer to the start of the list because of the case in which the first item is deleted—the program must know where the new first element is located.

Singly linked lists have one major drawback that prevents their extensive use: the list cannot be followed in reverse order. For this reason, doubly linked lists are generally used.

Doubly Linked Lists

Doubly linked lists consist of data and links to both the next item and the preceding item. Figure 3-8 shows how these links are arranged. A list that has two links instead of just one has two major advantages. First, the list can be read in either direction. This not only simplifies sorting the list but also, in the case of a database, allows a user to scan the list in either direction. Second, because either a forward link or a backward link can read the entire list, if one link becomes invalid, the list can be reconstructed using the other link. This is meaningful only in the case of equipment failure.

Three primary operations can be performed on a doubly linked list: insert a new first element, insert a new middle element, and insert a new last element. These operations are shown in Figure 3-9.

Building a doubly linked list is similar to building a singly linked list, except that the structure must have room to maintain two links. Using the mailing list example again, you can modify the structure **address** as shown here to accommodate this:

```
struct address {
        char name[40];
        char street[40];
        char city[20];
        char state[3];
        char zip[10];
        struct address *next;
        struct address *prior;
} info;
```

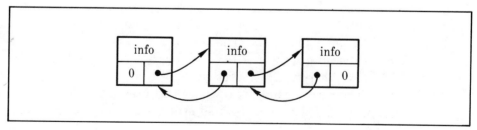

Figure 3-8. A doubly linked list

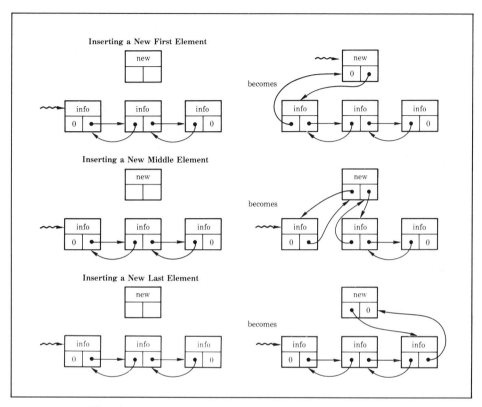

Figure 3-9. The three primary operations that can be performed on a doubly linked list

Using structure **address** as the basic data item, the function **dlstore( )** builds a doubly linked list:

```
dlstore(i)
struct address *i;
{
        static struct address *last=0; /* start with null link */

        if(last==0) last=i; /* first item in list */
        else last->next=i;
        i->next=0;
        i->prior=last;
        last=i;
}
```

This function places each new entry on the end of the list.

Like the singly linked list, a doubly linked list can have a function that stores each element in a specific location in the list as it is built, instead of always placing each new item on the end. The function **dls—store( )** creates a list that is sorted in ascending order.

```
struct address *dls_store(i,top)  /* store in sorted order */
struct address *i;  /* new element */
struct address *top;   /* start of list */
{
        static struct address *last=0; /* start with null link */
        struct address *old,*p;

        if(last==0) {  /* first element in list */
                i->next=0;
                i->prior=0;
                last=i;
                return i;
        }

        p=top; /* start at top of list */

        old=0;
        while(p) {
                if(strcmp(p->name,i->name)<0){  /* find
                        old=p;                  where it goes */
                        p=p->next;
                }
                else {
                        if(p->prior) {
                                p->prior->next=i;
                                i->next=p;
                                i->prior=p->prior;
                                p->prior=i;
                                return top;
                        }
                        i->next=p; /* new first element */
                        i->prior=0;
                        p->prior=i;
                        return i;
                }
        }
        old->next=i; /* put on end */
        i->next=0;
        i->prior=old;
        last=i;
        return start;
}
```

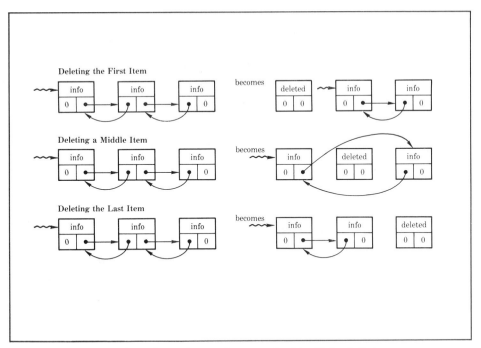

Figure 3-10. Deleting three items from a doubly linked list

Because an item may be inserted at the top of the list, this function must return a pointer to the first item so that other parts of the program will know where the list begins. As with the singly linked list, to retrieve a specific data item the program follows the links until the proper element is found.

There are three cases to consider when deleting an element from a doubly linked list: deleting the first item, deleting a middle item, and deleting the last item. Figure 3-10 shows how the links are rearranged.

The following function deletes an item of type **address** from a doubly linked list.

```
struct address *dldelete(i,top)
struct address *i; /* item to delete */
struct address *top;  /* first item in list */
{
        if(i->prior) i->prior->next = i->next;
        else { /* new first item */
                top=i->next;
                /* if deleting only element in list
                   skip */
                if(top) top->prior=0;
        }

        if(i->next) i->next->prior = i->prior;

        return top;
}
```

This function requires one less pointer to be passed to it than the singly linked list version required, because the data item being deleted already carries a link to the previous element and to the next element. Because the first element in the list could change, the pointer to the top element is passed back to the calling routine.

A Mailing List That Uses A Doubly Linked List

Here is a simple mailing-list program that shows the use of a doubly linked list. The entire list is kept in memory while in use; however, the program can save the mailing list in a disk file.

```
#include "stdio.h"

struct address {
        char name[30];
        char street[40];
        char city[20];
        char state[3];
        char zip[10]; /* hold US and Canadian zips */
        struct address *next;  /* pointer to next entry */
        struct address *prior;  /* pointer to previous record */
} list_entry;

struct address *start;  /* pointer to first entry in list */
struct address *last;  /* pointer to last entry */

main()
{
        char s[80], choice;
        struct address *info;
```

```
        start=0;  /* zero length list */
        for(;;) {
            switch(menu_select()) {
                case 1: enter();
                        break;
                case 2: delete();
                        break;
                case 3: list();
                        break;
                case 4: search(); /* find an street */
                        break;
                case 5: save();   /* save list to disk */
                        break;
            X   case 6: load();   /* read from disk */
                        break;
                case 7: exit(0);
            }
        }
    }
menu_select()
{
        char s[80];
        int c;

        printf("1. Enter a name\n");
        printf("2. Delete a name\n");
        printf("3. List the file\n");
        printf("4. Search\n");
        printf("5. Save the file\n");
        printf("6. Load the file\n");
        printf("7. Quit\n");
        do {
                printf("\nEnter your choice: ");
                gets(s);
                c=atoi(s);
        } while(c<0 || c>7);
        return c;
}
enter()
{
        struct address *info,*dls_store();

        for(;;) {
                info=malloc(sizeof(list_entry));
                if(info==0) {
                        printf("\nout of memory");
                        return;
                }

                inputs("enter name: ",info->name,30);
                if(!info->name[0]) break;  /* stop entering */
                inputs("enter street: ",info->street,40);
                inputs("enter city: ",info->city,20);
                inputs("enter state: ",info->state,3);
                inputs("enter zip: ",info->zip,10);

                start=dls_store(info,start);
```

```
        } /* entry loop */
}

inputs(prompt,s,count) /* this function will input a string up to
                the length in count.  This will prevent
                the string from overrunning its space and
                display a prompt message. */
char *prompt;
char *s;
int count;
{
        char p[255];

        do {
                printf(prompt);
                gets(p);
                if(strlen(p)>count) printf("\ntoo long\n");
        } while(strlen(p)>count);
        strcpy(s,p);
}

struct address *dls_store(i,top)  /* store in sorted order */
struct address *i;     /* new element */
struct address *top;  /* first element in list */
{
        static struct address *last=0; /* start with null link */
        struct address *old,*p;


        if(last==0) {  /* first element in list */
                i->next=0;
                i->prior=0;
                last=i;
                return i;
        }

        p=top; /* start at top of list */

        old=0;
        while(p) {
                if(strcmp(p->name,i->name)<0){
                        old=p;
                        p=p->next;
                }
                else {
                        if(p->prior) {
                                p->prior->next=i;
                                i->next=p;
                                p->prior=i;
                                return top;
                        }
                        i->next=p; /* new first element */
                        i->prior=0;
                        p->prior=i;
                        return  i;
                }
        }
        old->next=i; /* put on end */
```

```
        i->next=0;
        i->prior=old;
        last=i;
        return start;
}
delete()
{
        struct address *info, *find();
        char s[80];
        printf("enter name: ");
        gets(s);
        info=find(s);
        if(info) {
                if(start==info) {
                        start=info->next;
                        if(start) start->prior=0;
                        else last=0;
                }
                else {
                        info->prior->next=info->next;
                        if(info!=last)
                                info->next->prior=info->prior;
                        else
                                last=info->prior;
                }
                free(info);  /* return memory to system */
        }
}
struct address *find(name)
char *name;
{
        struct address *info;

        info=start;
        while(info) {
                if(!strcmp(name,info->name)) return info;
                info=info->next;  /* get next address */
        }
        printf("name not found\n");
        return 0;  /* not found */
}
list()
{
        register int t;
        struct address *info;

        info=start;
        while(info) {
                display(info);
                info=info->next;  /* get next address */
        }
        printf("\n\n");
}
display(info)
```

```
struct address *info;
{
                printf("%s\n",info->name);
                printf("%s\n",info->street);
                printf("%s\n",info->city);
                printf("%s\n",info->state);
                printf("%s\n",info->zip);
                printf("\n\n");
}
search()
{
        char name[40];
        struct address *info,*find();

        printf("enter name to find: ");
        gets(name);
        if(!(info=find(name))) printf("not found\n");
        else display(info);
}
save()
{
        register int t,size;
        struct address *info;
        char *p;

        FILE *fp;
        if((fp=fopen("mlist","w"))==0) {
                printf("cannot open file\n");
                exit(0);
        }
        printf("\nsaving file\n");
        size=sizeof(list_entry);
        info=start;
        while(info) {
                p=info;  /* convert to char pointer */
                for(t=0;t<size;++t)
                        putc(*p++,fp);  /* save byte at a time */
                info=info->next;  /* get next address */
        }
        putc(EOF,fp);  /* send an explicit EOF */
        fclose(fp);
}
load()
{
        register int t,size;
        struct address *info, *temp;
        char *p;
        FILE *fp;

        if((fp=fopen("mlist","r"))==0) {
                printf("cannot open file\n");
                exit(0);
        }

        printf("\nloading file\n");
```

```
    size=sizeof(list_entry);
    start=malloc(size);
    if(!start) {
            printf("out of memory\n");
            return;
    }
    info=start;
    p=info;   /* convert to char pointer */
    while((*p++=getc(fp))!=EOF) {
            for(t=0;t<size-1;++t)
                    *p++=getc(fp);   /* load byte at a time */
            info->next=malloc(size); /* get memory for next */
            if(!info->next) {

                    printf("out of memory\n");
                    return;
            }
            info->prior=temp;
            temp=info;
            info=info->next;
            p=info;
    }
    temp->next=0;   /* last entry */
    last=temp;

    start->prior=0;
    fclose(fp);
}
```

Binary Trees

The fourth data structure is the *binary tree*. Although there can be many types of trees, binary trees are special because, when they are sorted, they lend themselves to rapid searches, insertions, and deletions. Each item in a binary tree consists of information with a link to the left member and a link to the right member. Figure 3-11 shows a small tree.

The special terminology needed to discuss trees is a classic case of mixed metaphors. The *root* is the first item in the tree. Each data item is called a *node* (or sometimes a *leaf*) of the tree, and any piece of the tree is called a *subtree*. A node that has no subtrees attached to it is called a *terminal node*. The *height* of the tree equals the number of layers deep that its roots grow. Throughout this discussion, think of binary trees as appearing in memory as they do on paper, but remember that a tree is only a way to structure data in memory, which is linear in form.

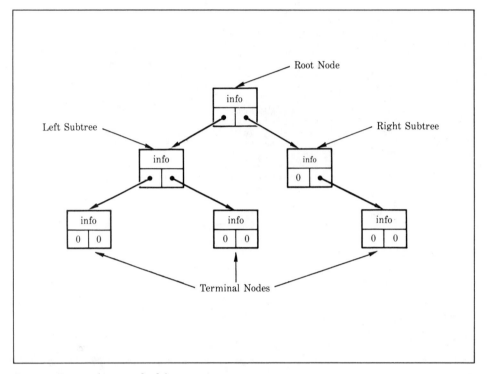

Figure 3-11.   A sample binary tree

The binary tree is a special form of linked list. Items can be inserted, deleted, and accessed in any order. In addition, the retrieval operation is nondestructive. Although they are easy to visualize, trees present difficult programming problems that this section will only introduce.

Most functions that use trees are recursive, because the tree itself is a recursive data structure; that is, each subtree is a tree. Therefore, the routines that are developed here are recursive as well. Nonrecursive versions of these functions do exist, but their code is much more difficult to understand.

The order of a tree depends on how the tree is going to be referenced. The process of accessing each node in a tree is called a *tree traversal* and is shown by this tree diagram:

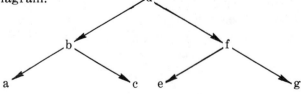

There are three ways to traverse a tree: *inorder, preorder,* and *postorder.* Using inorder, you visit the left subtree, visit the root, and then visit the right subtree. In preorder, you visit the root, then the left subtree, and then the right subtree. With postorder, you visit the left subtree, then the right subtree, and then the root. The order of access for the tree just shown, using each method, is as follows:

inorder	a b c d e f g
preorder	d b a c f e g
postorder	a c b e g f d

Although a tree need not be sorted, most uses require it. What constitutes a sorted tree depends on how you will be traversing the tree. The examples in the rest of this chapter access the tree inorder. In a sorted binary tree, the subtree on the left contains nodes that are less than or equal to the root, while those on the right are greater than the root. The following function, **stree( )**, builds a sorted binary tree:

```
struct tree {
        char info;
        struct tree *left;
        struct tree *right;
} t;
struct tree *stree(root,r,info)
struct tree *root;
struct tree *r;
char info;
{
        if(r==0) {    /* first node in subtree */
                r=malloc(sizeof(t));
                if(r==0) {
                        printf("out of memory\n");
                        exit(0);
                }
                r->left=0;
                r->right=0;
                r->info=info;
                if(root) {
                        if(info<root->info) root->left=r;
                        else root->right=r;
                }
                else {  /* first node in tree */
                        r->right=0;
                        r->left=0;
```

```
                }
                return r;
        }

        if(info<=r->info) stree(r,r->left,info);
        if(info>r->info) stree(r,r->right,info);
}
```

This algorithm simply follows the links through the tree, going left or right based on the **info** field. To use this function, you need a global variable that holds the root of the tree. This global must be set initially to 0, and a pointer to the root will be assigned on the first call to **stree( )**. Subsequent calls will not need to reassign the root. If you assume the name of this global is **rt**, then to call the **stree( )** function, you would use

```
/* call stree() */
if(!rt) rt=stree(rt,rt,info);
else stree(rt,rt,info);
```

In this way both the first and the subsequent elements can be inserted correctly.

The function **stree( )** is a recursive algorithm, as are most tree routines. The same routine would be several times longer if straight iterative methods were used. The function must be called with a pointer to the root, the left or right node, and information. Although a single character is used here as the information, for the sake of simplicity, you could substitute any simple or complex data type you like.

To traverse the tree built by using **stree( )** inorder and to print the **info** field of each node, you could use the function **inorder( )**.

```
inorder(root)
struct tree *root;
{
        if(!root) return;

        inorder(root->left);
        printf("%c ",root->info);
        inorder(root->right);
}
```

This recursive function returns when it encounters a terminal node (a null pointer). The functions to traverse the tree in preorder and in postorder are shown here.

```
preorder(root)
struct tree *root;
{
        if(!root) return;

        printf("%c ",root->info);
        preorder(root->left);
        preorder(root->right);
}

postorder(root)
struct tree *root;
{
        if(!root) return;

        postorder(root->left);
        postorder(root->right);
        printf("%c ",root->info);
}
```

You can write a short program that builds a sorted binary tree and prints the tree sideways on the screen of your computer. You need only a small modification to the **inorder( )** function. The new function, which is called **print_tree( )**, prints a tree in inorder fashion.

```
print_tree(r,l)
struct tree *r;
int l;
{
        int i;

        if(r==0) return;

        print_tree(r->left,l+1);
        for(i=0;i<l;++i) printf("   ");
        printf("%c\n",r->info);
        print_tree(r->right,l+1);
}
```

When testing the entire tree-printing program given here, try entering various trees to see how each one is built:

```
struct tree {
        char info;
        struct tree *left;
        struct tree *right;
}
```

```
struct tree *root;  /* first node in tree */

main()  /* treeprint program */

{
        char s[80];
        struct tree *stree();

        root=0;  /* initialize the root */

        do {
                printf("enter a letter: ");
                gets(s);
                if(!root) root=stree(root,root,*s)
                else stree(root,root,*s);
        } while(*s);

        print_tree(root,0);

}

struct tree *stree(root,r,info)
struct tree *root;
struct tree *r;
char info;
{

        if(r==0) {
                r=malloc(sizeof(t));
                if(r==0) {
                        printf("out of memory\n");
                        exit(0);
                }
                r->left=0;
                r->right=0;
                r->info=info;
                if(info<root->info) root->left=r;
                else root->right=r;
                return r;
        }

        if(info<r->info) stree(r,r->left,info);
        else
        if(info>r->info) stree(r,r->right,info);
}

print_tree(r,l)
struct tree *r;
int l;
{
        int i;

        if(r==0) return;

        print_tree(r->left,l+1);
        for(i=0;i<l;++i) printf("    ");
        printf("%c\n",r->info);
        print_tree(r->right,l+1);
}
```

The Treeprint program actually sorts the information you give it. This is a variation on the Insertion sort that was given in Chapter 2. For the average case, its performance can be quite good, but the Quicksort is still a better general-purpose sorting method because it uses less memory and has lower processing overhead. However, if you have to build a tree from scratch, or if you have to maintain an already sorted tree, you should always insert new entries in sorted order using the **stree( )** function.

If you have run the Treeprint program, you probably noticed that some trees are *balanced* — each subtree is the same or nearly the same height as any other — and that other trees are far out of balance. If you entered abcd as a tree, it would be built like this:

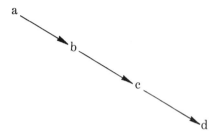

There would be no left subtrees. This is called a *degenerate tree* because it has degenerated into a linear list. In general, if the data you use to build a binary tree is fairly random, the tree produced will approximate a balanced tree. However, if the information used is already sorted, a degenerate tree will result. (It is possible to readjust the tree with each insertion to keep the tree in balance. The algorithms to do this are fairly complex; if you are interested in them, refer to books on advanced programming algorithms.)

Search functions are easy to implement for binary trees. This function returns a pointer to the node in the tree that matches the key; otherwise, it returns null:

```
struct tree *search_tree(root,key)
struct tree *root;
char key;
{
        if(!root) return root;   /* empty tree */
        while(root->info!=key) {
                if(key<root->info) root=root->left;
                else root=root->right;
                if(root==0) break;
        }
        return root;
}
```

Unfortunately, deleting a node from a tree is not as simple as searching the tree. The deleted node may be either the root, a left node, or a right node. The node may also have from zero to two subtrees attached to it. Rearranging the pointers lends itself to a recursive algorithm, as shown here:

```
struct tree *dtree(root,key)
struct tree *root;
char key;
{
        struct tree *p,*p2;

        if(root->info==key) { /* delete root */
                /* this means an empty tree */
                if(root->left==root->right){
                        free(root);
                        return 0;
                }
                /* or if one subtree is null */
                else if(root->left==0) {
                        p=root->right;
                        free(root);
                        return p;
                }
                else if(root->right==0) {
                        p=root->left;
                        free(root);
                        return p;
                }
                /* or both tree present */
                else {
                        p2=root->right;
                        p=root->right;
                        while(p->left) p=p->left;
                        p->left=root->left;
                        free(root);
                        return p2;
                }
        }
        if(root->info<key) root->right=dtree(root->right,key);
        else root->left=dtree(root->left,key);
        return root;
}
```

Remember to update the pointer to the root in the rest of your program, because the node deleted could be the root of the tree.

When used with database-management programs, binary trees offer power, flexibility, and efficiency because the information for these databases must reside on disk and because access times are important. Because a balanced binary tree has, as a worst case, $\log_2 n$ comparisons in searching, it performs far better than a linked list, which must rely on a sequential search.

Dynamic Allocation
C H A P T E R 4

Designing a computer program can be somewhat like designing a building, with numerous functional and aesthetic considerations that contribute to the final outcome. For example, some programs are functionally rigid like a house, with a certain number of bedrooms, a kitchen, two baths, and so on. Other programs must be open-ended like convention centers, with movable walls and modular flooring that enable them to be adapted to various needs. This chapter presents the storage mechanisms that allow you to write flexible programs.

There are two ways in which a C program can store information in the main memory of the computer. The first uses global and local variables — including arrays and structures — that are defined by the C language. For global variables, storage is fixed throughout the run time of your program. For local variables, storage is allocated from the stack space of the computer. Although global and local variables are efficiently implemented in C, they require that the programmer know in advance the amount of storage needed for every situation.

The second and more efficient way that information can be stored is by using C's dynamic allocation functions **malloc( )** and **free( )**. Storage for information is allocated from the free memory area that lies between your program's permanent storage area and the stack (which is used by C to store local variables). Figure 4-1 shows how a C program would appear in memory. The stack grows downward as it is used so that the amount of memory needed is determined by the way that your program is designed. For example, a program with many recursive functions makes much greater demands on stack memory than a program that does not have recursive functions, because local variables are stored on the stack. The memory required for the program and the global data is fixed during the execution of the program. Memory to satisfy a **malloc( )** request is taken from the free memory area, starting above the global variables and growing toward the stack. Under fairly extreme cases it is possible for the stack to run into allocated memory.

If you are not thoroughly familiar with **malloc( )** and **free( )**, here is a short review.

A Review of malloc( ) And free( )

The functions **malloc( )** and **free( )** form C's dynamic allocation system and are part of the standard C library. They work together, using the free memory region that lies between the end of your program and the top of the stack to establish and maintain a list of available storage. Each time a **malloc( )** memory request is made, a portion of the remaining free memory is allocated. Each time a **free( )** memory release call is made, memory is returned to the system. The most common way to implement **malloc( )** and **free( )** is to organize the free memory into a linked list.

The **malloc( )** function is C's general-purpose memory allocation function. Its general calling form is

```
char *malloc( ), *p;
int number_of_bytes;
p=malloc(number_of_bytes);
```

After a successful call, **p** holds a pointer to the first byte of the region of memory. If there is not enough available memory to satisfy the **malloc( )** request, an allocation failure occurs and **malloc( )** returns a zero value. The **malloc( )** function always needs to know the number of bytes to allocate—even if the information you need to store is some other data type, such as an integer or a structure. You can use **sizeof** to determine the exact number of bytes needed for each type of data. This helps to make your programs portable to a variety of systems. Even though a character pointer is returned, it can be assigned to a pointer of the proper type to satisfy any programming need. Before you use the pointer returned by **malloc( )** always make sure that your allocation request succeeded by testing the return value against 0. Do not use a pointer of value 0—it will probably crash your system.

The **free( )** function is the opposite of **malloc( )**: it returns previously allocated memory to the system. That part of memory may be reused by a

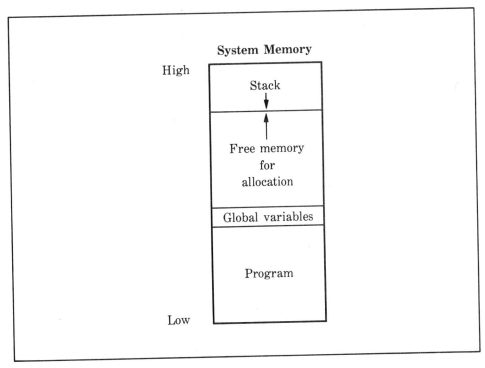

Figure 4-1. A C program's use of memory

subsequent call to **malloc( )**. The general form of **free( )** is

```
char *p;
/* assume that p holds a valid pointer address */
free(p);
```

Remember that you must *never* call **free( )** with an invalid argument, because the free list would be destroyed.

The following short program allocates enough storage for 40 integers, prints their values, and releases the memory back to the system. The **sizeof** is used here to ensure portability to other computer types.

```
main()   /* short allocation example */
{
        int *p, t;

        p=malloc(40*sizeof(int));
        if(p==0) {
                printf("out of memory\n");
                exit(0);
        }

        for(t=0;t<40;++t) *(p+t)=t;

        for(t=0;t<40;++t) printf("%d ",*(p+t));

        free(p);

}
```

Sparse-Array Processing

One major use of dynamic allocation is for processing a *sparse array*. In a sparse array, not all of the elements are actually present. You may want to create an array like this when the array dimensions you need are larger than will fit in the memory of your machine and when not all array locations will be used. Multidimensional arrays can consume vast quantities of memory because their storage needs are exponentially related to their size. For example, a character array of 10×10 only needs 100 bytes of memory, and one that is a 100×100 needs 10,000, but a 1000×1000 character array needs 1,000,000 bytes of memory.

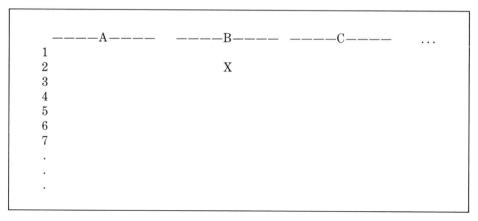

Figure 4-2.   The organization of a sample spreadsheet

A spreadsheet program is a good example of a sparse array. Even though the matrix is large—say, 999 by 999—only a portion of it may actually be in use at any one time. Spreadsheets use the matrix to hold formulas, values, and strings associated with each location. In a sparse array, storage for each element is allocated from the pool of free memory as needed. Although only a small portion of the elements is actually in use, the array may appear to be very large—larger than would normally fit in the memory of the computer.

In this section, three distinct techniques will be used to create a sparse array: a linked list, a binary tree, and a pointer array. All of these examples assume that the spreadsheet matrix is organized as shown in Figure 4-2, with **X** located in cell B2.

The Linked-List Approach
To Sparse Arrays

When you implement a sparse array that uses a linked list, a structure is used to hold the information for each element in the array, including its logical position in the array and links to both the previous element and the next element. Each structure is placed in the list with the elements in a sorted order that is based on the array index. The array is accessed by following the links.

For example, you could use the following structure to create a sparse array for use in a spreadsheet program:

```
struct cell {
        char cell_name[9];   /* cell name i.e A1, B34 */
        char  formula[128]; /* info i.e. 10/B2 */
        struct cell *next;   /* pointer to next entry */
        struct cell *prior;   /* pointer to previous record */
} list_entry;
```

The field **cell—name** holds a string that contains the cell name (such as A1, B34, or Z19). The **formula** string holds the formula that is assigned to each spreadsheet location.

Here are a few sample functions that would be used by the spreadsheet, which uses a linked-list sparse array. Remember that there are many ways to implement a spreadsheet program, and the data structure and routines used in these samples should serve only as examples of sparse-array techniques. The following global variables will be used to point to the beginning and the end of the linked array list:

```
struct cell *start;   /* first element in list */
struct cell *last;    /* last element in list */
```

When you enter a formula into a cell on a typical spreadsheet, you are in effect creating a new element in the sparse array. If the spreadsheet uses a linked list, that new cell is inserted by using **dls—store( )**, which was developed in Chapter 3. (Thanks to C's ability to create and stand-alone, reusable functions, you can use it here with no fundamental changes.) Remember, the list is sorted by cell name—A12 precedes A13, and so on.

```
struct cell *dls_store(i)   /* store in sorted order */
struct cell *i;              /* based on cell name   */
{
        static struct cell *last=0; /* start with null link */
        struct cell *old,*p;

        if(last==0) { /* first element in list */
                i->next=0;
                i->prior=0;
                last=i;
                return i;
        }

        p=start; /* start at top of list */

        old=0;
        while(p) {
```

```
        if(strcmp(p->cell_name,i->cell_name)<0){
                old=p;
                p=p->next;
        }
        else {
                if(p->prior) {
                        p->prior->next=i;
                        i->next=p;
                        i->prior=p->prior;
                        p->prior=i;
                        return start;
                }
                i->next=p; /* new first element */
                i->prior=0;
                p->prior=i;
                return i;
        }
}
old->next=i; /* put on end */
i->next=0;
i->prior=old;
last=i;
return start;
}
```

To remove a cell from the spreadsheet, you must remove the proper structure from the list and allow the memory it occupies to be returned to the
system by using **free( )**. The **delete( )** function shown here removes a cell
from the list when given the cell name:

```
delete(cell_name)
char *cell_name;
{
        struct cell *info, *find();

        info=find(cell_name);
        if(info) {
                if(start==info) {
                        start=info->next;
                        if(start) start->prior=0;
                        else last=0;
                }
                else {
                        info->prior->next=info->next;
                        if(info!=last)
                            info->next->prior=info->prior;
                        else
                                last=info->prior;
                }
                free(info);  /* return memory to system */
        }
}
```

The function **find( )** locates any specific cell. It is an important function because many spreadsheet formulas have references to other cells that must be found so that their values can be updated. The **find( )** requires the use of a linear search to locate each item, and, as shown in Chapter 2, the average number of comparisons in a linear search is $n/2$, where n is the number of elements in the list. In addition, a significant loss of performance occurs because each cell may contain references to other cells in the formula, and each of these cells must be found. Here is an example of **find( )**.

```
struct cell *find(cell)
char *cell;
{
        struct cell *info;

        info=start;
        while(info) {
                if(!strcmp(cell,info->cell)) return info;
                info=info->next;  /* get next cell */
        }
        printf("cell not found\n");
        return 0;  /* not found */
}
```

The linked-list approach to creating, maintaining, and processing a sparse array has one major drawback—it must use a linear search to access each cell in the list. Without using additional information, which requires more memory overhead, you cannot perform a binary search to locate a cell. Even the store routine uses a linear search to find the proper location to insert a new cell into the list. You can solve these problems by using a binary tree to support the sparse array.

The Binary Tree Approach
To Sparse Arrays

In essence, the binary tree is simply a modified doubly linked list. Its major advantage over a list is that it can be searched quickly, which means that insertions and lookups can be very fast. In applications in which you want a linked-list structure but need fast search times, the binary tree is the solution.

To use a binary tree to support the spreadsheet example, you must change the structure **cell** as shown:

```
struct cell {
        char cell_name[9];  /* cell name i.e A1, B34 */
        char  formula[128]; /* info i.e. 10/B2 */
        struct cell *left;  /* pointer to left subtree */
        struct cell *right;  /* pointer to right subtree */
} list_entry;
```

You can modify the **stree( )** function from Chapter 3 so that it builds a tree based on the cell name. Notice that it assumes that the parameter **new** is a pointer to a new entry in the tree.

```
struct cell *stree(root,r,new)
struct cell *root;
struct cell *r;
struct cell *new;
{
        if(r==0) {      /* first node in subtree */
                new->left=0;
                new->right=0;
                if(root) {
                        if(strcmp(new->cell_name,root->cell_name)<0)
                                root->left=new;
                        else root->right=new;
                }
                else {  /* first node in tree */
                        new->right=0;
                        new->left=0;
                }
                return new;  /* root of tree */
        }

        if(strcmp(new->cell_name,r->cell_name)<=0)
                stree(r,r->left,new);
        if(strcmp(new->cell_name,r->cell_name)>0)
                stree(r,r->right,new);

        return root;
}
```

The **stree( )** must be called with a pointer to the root node for the first two parameters, and a pointer to the new cell for the third. It returns a pointer to the root.

To delete a cell from the spreadsheet, you should modify **dtree( )** as shown
here to accept the name of the cell as a key:

```
struct cell *dtree(root,key)
struct cell *root;
char *key;
{
        struct tree *p,*p2;

        if(!strcmp(root->cell_name==key)) { /* delete root */
                /* this means an empty tree */
                if(root->left==root->right){
                        free(root);
                        return 0;
                }
                /* or if one subtree is null */
                else if(root->left==0) {
                        p=root->right;
                        free(root);
                        return p;
                }
                else if(root->right==0) {
                        p=root->left;
                        free(root);
                        return p;
                }
                /* or both tree present */
                else {
                        p2=root->right;
                        p=root->right;
                        while(p->left) p=p->left;
                        p->left=root->left;
                        free(root);
                        return p2;
                }
        }
        if(strcmp(root->cell_name,key)<0)
                root->right=dtree(root->right,key);
        else root->left=dtree(root->left,key);
        return root;
}
```

Finally, you can use a modified **search( )** function to locate any cell in the
spreadsheet quickly, given its cell name.

```
struct cell *search_tree(root,key)
struct cell *root;
char *key;
{
        if(!root) return root;  /* empty tree */
        while(strcmp(root->cell,key)) {
                if(strcmp(root->cell_name,key)<0)
                        root=root->left;
                else root=root->right;
                if(root==0) break;
        }
        return root;
}
```

The most important aspect of using a binary tree instead of a linked list is that it results in much faster search times. (Remember, a sequential search requires $n/2$ comparisons on average, where n is the number of elements in the list, whereas a binary search requires only $\log_2 n$ comparisons.) However, in some situations there is an even better alternative.

The Pointer-Array Approach
To Sparse Arrays

Suppose that your spreadsheet's dimensions were 26 by 100 (A1 through Z100), or a total of 2600 elements. In theory, then, the following array of structures could be used to hold the spreadsheet entries:

```
struct cell {
        char cell_name[9];
        char  formula[128];
} list_entry[2600];          /* 2,600 cells */
```

However, 2600 cells multiplied by 128 (the formula field alone) requires 332,800 bytes of memory for a fairly small spreadsheet. This approach is obviously not practical. Instead, you could create an array of pointers to structures. This method would require significantly less permanent storage than would the creation of an entire array and would offer performance far superior to that of the linked-list and binary tree methods. The declaration would look as shown here.

```
struct cell {
        char cell_name[9];
        char  formula[128];
} list_entry;

struct cell *sheet[10000];        /* array of 10,000 pointers */
```

You can use this smaller array to hold pointers to the information that is actually entered by the user of the spreadsheet. As each entry is made, a pointer to the cell information is stored in the proper location in the array. Figure 4-3 shows how this process might appear in memory, with the pointer array providing support for the sparse array.

Before you can use the pointer array, you must initialize each element to null, which indicates that there is no entry in that location. Use the following function:

```
init_sheet()
{

        register int t;

        for(t=0;t<10000;++t) sheet[t]=0;

}
```

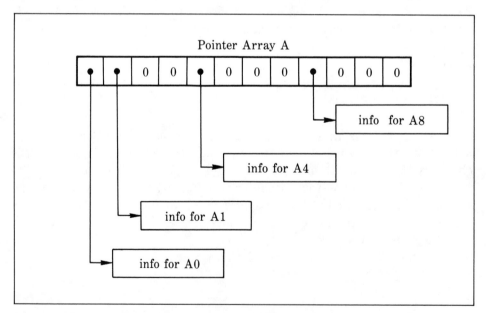

Figure 4-3. A pointer array as support for a sparse array

When the user enters a formula for a cell in the spreadsheet, the cell location, defined by its name, produces an index for the pointer array **sheet**. The index is derived from the cell name by converting the name into a number, as shown here in the **store( )**. When **store( )** computes the index, it assumes that all cell names begin with a capital letter followed by an integer — for example, B34 or C19.

```
store(i)
struct cell *i;
{
        int loc;
        char *p;

        loc=(*(i->cell_name)-'A');
        p=&(i->cell_name[1]);
        loc+=atoi(p)*26;    /* 26 columns * num rows */

        if(loc>=10000) {
                printf("cell out of bounds\n");
                return;
        }

        sheet[loc]=i; /* place pointer in the array */

}
```

Because each cell name is unique, each index is also unique; because the ASCII collating sequence is used, the pointer to each entry is stored into the proper array element. If you compare this procedure to the linked-list version, you will see how much shorter and simpler it is.

The **delete( )** function also becomes short. When called with the index of the cell, **delete( )** zeros the pointer to the element and returns the memory to the system:

```
delete(cell_index)
int cell_index;
{
        free(sheet[cell_index]);  /* return memory to system */
        sheet[cell_index]=0;
}
```

Again, when you compare this to the linked-list version you can see that this code is much faster and simpler.

With this procedure, locating a cell given its name is trivial because the name itself directly produces the array index; therefore, the **find( )** function changes, as shown here.

```
struct cell *find(cell_name)
char *cell_name;
{
        int loc;
        char *p;

        loc=(*(i->cell_name)-'A');
        p=&(i->cell_name[1]);
        loc+=atoi(p)*26;      /* 26 columns * num rows */

        if(loc>=10000 || !sheet[loc]) {   /* no entry in that cell */
                printf("cell not found\n");
                return -1;  /* not found */
        }
        else return sheet[loc];
}
```

Remember that the pointer array itself uses some memory for every location—whether or not that location is used. This can be a serious limitation for certain applications.

Comparing the Linked-List, Binary Tree, And Pointer-Array Approaches

When deciding whether to use a linked-list, binary tree, or pointer-array approach to implement a sparse array, you should consider memory efficiency and speed.

When the array is very sparse, the most memory-efficient approaches are the linked-list and binary tree implementations, because only those array elements that are actually in use have memory allocated to them. The links themselves require little additional memory and generally have a negligible effect. The pointer-array design requires that each array element have a pointer allocated to it, whether or not its entry exists. Not only must the entire pointer array fit in memory, but there must be enough memory left over for the application to use. This could be a serious problem for certain applications, whereas it may not be a problem for others. You can usually decide this by calculating the approximate amount of free memory and determining whether it is sufficient for your program.

When the array is fairly full, however, the situation changes. In this case, the pointer-array approach makes better use of memory because both the linked-list and binary tree implementations need two pointers, whereas the pointer array only needs one pointer. For example, if a 1000-element array was full and pointers were two bytes long, then both the binary tree and the linked list would use 4000 bytes for pointers—but the pointer array would only need 2000, a savings of 2000 bytes.

The fastest-executing approach is the pointer array. As in the spreadsheet example, there is often an easy method that indexes the pointer array and links it with the sparse-array elements. This method makes accessing the elements of the sparse array nearly as fast as accessing the elements of a normal array. The linked-list version is very slow by comparison, because it must use a linear search to locate each element. Even if extra information were added to the linked list to allow faster accessing of elements, it would still be slower than the pointer array's direct accessing capability. The binary tree certainly speeds up the search time, but when compared with the pointer array's direct indexing capability, it still seems sluggish.

Whenever possible, a pointer-array implementation is the best because it is much faster. If memory usage is critical, however, you have no choice but to use the linked-list or binary tree approach.

Reusable Buffers

When memory is scarce, dynamic allocation can be used in place of normal variables. As an example, imagine two processes, **A( )** and **B( )**, inside one program. Assume that **A( )** requires 60% of free memory and that **B( )** needs 55%. If both **A( )** and **B( )** derive their storage needs from local variables, then **A( )** cannot call **B( )** and **B( )** cannot call **A( )**—more than 100% of memory would be required. If **A( )** never calls **B( )**, then there is no trouble, but the problem arises when you want **A( )** to be able to call **B( )**. The only way this can occur is to use dynamic storage for both and to free that memory before calling the other. In other words, if both **A( )** and **B( )** require more than one-half of available free memory while executing, and if **A( )** must call **B( )**, then they *must* use dynamic allocation. In this way, both **A( )** and **B( )** will have the memory they need when they need it.

Imagine that there are 100,000 bytes of free memory left in a computer that is running a program with the following two functions in it:

```
A( )
{
          char a[60000];
          .
          .
          .
          B( );
          .
          .
          .
}

B( )

{
          char b[55000];
          .
          .
          .
}
```

Here, **A( )** and **B( )** both have local variables requiring more than one-half of free memory each. There is no way that **B( )** can execute, because there is not enough memory available to allocate the 55,000 bytes needed for the local array **b**.

A situation like this is sometimes insurmountable, but in certain instances you can work around it. If **A( )** did not need to preserve the contents of the array **a** while **B( )** was executing, then both **A( )** and **B( )** could share the memory. You can do this by allocating **A( )** and **B( )**'s array dynamically. Then **A( )** could free memory prior to the call to **B( )** and reallocate it later if necessary. The code would look like this:

```
A( )
{
 char *s;
          s=malloc(60000);
          .
          .
          free(s); /* free memory for B( ) */
```

```
                    B( );
                    s=malloc(60000);
                    .
                    .
                    .
                    free(s); /* all done */
    }

    B( )
    {

                    char *b;
                    b=malloc(55000);
                    .
                    .
                    free(55000);
    }
```

Only the pointer **s** is in existence while **B( )** is executing.

Although you will only need to do something like this occasionally, the technique is useful to master because it is often the only way around this type of problem.

The "Unknown Memory" Dilemma

If you are a professional programmer, you probably have faced the "unknown memory" dilemma. This occurs when you write a program that has some of its performance based on the amount of memory inside the computer that is running it. Examples of programs that can have this problem are spreadsheets, in-RAM mailing-list programs, and sorts. For example, an in-memory sort that can handle 10,000 addresses in a 256K machine may be able to sort only 5,000 addresses in a 128K computer. If this program were going to be used on computers of unknown memory sizes, it would be difficult to determine the optimum fixed-size array to hold the sort information for two reasons: either the program would not work on machines whose memory capabilities were too small to fit the array, or you would have to create an array for the worst case and not allow users who had more memory to use it. The solution is to use allocated memory to hold the information.

A text editor is a program that illustrates the memory dilemma and solution well. Most text editors do not limit the number of characters that they can hold, but rather use all of the computer's available memory to store the text that the user types in. For example, as each line is entered, storage is allocated and a linked list is maintained. When a line is deleted, memory is returned to the system. One way to implement such a text editor would be to use the following structure for each line:

```
struct line {
        char text[81];  /* this holds the actual text */
        int num;        /* line number of line */
        struct line *next;  /* pointer to next entry */
        struct line *prior;  /* pointer to previous record */
} list_entry;

struct line *start;  /* pointer to first entry in list */
struct line *last;  /* pointer to last entry */
```

For simplicity, this structure always allocates enough memory for each line to be 80 characters long with a null terminator. In reality, only the exact length of the line would be allocated and additional overhead would be incurred if the line were altered. The element **num** holds the line number for each line of text. This allows you to use the standard sorted, doubly linked list-storage function **dls_store( )** to create and maintain the text file as a linked list.

The program for a simple text editor, shown next, supports the insertion of lines at any point based on the line number specified and supports the deletion of any line. You may also list the text and store it in a disk file.

The general means of operation for the editor is based on a sorted, linked list of lines of text. The sort key is the line number of each line. Not only can you insert text easily at any point by specifying the starting line number, but you can also delete text easily. The only function that may not be intuitive is **patchup( )**. It renumbers the element **num** for each line of text when insertions or deletions make this necessary.

In this example the amount of text that the editor can hold is directly based on the amount of free memory in the user's system. Thus, the editor automatically uses additional memory without having to be reprogrammed. This is the most important reason for using dynamic allocation when you are faced with the memory dilemma.

The program as shown is limited, but the basic text-editing support is solid. You may enhance it to create a customized text editor.

```
#include "stdio.h"

struct line {
        char text[81];
        int num;             /* line number of line */
        struct line *next;   /* pointer to next entry */
        struct line *prior;  /* pointer to previous record */
} list_entry;

struct line *start;  /* pointer to first entry in list */
struct line *last;   /* pointer to last entry */

main(argc,argv)
int argc;
char *argv[];
{
        char s[80], choice,fname[80];
        struct line *info;
        int linenum=1;

        start=0; last=0; /* zero length list */
        if(argc==2) load(argv[1]); /* read file on command line */

        do {
            choice=menu_select();
            switch(choice) {
                case 1: printf("Enter line number: ");
                        gets(s);
                        linenum=atoi(s);
                        enter(linenum);
                        break;
                case 2: delete();
                        break;
                case 3: list();
                        break;
                case 4: printf("enter filename: ");
                        gets(fname);
                        save(fname);   /* write to disk */
                        break;
                case 5: printf("enter filename: ");
                        gets(fname);
                        load(fname);   /* read from disk */
                        break;
                case 6: exit(0);
            }
        } while(1);

}
menu_select()
{
        char s[80];
        int c;
        printf("1. Enter text\n");
        printf("2. Delete a line\n");
        printf("3. List the file\n");
        printf("4. Save the file\n");
        printf("5. Load the file\n");
        printf("6. Quit\n");
        do {
```

```
                        printf("\nEnter your choice: ");
                        gets(s);
                        c=atoi(s);
                } while(c<0 || c>6);
                return c;
}

enter(linenum)   /* enter text at linenum */
int linenum;
{
        struct line *info,*dls_store(),*find();
        char t[81];

        do {
                info=malloc(sizeof(list_entry));
                if(info==0) {
                        printf("\nout of memory");
                        return;
                }

                printf("%d : ",linenum);
                gets(info->text);
                info->num=linenum;
                if(find(linenum)) patchup(linenum,1); /* fix up
                                                 old line nums */
                if(*info->text) start=dls_store(info);
                else break;
                linenum++;

        } while(1); /* entry loop */
        return linenum;
}

patchup(n,incr) /* when text is inserted into middle of file
            line numbers below it must be increased by one
            and deleted lines need others decrement by one */
int n;
int incr;
{
        struct line *i,*find();

        i=find(n);

        while(i) {
                i->num=i->num+incr;
                i=i->next;
        }
}
struct line *dls_store(i)   /* store in sorted order */
struct line *i;             /* based on line number  */
{
        struct line *old,*p;

        if(last==0) {  /* first element in list */
                i->next=0;
                i->prior=0;
                last=i;
                return i;
```

```
        }

        p=start; /* start at top of list */

        old=0;
        while(p) {
                if(p->num < i->num){
                        old=p;
                        p=p->next;
                }
                else {
                        if(p->prior) {
                                p->prior->next=i;
                                i->next=p;
                                p->prior=i;
                                return start;
                        }
                        i->next=p; /* new first element */
                        i->prior=0;
                        p->prior=i;
                        return  i;
                }
        }
        old->next=i; /* put on end */
        i->next=0;
        i->prior=old;
        last=i;
        return start;
}

delete()
{
        struct line *info, *find();
        char s[80];
        int linenum;

        printf("enter line number ");
        gets(s);
        linenum=atoi(s);
        info=find(linenum);
        if(info) {
                if(start==info) {
                        start=info->next;
                        if(start) start->prior=0;
                        else last=0;
                }
                else {
                        info->prior->next=info->next;
                        if(info!=last)
                            info->next->prior=info->prior;
                        else
                                last=info->prior;
                }
                free(info);  /* return memory to system */
                patchup(linenum+1,-1); /* decrement line numbers */
        }
}

struct line *find(linenum)
int linenum;
```

```
        {
                struct line *info;

                info=start;
                while(info) {
                        if(linenum==info->num) return info;
                        info=info->next;  /* get next address */
                }
                return 0;  /* not found */
        }

list()
{
                struct line *info;

                info=start;

                while(info) {
                        printf("%d: %s\n",info->num,info->text);
                        info=info->next;  /* get next address */
                }
                printf("\n\n");
        }


save(fname)
char *fname;
{
                register int t,size;
                struct line *info;
                char *p;

                FILE *fp;

                if((fp=fopen(fname,"w"))==0) {
                        printf("cannot open file\n");
                        exit(0);
                }
                printf("\nsaving file\n");

                size=sizeof(list_entry);
                info=start;
                while(info) {
                        p=info->text; /* convert to char pointer */
                        while(*p) putc(*p++,fp);  /* save byte at a time */
                        putc('\r',fp);  /* terminator */
                        putc('\n',fp);  /* terminator */
                        info=info->next; /* get next line */
                }
                putc(EOF,fp); /* send an explicit EOF */
                fclose(fp);

        }
```

```
load(fname)
char *fname;
{
        register int t,size,lnct;
        struct Line *info, *temp;
        char *p;
        FILE *fp;

        if((fp=fopen(fname,"r"))==0) {
                printf("cannot open file\n");
                return;
        }
        while(start)  {    /* free any previous edit */
                p=start;
                start=start->next;
                free(p);
        }

        printf("\nloading file\n");

        size=sizeof(List_entry);
        start=malloc(size);
        if(!start) {
                printf("out of memory\n");
                return;
        }
        info=start;
        p=info->text;  /* convert to char pointer */
        lnct=1;
        while((*p=getc(fp))!=EOF) {
                while(*p++!='\r') *p=getc(fp);
                getc(fp);  /* read the linefeed */
                p--;   /* insert null terminator */
                *p='\0';
                info->num=lnct++;
                info->next=malloc(size); /* get memory for next */
                if(!info->next) {

                        printf("out of memory\n");
                        return;

                }
                info->prior=temp;
                temp=info;
                info=info->next;
                p=info->text;
        }
        temp->next=0;  /* last entry */
        last=temp;
        free(info);
        start->prior=0;
        fclose(fp);
}
```

Fragmentation

Because **malloc( )** and **free( )** are not technically part of the C language, but rather part of the C library, their exact implementation varies from compiler to compiler. The developers of some compilers have put a great deal of effort into these dynamic allocation routines, while others have done a minimally acceptable job. Under all implementations of **malloc( )** and **free( )**, *fragmentation* of memory can occur, which can gradually cause allocation requests to fail even though enough free memory actually exists. In some C compilers this can occur quickly.

Fragmentation occurs when pieces of free memory lie between blocks of allocated memory. Although the free memory is usually large enough to fill allocation requests, a problem develops when the individual pieces are too small to fill a request, even though there would be sufficient memory if they were added together. Figure 4-4 shows how a sequence of calls to **malloc( )** and **free( )** can produce this situation.

You can avoid some types of fragmentation if the dynamic allocation functions combine adjacent regions of memory. For example, if memory regions A, B, C, and D (shown here) were allocated and then regions B and C were freed, B and C theoretically could be combined because they are next to each other. However, if B and D were freed, there is no way to combine them, because C lies between them and is still in use.

A	B	C	D

At first you might wonder why, since B and D were free while C was allocated, you couldn't just move C's contents to D and combine B and C. The problem is that your program would have no way of knowing that what was in C had been moved to D.

One way to avoid excess fragmentation is always to allocate equal amounts of memory: all de-allocated regions can be re-allocated to subsequent requests and all of free memory can be used. If this is not possible, try to limit the different sizes to just a few. This can sometimes be accomplished by compacting several small requests into a large request. Of course, you should never allocate a lot more memory than you need just to avoid fragmentation,

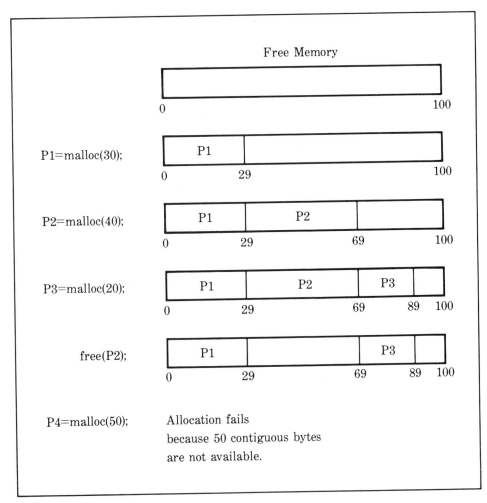

Figure 4-4. Fragmentation in dynamic allocation

because the amount of wasted memory will far outweigh any gains you receive from avoiding fragmentation. Here is another solution: upon receipt of a null pointer from **malloc( )**, write out all of the information stored in dynamic memory regions to a temporary disk file, use **free( )** to free all memory, and then read the information back in. This generally works, since most dynamic allocation routines combine adjacent free memory regions.

Dynamic Allocation
And Artificial Intelligence

Although C is not a mainstream artificial intelligence development language, you can use it to experiment. A common trait of many artificial intelligence programs is the existence of a list of information items that can be extended by the program automatically as it "learns" new things. In a language like LISP, considered to be the premier artificial intelligence language, the language itself performs list maintenance. In C you have to program such procedures by using linked lists and dynamic allocation. Although the example here is very simple, the concepts can be applied to more sophisticated "intelligent" programs.

One interesting area of AI covers programs that seem to behave like people. The famous Eliza program, for example, appeared to be a psychiatrist. It would be wonderful to have a computer program that would carry on a conversation about anything—a great program to run when you're tired of programming and feeling lonely! The example used here is an extremely simple version of such a program. It uses words and their definitions to carry on a conversation with the user. One common device of many AI programs is to link an informational item with its meaning; in this case, the program links words with their meanings. The following structure holds each word, its definition, its part of speech, and its connotation:

```
struct vocabulary {
        char type[3];  /* noun, verb, article */
        char word[30]; /* string containing the word */
        char connotate[3]; /* good, bad, neutral */
        char def[128]; /* meaning */
        struct vocabulary *next;  /* pointer to next entry */
        struct vocabulary *prior;  /* pointer to previous record */
} smart;

struct vocabulary *start;  /* pointer to first entry in list */
struct vocabulary *last;  /* pointer to last entry */
```

In the program that follows, you enter a word, its definition, what type of word it is, and its connotation of good, bad, or indifferent. To hold these dictionary entries, a linked list is then built by using dynamic allocation. The **dls—store( )** creates and maintains a sorted, doubly linked list of the dictionary. After you have entered a few words into the dictionary, you can begin to have a conversation with the computer. For example, you type in a sentence,

such as **It is a nice day.** The program scans the sentence looking for a word
that it knows. If it finds one, it makes a comment about the word based on its
meaning. If the program encounters a word that it does not know, it prompts
you to enter that word with its definition. You type **quit** to exit conversation
mode.

The function **talk( )** is the part of the program that carries on the conversation. A support function called **dissect( )** looks at your input sentence a
word at a time. The global variable **token** holds your input sentence because
dissect( ) returns only one word at a time, so the variable that holds your
sentence must be stable between calls and shared between two functions.
Here are the functions **talk( )** and **dissect( ):**

```
talk()
{

        char w[128],*s, *dissect();
        struct vocabulary *word;

        printf("Conversation mode (Quit to exit)\n");
        do {
                s=token;
                printf(": ");
                gets(token);
                do {
                        s=dissect(s,w);   /* find first noun */
                        if(!*w) break;
                        word=find(w);
                        if(*word->type=='n') {
                                switch(*word->connotate) {
                                    case 'g':
                                        printf("I like ");
                                        break;
                                    case 'b':
                                        printf("I don't like ");
                                        break;
                                    case 'n':
                                        break;
                                }
                                printf(word->def);
                                printf("%\n");
                        }
                } while(strcmp(w,"quit"));
        } while (strcmp(w,"quit"));
}

char *dissect(s,w)
char *s,*w;
{

        while(*s==' ') ++s;

        while(isalpha(*s)) *w++=*s++;
        *w=0;  return s;
}
```

The entire program is shown here:

```
#include "stdio.h"
#include "ctype.h"

struct vocabulary {
        char word[30];
        char def[128];
        char connotate;
        char type;
        struct vocabulary *next;  /* pointer to next entry */
        struct vocabulary *prior;  /* pointer to previous record */
} smart;

struct vocabulary *start;  /* pointer to first entry in list */
struct vocabulary *last;  /* pointer to last entry */

char token[256];

main()
{
        char s[80], choice;
        struct vocabulary *info;

        start=0;  /* zero length list */
        last=0;
        for(;;) {
            choice=menu_select();
            switch(choice) {
                case 1: enter();
                        break;
                case 2: delete();
                        break;
                case 3: list();
                        break;
                case 4: search(); /* find a word */
                        break;
                case 5: save();  /* save list to disk */
                        break;
                case 6: load();  /* read from disk */
                        break;
                case 7: talk();
                        break;
                case 8: exit(0);
            }
        }
}
menu_select()
{
        char s[80];
        int c;

        printf("1. Enter a word\n");
        printf("2. Delete a word\n");
        printf("3. List the file\n");
        printf("4. Search\n");
        printf("5. Save the file\n");
        printf("6. Load the file\n");
        printf("7. Converse\n");
```

```
        printf("8. Quit\n");
        do {
                printf("\nEnter your choice: ");
                gets(s);
                c=atoi(s);
        } while(c<0 || c>8);
        return c;
}

enter()
{
        struct vocabulary *info,*dls_store();
        char t[10];

        for(;;) {
                info=malloc(sizeof(smart));
                if(info==0) {
                        printf("\nout of memory");
                        return;
                }

                inputs("enter word: ",info->word,30);
                if(!info->word[0]) break;  /* stop entering */
                inputs("enter type (n,v,a): ",t,3);
                info->type=*t;
                inputs("enter conotation (g,b,n): ",t,3);
                info->connotate=*t;
                inputs("enter definition: \n",info->def,128);
                start=dls_store(info);
        }  /* entry loop */
}

inputs(prompt,s,count) /* this function will input a string up to
                the lenght in count.  This will prevent
                the string from overrunning its space and
                display a prompt message. */
char *prompt;
char *s;
int count;
{
        char p[255];

        do {
                printf(prompt);
                gets(p);
                if(strlen(p)>count) printf("\ntoo long\n");
        } while(strlen(p)>count);
        strcpy(s,p);
}

struct vocabulary *dls_store(i)  /* store in sorted order */
struct vocabulary *i;
{
        struct vocabulary *old,*p;
        if(last==0) {  /* first element in list */
                i->next=0;
                i->prior=0;
                last=i;
                return i;
        }
```

```
                    p=start; /* start at top of list */

                    old=0;
                    while(p) {
                            if(strcmp(p->word,i->word)<0){
                                    old=p;
                                    p=p->next;
                            }
                            else {
                                    if(p->prior) {
                                            p->prior->next=i;
                                            i->next=p;
                                            p->prior=i;
                                            return start;
                                    }
                                    i->next=p; /* new first element */
                                    i->prior=0;
                                    p->prior=i;
                                    return  i;
                            }
                    }
                    old->next=i; /* put on end */
                    i->next=0;
                    i->prior=old;
                    last=i;
                    return start;
            }

    delete()
    {
            struct vocabulary *info, *find();
            char s[80];

            printf("enter word: ");
            gets(s);
            info=find(s);
            if(info) {
                    if(start==info) {
                            start=info->next;
                            if(start) start->prior=0;
                            else last=0;
                    }
                    else {
                            info->prior->next=info->next;
                            if(info!=last)
                                info->next->prior=info->prior;
                            else

                                    last=info->prior;
                    }
                    free(info);  /* return memory to system */
            }
    }

struct vocabulary *find(word)
char *word;
{
        struct vocabulary *info;
        char s[80];
```

```
        info=start;
        while(info) {
                if(!strcmp(word,info->word)) return info;
                info=info->next;  /* get next vocabulary */
        }
        printf("%s unknown, please enter.\n",word);
        enter();
        return 0;  /* not found */
}

list()
{
        register int t;
        struct vocabulary *info;

        info=start;
        while(info) {
                display(info);
                info=info->next;  /* get next address */
        }
        printf("\n\n");
}

display(info)
struct vocabulary *info;
{
                printf("word: %s\n",info->word);
                printf("type: %c\n",info->type);
                printf("connotation:%c\n",info->connotate);
                printf("definition: %s\n",info->def);
                printf("\n\n");
}

search()
{
        char word[40];
        struct vocabulary *info,*find();

        printf("enter word to find: ");
        gets(word);
        if(!(info=find(word))) printf("not found\n");
        else display(info);
}

save()
{
        register int t,size;
        struct vocabulary *info;
        char *p;

        FILE *fp;
        if((fp=fopen("smart.dic","w"))==0) {
                printf("cannot open file\n");
                exit(0);
        }
        printf("\nsaving file\n");
        size=sizeof(smart);
        info=start;
        while(info) {
```

```
                    p=info;   /* convert to char pointer */
                    for(t=0;t<size;++t)
                            putc(*p++,fp);   /* save byte at a time */
                    info=info->next;   /* get next address */
            }
            putc(EOF,fp);   /* send an explicit EOF */
            fclose(fp);
    }

    load()
    {
            register int t,size;
            struct vocabulary *info;
            char *p;
            FILE *fp;

            if((fp=fopen("smart.dic","r"))==0) {
                    printf("cannot open file\n");
                    return;
            }

            while(start) {   /* free any previous lists */
                    p=start;
                    start=start->next;
                    free(start);
            }
            last=0;   /* reset the last pointer as well */
            printf("\nloading file\n");

            size=sizeof(smart);
            start=malloc(size);
            if(!start) {
                    printf("out of memory\n");
                    return;
            }
            info=start;
            p=info;   /* convert to char pointer */
            while((*p++=getc(fp))!=EOF) {
                    for(t=0;t<size-1;++t)
                            *p++=getc(fp);   /* load byte at a time */
                    dls_store(info);
                    info=malloc(size); /* get memory for next */
                    if(!info) {
                            printf("out of memory\n");
                            return;
                    }
                    p=info;
            }
            start->prior=0;
            fclose(fp);
    }


    talk()
    {
```

```
            char w[128],*s, *dissect();
            struct vocabulary *word;

            printf("Conversation mode (Quit to exit)\n");
            for(;;) {
                    s=token;
                    printf(": ");
                    gets(token);
                    if(!strcmp(token,"quit")) return;
                    for(;;) {
                            s=dissect(s,w);   /* find first noun */
                            if(!*w) break;
                            word=find(w);
                            if(word->type=='n') {
                                    switch(word->connotate) {
                                        case 'g':
                                            printf("I like ");
                                            break;
                                        case 'b':
                                            printf("I don't like ");
                                            break;
                                        case 'n':
                                            break;
                                    }
                                    printf(word->def);
                                    printf("%\n");
                            }
                            else
                                    printf("%s ",word->def);

                    }
            }
    }

char *disect(s,w)
char *s,*w;
{
        while(*s==' ') ++s;

        while(isalpha(*s)) *w++=*s++;
        *w=0;  return s;
}
```

This program is fun and easy to write. You should be able to make it appear quite a bit smarter. One way to do so would be to have the program scan your sentence for verbs and then have it substitute an alternate verb in its comment. You could also make it ask questions now and then.

Interfacing to Assembly Language Routines And the Operating System

CHAPTER 5

As powerful as C is, there are times when you must either write a routine using assembler or use a system call in the operating system. The way to do both of these varies somewhat among compilers, but the general procedures described in this chapter apply to most C compilers.

Each processor has a different assembly language, and each operating system has a different interface structure. In addition, various C compilers have different "calling conventions" that define how information is passed to and from a function. This chapter is based on the IBM PC-DOS operating system, the Aztec C compiler, and the 8086 assembly language. Even if you have different equipment, you can use the following discussions as a guide.

Assembly Language Interfacing

There are three reasons to use a routine written in assembler:

- To enhance speed and efficiency

- To perform a machine-specific function that is unavailable in C

- To use a general-purpose, packaged assembly language routine.

Although C compilers can produce extremely fast, compact object code, no compiler consistently creates code that is as fast or compact as that written by a competent programmer using assembler. The small difference usually does not matter and does not warrant the extra time needed to write in assembler. However, there are special cases in which a specific function must be coded in assembler so that it will run quickly. This is true of a function if it will be used frequently and will greatly affect the ultimate execution speed of a program. A good example is a floating-point math package. Also, special hardware devices sometimes need exact timing, and you must code in assembler to meet such a strict timing requirement.

Many computers, including 8086-based machines, have useful capabilities that cannot be directly executed by using standard C operators. For example, you cannot change data segments with any C instruction, and you also cannot issue a software interrupt or control the contents of specific registers by using C.

In professional programming environments, subroutine libraries are often purchased for such commonly needed capabilities as graphics and floating-point math. Sometimes you must take these in object format because the developer will not sell the source code. Occasionally, you can simply link these routines with code compiled by your compiler; at other times, you must write an interface module to correct any differences in the interface used by your compiler and the routines you purchased.

There are primarily two ways to integrate assembly code modules into your C programs. The first is to code the routine separately, assemble it with a stand-alone assembler, and link it with the rest of your program. The second is to use the in-line assembly code capabilities of many C compilers.

It is not within the scope of this book to teach assembly language programming. This chapter assumes that you are already familiar with your computer's assembly language; the examples presented serve only as guides.

Calling Conventions of a C Compiler

A *calling convention* is the method by which a C compiler passes parameter values to functions and returns values from the functions. The usual solutions use either the internal registers of the CPU or the system stack to pass information between independent functions. Generally, C compilers use the stack to pass arguments to functions. If the argument is one of the seven built-in data types (**char**, **short int**, **int**, **long int**, **unsigned int**, **float**, or **double**), then the data's actual value is placed on the stack. If the argument is an array or a structure, its address is placed on the stack. When a C function begins execution, it gets the argument values from the stack. When a C function terminates, it passes a return value back to the calling routine. This return value is usually placed in a register, although theoretically it could be passed on the stack.

An interesting aspect to the calling convention concerns exactly which registers must be preserved by a function as it executes and which ones can be used freely. Often a compiler requires that certain processor registers be left intact. Assembly language modules must preserve the contents of the registers either by not using them or by pushing their contents onto the stack before use. Any other registers are generally free for your use.

When you write an assembly language module that must interface to code compiled by your C compiler, you must follow all of the conventions that are defined and used by your compiler. Only by doing so can you have assembly language routines correctly interface to your C code.

Creating an Assembly Code Function

Your C compiler manual should have a section in it that describes how parameters are passed to functions, which registers must be saved and re-·stored, and how the return value of the function is passed back to the calling routine. Before you try to write an assembly language function for your C compiler, you must have access to this information. After you know the calling conventions of your compiler, you simply write the assembly language function and link it with your program by using the linker.

For example, assume that for some reason it is necessary to code the following function in assembler:

```
sample(a,b)
int a,b;
{
        a=a+b;
        return a;
}
```

Since this function will be called from a C program, your first step is to determine how the arguments will be passed into the function (you will find the information in the C compiler manual). In almost all C compilers, the arguments are passed on the stack. In the Aztec compiler, the arguments are pushed on the stack in the reverse of the order in which they appeared in the call. For example, if **sample( )** is called with

```
sample(10,20);
```

the value 20 is pushed first and the value 10 is pushed second. Remember that if the calling arguments are simple variables, their values are passed onto the stack. For a string or an array, a pointer (an address) is passed onto the stack.

Your second step is to know what registers must be preserved by your assembly language function. If you use the Aztec compiler on the IBM PC, the segment registers—as well as BP, BX, SI, and DI—must be preserved. You can do this by pushing them onto the stack and popping them off of the stack just before the return.

Your last step is to know how to return a value from a function. The Aztec compiler requires that the value be placed in AX and the Z flag set according to this value.

The function **sample( )** in assembly language is

```
codeseg segment para public 'code'
dataseg segment para public 'data'
dataseg ends
```

```
          assume cs:codeseg,ds:dataseg,es:dataseg,ss:dataseg
          public sample_
sample_ proc     near
          push bx
          push bp
          push si
          push di
          mov bx,sp    ; put current tos into bx
          mov ax,word ptr10[bx]  ; this is parameter a
          add ax,word ptr 12[bx] ; this adds in parameter b
          mov word ptr 10[bx],ax  ; result in a as well as ax
          pop di
          pop si
          pop bp
          pop bx
          ret
sample_ endp
codeseg ends
dataseg segment para public 'data'
dataseg ends
          end
```

Notice that all appropriate registers are saved with **push** and **pop** instructions and that the arguments are accessed on the stack. If you are unfamiliar with 8086 assembly code, here is an example. The code

```
mov bx,sp    ; put current tos into bx
mov ax,word ptr 10[bx]  ; this is parameter a
```

puts the address of the top of the stack into register **bx** and then moves the tenth word down on the stack, which is parameter **a**, into the **ax** register. Parameters are the tenth and twelfth words down because the return address and the **push** instructions to save the registers use ten bytes; therefore, the parameters are found starting at byte 10 down from the stack.

You can use the short program

```
main()
{
        printf("%d ",sample(10,20));

        printf("%d\n",sample(30,40));

}
```

as long as **sample( )** is included in the link line. If you do this and execute the program, the numbers **30** and **70** will be printed on the screen.

Remember, however, that every compiler is different and every processor is different. You must study your user manuals.

Using #asm and #endasm

Many C compilers have added an extension to the C preprocessor directives that allow in-line assembly code to be made a part of otherwise standard C functions. (The UNIX compiler does not support this extension.) There are two advantages: first, the programmer is not required to write all of the interface code needed to make an assembly module act as a C function; second, all of the code is in one place, making support easier.

The two preprocessor directives that make this possible are **#asm** and **#endasm**: **#asm** begins a block of assembly code and **#endasm** ends the block. All code inside a **#asm** block must be the correct assembly code for your computer. The C compiler simply passes this code, untouched, through to the assembler phase of the compiler.

For example, the function **init‒port1( )** sends 255 and then 0 to port 26 using 8086 assembly code.

```
init_port1()
{
        printf("Initializing Port\n");
#asm
        out 26,255
        out 26,0
#endasm
}
```

The C compiler automatically produces the appropriate code to save registers and to return any needed values from the function.

If you wish to use this method to code **sample( )**, you could use the C compiler to fill in all of the support. You would only need to provide the body of the function, as shown next.

```
sample(a,b)
int a,b;
{
#asm
        mov ax,word ptr 8[bp]
        add ax,word ptr 10[bp]
        mov word ptr 8[bp],ax
        mov ax,word ptr 8[bp]
#endasm
}
```

The C compiler provides all customary support for setting up and returning from a function call. All you have to do is provide the body of the function and follow the calling conventions to access the arguments.

Whatever method you use, you are creating machine dependencies that will make your program difficult to port to a new machine. For demanding situations that require assembly code, however, it is usually worth the effort.

When to Code in Assembler

Most programmers only code in assembler when absolutely necessary, because such coding is difficult. As a general rule, don't use it—it creates too many problems. However, there are two cases in which coding in assembler makes sense. One case is when there is absolutely no other way to do it—for example, when you need to interface directly to a hardware device that cannot be handled using C.

Another case for assembler is when a C program's execution time must be reduced. In this case, you should carefully choose the functions you code in assembler. If you code the wrong ones, you will see little increase in speed. If you choose the right one, your program will fly! To determine which functions need recoding, you must review the operational flow of your program. The functions used inside loops are generally the ones you should program in assembler because they are executed repeatedly. Using assembler to code a function that is used only once or twice may not offer significant speed improvements, but using assembler to code a function that is used several times may. For example, consider the following **main( )** function.

```
main()
{
        register int t;

        init();

        for(t=0;t<1000;++t) {
                phase1();
                phase2();
                if(t==10) phase3();
        }

        byebye();

}
```

Recoding **init( )** and **byebye( )** may not measurably affect the speed of this program, because they are executed only once. Both **phase1( )** and **phase2( )** are executed 1000 times, and recoding them is more likely to have a major effect on the run time of this program. The **phase3( )** is only executed once, even though it is inside the loop, so recoding this function into assembler would probably not be worth the effort.

With careful thought you can improve the speed of your program by recoding only a few functions in assembler.

Operating-System
Interfacing

Because many C programs fall into the category of systems programs, it is often necessary to interface directly to the operating system, bypassing C's normal interface, to perform I/O operations. There also may be special operating system functions, which cannot be accessed by your C compiler, that you want to make use of. For these reasons, using the low-level resources of the operating system is a common occurrence in C programming.

Several operating systems in wide use today on microcomputers include

- PC-DOS or MS-DOS
- CP/M
- UNIX
- Apple DOS.

All operating systems have a set of functions that can be used, for example, to open disk files, read and write characters to and from the console, and allocate memory for the program to run in. The way these functions are accessed varies from system to system, but they tend to use the general concept of a *jump table*. In an operating system like CP/M, system calls are executed by using a CALL instruction to a specific region of memory, with the desired function code in a register. In PC-DOS, a software interrupt is used. In either case, the jump table routes the proper function to your program. Figure 5-1 shows how an operating system and its jump table might appear in memory.

It is not possible to discuss all operating systems here. This chapter focuses only on PC-DOS because it is most widely used. However, the general techniques applied here are applicable to most operating systems.

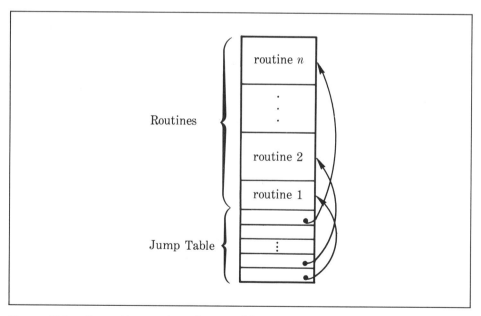

Figure 5-1. Operating-system jump table

Accessing System Resources
In PC-DOS

In PC-DOS the operating-system functions are accessed through software interrupts. Each interrupt has its own category of functions that it accesses, and the value of the AH register determines these functions. If additional information is needed, it is passed via the AL, BX, CX and DX registers. The PC-DOS operating system is divided into the BIOS (Basic I/O System) and DOS (Disk Operating System). The BIOS provides the lowest-level routines that DOS uses to provide the higher-level functions. However, the two overlap. Fortunately for our purposes, they are accessed in basically the same way. A partial list of these interrupts is shown here:

Interrupt	Function
10h	Video I/O
13h	Disk I/O
16h	Keyboard I/O
17h	Printer I/O
21h	DOS calls

For a complete list and explanation, refer to the IBM *Technical Reference* manual.

Each of these interrupts is associated with a number of options that can be accessed, depending upon the value of the AH register when called. Table 5-1 shows a partial list of the options available for each of these interrupts.

Table 5-1. Options Available for Some Interrupts

AH register	Function
	BIOS Video I/O Functions — Interrupt 10h
0	Set video mode
	if AL=0: 40×25 BW
	1: 40×25 color
	2: 80×25 BW
	3: 80×25 color
	4: 320×200 color graphics
	5: 320×200 BW graphics
	6: 340×200 BW graphics

Table 5-1. Options Available for Some Interrupts (*continued*)

AH register	Function
1	Set cursor lines
	CH bits 0-4 contain start of line
	bits 5-7 are 0
	CL bits 0-4 contain end of line
	bits 5-7 are 0
2	Set cursor position
	DH: row
	DL: column
	BH: video page number
3	Read cursor position
	BH: video page number
	Returns:
	DH: row
	DL: column
	CX: mode
4	Read light-pen position
	Returns:
	if AH=0 pen not triggered
	if AH=1 pen triggered
	DH: row
	DL: column
	CH: raster line (0-199)
	BX: pixel column (0-319 or 0-639)
5	Set active video page
	AL may be 0-7
6	Scroll page up
	AL: number of lines to scroll, 0 for all
	CH: row of upper-left corner of scroll
	CL: column of upper-left corner of scroll
	DH: row of lower-right corner of scroll
	DL: column of lower-right corner of scroll
	BH: attribute to be used on blank line
7	Scroll page down
	same as 6
8	Read character at cursor position
	BH: video page
	Returns
	AL: character read
	AH: attribute

Table 5-1. Options Available for Some Interrupts (*continued*)

AH register	Function

9	Write character and attribute at cursor position
	    BH: video page
	    BL: attribute
	    CX: number of characters to write
	    AL: character

10	Write character at current cursor position
	    BH: video page
	    CX: number of characters to write
	    AL: character

11	Set color palette
	    BH: palette number
	    BL: color

12	Write a dot
	    DX: row number
	    CX: column number
	    AL: color

13	Read a dot
	    DX: row number
	    CX: column number
	Returns
	    AL: dot read

14	Write character to screen and advance cursor
	    AL: character
	    BL: foreground color
	    BH: video page

15	Read video state
	Returns
	    AL: current mode
	    AH: number of columns on screen
	    BH: current active video page

BIOS Disk I/O Functions—Interrupt 13h	
0	Reset disk system
1	Read disk status Returns AL: status (see IBM *Technical Reference* manual)

Table 5-1.   Options Available for Some Interrupts (*continued*)

AH register	Function
2	Read sectors into memory DL: drive number DH: head number CH: track number CL: sector number AL: number of sectors to read ES:BX: address of buffer Returns AL: number of sectors read AH: 0 on success, otherwise status
3	Write sectors to disk (same as Read above)
4	Verify (same as Read above)
5	Format a track DL: drive number DH: head number CH: track number ES:BX: sector information

BIOS Keyboard I/O Functions—Interrupt 16h

0	Read scan code Returns AH: scan code AL: character code
1	Get status of buffer Returns ZF: 1 then buffer empty 0 then characters waiting with next char in AX as described above
2	Get status of keyboard (see IBM *Technical Reference* manual)

BIOS Printer I/O Functions—Interrupt 17h

0	Print a character AL: character DX: printer number Returns AH: status

Table 5-1. Options Available for Some Interrupts (*continued*)

AH register	Function

1	Initialize printer
	    DX: printer number
	Returns
	    AH: status

2	Read status
	    DX: printer number
	Returns
	    AH: status

High-Level DOS Functions Calls—Interrupt 21h (Partial List)

AH register	Function
1	Read character from the keyboard Returns AL: character
2	Display a character on the screen DL: character
3	Read a character from async port Returns AL: character
4	Write a character to async port DL: character
5	Print a character to list device DL: character
7	Read character from keyboard but do not display it Returns AL: character
B	Check keyboard status Returns AL: 0FFH if key struck; 0 otherwise
D	Reset disk
E	Set default drive DL: Drive number (0=A, 1=B,...)

11
(4E under 2.X)
	Search for file name
	    DX: Address of FCB
	Returns
	    AL: 0 if found, FFh if not with name in disk
	        transfer address

12 (4F under 2.X)	Find next occurrence of file name same as 11

Table 5-1. Options Available for Some Interrupts (*continued*)

AH register	Function
1A	Set disk transfer address DX: disk transfer address

2A	Get system date
	Returns
	    CX: year (1980-2099)
	    DH: month (1-12)
	    DL: day (1-31)

2B	Set system date
	    CX: year (1980-2099)
	    DH: month (1-12)
	    DL: day (1-31)

2C	Get system time
	Returns
	    CH: hours (0-23)
	    CL: minutes (0-59)
	    DH: seconds (0-59)
	    DL: hundredths of seconds (0-99)

2D	Set system time
	    CH: hours (0-23)
	    CL: minutes (0-59)
	    DH: seconds (0-59)
	    DL: hundredths of seconds (0-99)

There are basically two ways to access the functions found in Table 5-1. The first is through the use of built-in system call functions, often called **dos( )** or **bdos( )**, which are supplied with most compilers. The second is through the use of assembly language interfacing.

Using **dos( )** to Access System Functions

Most compilers for the PC-DOS operating system provide a function in the standard library called **dos( )** or **bdos( )**. It is used to perform an interrupt 21h call to access one of the higher-level functions in the operating system. This function is machine dependent; read your compiler's user manual to determine the exact calling sequence. This discussion uses Aztec C's **dos( )** function. It takes the general form

dos(*functionnumber*, **BX, CX, DX, DI, SI)**

where *functionnumber*, **BX, CX, DX, DI**, and **SI** are integers that hold the values to be placed into these registers at the time of the call. The return value of **dos( )** is the value of the AL register.

An earlier chapter made use of a system call to see if a key had been struck on the keyboard. Here is a function called **kbhit( )** that returns TRUE if a key has been pressed, and FALSE if not, by using interrupt 21h number Bh as shown here. Remember that hex numbers are preceded by **0x**, which tells the compiler that a hex number follows.

```
kbhit()   /* PCDOS specific */
{
        return(dos(0xB,0,0,0,0,0));
}
```

Notice that zeros were used for all but the first argument because no other information was needed. Generally, when a specific register is not used in the call, it may have any value assigned to it as a placeholder.

You will often need to interface to the operating system to use a function that is not in the standard C library. One function that seems to be left out of many C compilers for the IBM PC is a function for printing characters to the printer! However, you can develop a function to do this by using the DOS function call number 5, which prints one character to the printer. This short function prints a standard C null-terminated string to the standard printing device:

```
prints(s)
char *s;
{
        while(*s) dos(0x5,0,0,*s++,0,0);
}
```

Another function commonly missing from the standard library is one that would read or write characters to the async serial port. You use this port if you want to write a modem program, for example. Here are two functions you could use to access the serial port using DOS function 3 to read a character and function 4 to write a character:

```
put_async(ch)
char ch;
{
        dos(0x4,0,0,ch,0,0);
}

get_async()
{
        return(dos(0x3,0,0,0,0,0));
}
```

A more complex example using the interrupt 21h system calls is the function **dir—list( )** shown here. It lists all files in the current working directory. It works for 2.X and greater PC-DOS systems.

```
dir_list()   /* list entire directory for PCDOS 2.X */
{
        char pp[44];
        char done;

        dos(0x1a, 0,0,pp,0,0);

        dos(0x4e,bx,0,"*.*",di,si);
        printf("%s\n",&pp[30]);
        do {
                done=dos(0x4f,bx,cx,dx,di,si);
                if(done==-1) break;
                printf("%s\n",&pp[30]);
        } while( 1);
}
```

This function works as follows. According to the IBM *Technical Reference* manual, a disk transfer buffer must be initialized first. You can do this by passing the address of array **pp** to DOS via the call in which the address is passed in the DX register.

```
dos(0x1a,0,0,pp,0,0);
```

Because the rest of the registers are not used, zeros are substituted.

Next execute this call to function 4Eh to find the first file that matches the *.* wild card:

```
dos(0x4e,0,0,"*.*",0,0);
```

Subsequent files are found using the 4Fh function as follows:

```
done=dos(0x4f,0,0,0,0,0);
```

When the function returns −1, the last file name has been found. The file names are placed in the disk transfer buffer defined by the first DOS call. The file names are printed by a normal **printf( )** statement, except that you must do a little pointer arithmetic because the file name starts at byte 30 in the disk transfer buffer.

You can use **dos( )** to execute any 21h interrupt, but those interrupts that return information in registers other than AL will not work—the information will be lost. Although some C compilers also have a type of **bios( )** function call to execute the BIOS routines, many do not, so to interface to DOS calls that return multiple values in various registers and to use the BIOS routines, you must use an assembly language interface.

Using Assembly to Interface To BIOS and DOS Functions

Suppose that you wish to change the screen mode during the execution of a program. For PC-DOS, the seven modes that the color graphics adapters can have are

0	40×25 BW
1	40×25 color
2	80×25 BW
3	80×25 color
4	320×200 color graphics
5	320×200 BW graphics
6	340×200 BW graphics

Although some C compilers may have special functions that change screen modes, many do not. The function **mode( )**, shown here, executes a BIOS call to interrupt 10h number 1—set mode—using the parameter **c** as the mode to change to. This code only works for Aztec C, but you should be able to modify it so that it conforms to your compiler's calling conventions.

```
mode(c)
char c;
{
#asm
        mov bp,sp
        mov ax,word ptr 8[bp]
        mov ah,0
        int 010h
#endasm

}
```

The mode clears the screen by using the BIOS interrupt 10h function 6:

```
clear()
{
#asm
        mov al,0
        mov ah,6
        int 010h
#endasm

}
```

Another example of interfacing to BIOS through assembly language is the function **goto_xy( )**, which positions the cursor at the specified X and Y coordinates:

```
goto_xy(c,r)
char c,r;
{
#asm
        mov dl, 8[bp]
        mov cl, 10[bp]
        mov ah,2
        mov bh,0
        int 010h
#endasm

}
```

For the IBM PC, (0,0) is the upper-left corner of the screen.

Using the Scan Codes
From the PC Keyboard

One of the most frustrating experiences you can encounter while working with the IBM PC or a clone is trying to use the arrow keys (as well as INS, DEL, PGUP, PGDN, END, and HOME) and the function keys. These keys do not return the normal 8-bit characters in the way that the rest of the keys do. When you press a key, the PC actually generates a 16-bit value called a *scan code*. The scan code consists of the low-order byte, which, if a normal key, contains the ASCII code for the key; and a high-order byte that contains the key's position on the keyboard. For most keys, these scan codes are converted into 8-bit ASCII values by the operating system. But for such keys as the function keys and arrow keys this is not done, because the character code for a special key is 0. This means that you must use the position code to determine which key was pressed. The routine to read a character from the keyboard, which is supported by DOS function call number 1, does not allow you to read the special keys. Although a few C compilers have built-in routines to read these special keys, most do not.

The easiest way to access these keys from C is to write an assembly language function that calls interrupt 16h to read the scan code.

```
getarrow()
{
#asm
        mov ah,0
        int 016h
#endasm

}
```

After the call, the scan code and character code are already in AX, which is the correct register for returning information. After a call to interrupt 16h function 0, the position code is in AH and the character code is in AL.

The trick to using **getarrow( )** is knowing that when a special key is struck, the character code is 0. In such a case you then decode the position code to determine which key was actually typed. Using **getarrow( )** to do all keyboard input requires that the calling routine make decisions based on the contents of AH and AL. Here is a short program that illustrates one way to do this.

```
main()  /* scan code example */
{
        union scan {
                int c;
                char ch[2];
        } sc;

        do { /* read the keyboard */
                sc.c=getarrow();
                if(sc.ch[0]==0) {  /* is special key */
                        printf("special key number %d",sc.ch[1]);
                }
                else putchar(sc.ch[0]);
        } while(sc.ch[0]!='q');
}
```

The use of the **union** allows you to decode the two halves of the scan code returned by **getarrow( )**.

You can determine scan codes either by looking in the IBM *Technical Reference* manual or by using the short program just shown to determine the values experimentally (the latter method is more fun). To help you get started, here are the scan codes for the arrow keys:

Left arrow	75
Right arrow	77
Up arrow	72
Down arrow	80

To integrate completely the special keys with the normal keys requires writing special input functions and bypassing the normal **gets( )** functions found in the standard library. While this is unfortunate, it is the only way. However, the reward is that your program can then allow the user to work with the full PC keyboard.

Music

The IBM PC has a speaker that is usually used to beep on error conditions. You can also make this speaker produce musical tones. The method shown here produces an interesting timbre and can be used to provide unique special effects.

To produce a tone, you must create a pulsation: When a current is applied to the speaker coils, the speaker physically moves in; when the current is turned off, the speaker moves out. If you cause a series of on/off signals to be sent at, say, 100 times per second, then a 100hz tone is produced.

On the IBM PC, the speaker is turned on by sending a value of 2 to port 61h. The speaker is turned off by sending a 0 to port 61h. Most C compilers have functions in the standard library to output a byte to a port. The function used here has the general form

$$\textbf{outportb}(port, value);$$

where *port* is the port number and *value* is the byte to send. The short program shown here converts what you type at the keyboard into musical tones of varying pitch. You can easily change the **play( )** function to alter the duration or pitch.

```
main()   /* music  */
{
        int note, length;

        length=10;
        do {
                note=getchar();
                play(note,length);
        } while(note!='q');
}

play(note,l)
int note,l;
{
        int t,tone;

        l=l+1000/note;
        for(;l;l--){
                tone=note;
                outportb(0x61,2);   /* turn on speaker */
                outportb(0x61,0);   /* turn off speaker */
                for(;tone;--tone);
        }
}
```

With a little experimenting, you could learn to play tunes on the keyboard.

Final Thoughts
On Operating-System
Interfacing

This chapter has only scratched the surface of what can be done by using system resources creatively. To integrate your program with the operating system completely, you need to have access to information that describes all of the functions in detail.

There are several advantages to using operating-system functions. The first is that they can make better use of the special features of a given computer system, thus making your programs look and feel more professional. Second, bypassing some of C's built-in functions in favor of the operating-system functions can create programs that run faster and use less memory. Third, you have access to functions that are not available through C's standard library.

However, using the operating-system functions carries a price. You are creating more trouble for yourself when you use the operating-system functions instead of C's standard functions, because your code is no longer portable. You may also become dependent on specific versions of a given operating system and a C compiler, which will create compatibility problems when you distribute your programs. Only you can decide when and if you should introduce machine and operating-system dependencies into your programs.

Statistics

CHAPTER 6

Everyone who owns or has frequent access to a computer uses it at some point to perform *statistical analysis*. This analysis could take the form of monitoring or trying to predict the movement of stock prices in a portfolio, performing clinical testing to establish safe limits for a new drug, or even providing batting averages for the Little League team. The branch of mathematics that deals with the condensation, manipulation, and extrapolation of data is called *statistics*.

As a discipline, statistical analysis is quite young. It was born in the 1700s out of studies of games of chance. Indeed, probability and statistics are closely related. Modern statistical analysis began around the turn of this century when it became possible to sample and work with large sets of data. The computer made it possible to correlate and manipulate even larger amounts of data rapidly and to convert this data into a readily usable form. Today, because of the ever-increasing amount of information created and used by the government and the media, every aspect of life is adorned with reams of statistical information. It is difficult to listen to the radio or TV news, or to read a newspaper article, without being informed of some statistic.

Although C was not designed specifically for statistical programming, it adapts to the task quite well. It even offers some flexibility not found in more common business languages such as COBOL or BASIC. One advantage of C over COBOL is the speed and ease with which C programs can interface to the graphics functions of the system to produce charts and graphs of data. Also, depending on the compiler you have, C's math routines can be much faster than those commonly found in interpretive BASIC.

This chapter focuses on various concepts of statistics, including

- Mean

- Median

- Standard deviation

- Regression equation (line of best fit)

- Coefficient of correlation.

It also explores some simple graphing techniques.

Samples, Populations, Distributions, and Variables

Before you use statistics, you must understand a few key concepts. Statistical information is derived first by taking a *sample* of specific data points and then drawing generalizations about them. Each sample comes from the *population*, which consists of all of the possible outcomes for the situation under study. For example, if you wished to measure the output of a box factory over a year by using only the Wednesday output figures and generalizing from them, then your sample would consist of a year's worth of Wednesday figures taken from the larger population of each day's output in the year.

It is possible for the sample to equal the population if the sample is exhaustive. In the case of the box factory, your sample would equal the population if you used the actual output figures—five days a week for the entire year. When the sample is less than the population, there is always room for error; however, in many cases you can determine the probability for this error. This chapter assumes that the sample is the same as the population, and hence does not cover the problem of sample error.

For election projections and opinion polls, a proportionately small sample is used to project information about the population as a whole. For example, you might use statistical information about the Dow Jones stocks to make an inference about the stock market in general. Of course, the validity of these conclusions varies widely. In other uses of statistics, a sample that equals or nearly equals the population is used to summarize a large set of numbers for easier handling. For example, a board of education usually reports on the *average grade point* for a class, rather than on each student's individual grade.

Statistics are affected by the way that events are distributed in the population. Of the several common distributions in nature, the most important (and the only one used in this chapter) is the *normal distribution curve*, or the familiar "bell-shaped curve" as shown in Figure 6-1. As suggested by the graph in Figure 6-1, the elements in a normal distribution curve are found

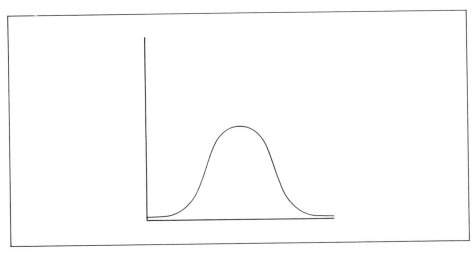

Figure 6-1. The normal distribution curve

mostly in the middle. In fact, the curve is completely symmetrical around its peak—which is also the average for all the elements. The further from the middle in either direction on the curve, the fewer elements there are.

In any statistical process there is always an *independent variable*, which is the number under study, and a *dependent variable*, which is the factor that determines the independent variable. This chapter uses *time*—the stepwise incremental passage of events—for the dependent variable. For example, when watching a stock portfolio you may wish to see the movement of the stock on a daily basis. You would therefore be concerned with the movement of stock prices over a given period of time, not with the actual calendar date of each price.

Throughout this chapter, individual statistical functions will be developed and then assembled into a single menu-driven program. You can use this program to perform a wide variety of statistical analyses, as well as to plot information on the screen.

Whenever the elements of a sample are discussed, they will be called *D* and indexed from 1 to *N*, where *N* is the number of the last element.

The Basic Statistics

Three important values form the basis of many statistical analyses and are also useful individually. They are the *mean*, the *median*, and the *mode*.

The Mean

The mean, or the arithmetic average, is the most common of all statistics. This single value number can be used to represent a set of data—the mean can be called the set's "center of gravity." To compute the mean, all elements in the sample are added together and the result is divided by the total number of elements. For example, the sum of the set

$$1\ 2\ 3\ 4\ 5\ 6\ 7\ 8\ 9\ 10$$

equals 55. When that number is divided by the number of elements in the sample, which is 10, the mean is 5.5.

The general formula for finding the mean is

$$M = \frac{D_1+D_2+D_3+\ldots+D_N}{N}$$

or

$$M = \frac{1}{N}\ \sum_{i=1}^{N}\ D_1$$

The symbol Σ indicates the summation of all elements between 1 and N.

As the statistical functions are developed in C, you should assume that all data is stored in an array of floating-point numbers and that the number of sample elements is known. The following function computes the mean of an array of **num** floating-point numbers and returns the floating-point average:

```
float mean(data,num)
float *data;
int num;
{
        int t;
        float avg;

        avg=0;
        for(t=0;t<num;++t)
                avg+=data[t];

        avg/=num;

        return avg;
}
```

For example, if you called **mean( )** with a 10-element array that contained the numbers 1 through 10, then **mean( )** would return the result 5.5.

The Median

The median of a sample is the middle value based on order of magnitude. For example, in the sample set

$$1\ 2\ 3\ 4\ 5\ 6\ 7\ 8\ 9$$

5 is the median because it is in the middle. In the set

$$1\ 2\ 3\ 4\ 5\ 6\ 7\ 8\ 9\ 10$$

you could use either 5 or 6 as the median. In a well-ordered sample that has a normal distribution, the median and the mean are very similar. However, as the sample moves further from the normal distribution curve, the difference between the median and the mean increases. Calculating the mean of a sample is as simple as sorting the sample into ascending order and then selecting the middle element, which is indexed as $N/2$.

The function **median( )** shown here returns the value of the middle element in a sample. A modified version of Quicksort, developed in Chapter 2, is used to sort the data array.

```
float median(data,num)
float *data;
int num;
{
        register int t;
        float dtemp[MAX];

        for(t=0;t<num;++t) dtemp[t]=data[t]; /* copy data to sort */
        quick(dtemp,num);   /* sort data into ascending order */
        return dtemp[num/2];
}

quick(item,count)  /* quick sort for floating point numbers */
float *item;
int count;
{

        qs(item,0,count-1);

}

qs(item,left,right)  /* quick sort */
```

```
float *item;
int left,right;
{
        register int i,j;
        float x,y;

        i=left; j=right;
        x=item[(left+right)/2];

        do {
                while(item[i]<x && i<right) i++;
                while(x<item[j] && j>left) j--;

                if(i<=j) {
                        y=item[i];
                        item[i]=item[j];
                        item[j]=y;
                        i++; j--;
                }
        } while(i<=j);

        if(left<j)  qs(item,left,j);
        if(i<right) qs(item,i,right);
}
```

The Mode

The mode of a sample is the value of the most frequently occurring element.
For example, in the set

$$1\ 2\ 3\ 3\ 4\ 5\ 6\ 6\ 6\ 7\ 8\ 9$$

the mode would be 6 because it occurs three times. There may be more than
one mode; for example, the sample

$$10\ 20\ 30\ 30\ 40\ 50\ 60\ 60\ 70$$

has two modes—30 and 60—because they both occur twice.

The following function, **find_mode( )**, returns the mode of a sample. (Be
careful; *mode* is a common function name in many C libraries.) If there is
more than one mode, then it returns the last one found.

```
float find_mode(data,num)
float *data;
int num;
{
        register int t,w;
        float md,oldmode;
        int count,oldcount;

        oldmode=0; oldcount=0;
        for(t=0;t<num;++t) {
                md=data[t];
                count=1;
                for(w=t+1;w<num;++w)
                        if(md==data[w]) count++;
                if(count>oldcount) {
                        oldmode=md;
                        oldcount=count;
                }
        }
        return oldmode;
}
```

Using the Mean, the Median, And the Mode

The mean, the median, and the mode share the same purpose: to provide one value that is the condensation of all the values in the sample. However, each represents the sample in a different way. The mean of the sample is generally the most useful value. Because it uses all values in its computation, the mean reflects all elements of the sample. The main disadvantage to the mean is its sensitivity to one extreme value. For example, in an imaginary business called Widget, Incorporated, the owner's salary is $100,000 per year, while the salary of each of the nine employees is $10,000. The average wage at Widget is $19,500, but this figure does not fairly represent the actual situation.

In samples like the salary dispersion at Widget, the mode is sometimes used instead of the mean. The mode of the salaries at Widget is $10,000—a figure that reflects more accurately the actual situation. However, the mode can be misleading. Consider a car company that makes cars in five different colors. In a given week, they made

100 green cars
100 orange cars
150 blue cars
200 black cars
190 white cars

Here, the mode of the sample is black, because 200 black cars were made, more than any other color. However, it would be misleading to suggest that the car company primarily makes black cars.

The median is interesting because its validity is based on the *hope* that the sample will reflect a normal distribution. For example, if the sample is

$$1\ 2\ 3\ 4\ 5\ 6\ 7\ 8\ 9\ 10$$

then the median is 5 or 6, and the mean is 5.5. Hence, the median and mean are similar in this case. However, in the sample

$$1\ 1\ 1\ 1\ 5\ 100\ 100\ 100\ 100$$

the median is still 5, but the mean is about 46.

In certain circumstances, neither the mean, the mode, nor the median can be counted on to give a meaningful value. This leads to two of the most important values in statistics—the *variance* and the *standard deviation*.

Variance and Standard Deviation

Although the one-number summary (such as the mean or median) is convenient, it can easily be misleading. Giving a little thought to this problem, you can see that the cause of the difficulty is not in the number itself, but in the fact that it does not convey any information about the variations of the data. For example, in the sample

$$1\ 1\ 1\ 1\ 9\ 9\ 9\ 9$$

the mean is 5; however, there is no element in the sample that is close to 5. What you would probably like to know is how close each element in the sample is to the average. If you know how much the data varies, you can better interpret the mean, median, and mode. You can find the variability of a sample by computing its variance and its standard deviation.

The variance and its square root, the standard deviation, are numbers that tell you the average deviation from the sample mean. Of the two, the standard deviation is the most important. It can be thought of as the average of the distances between the elements and the mean of the sample. The variance is computed as

$$V = \frac{1}{N} \sum_{i=1}^{N} (D_i - M)^2$$

where N is the number of elements in the sample and M is the sample mean. It is necessary to square the difference of the mean and each element in order to produce only positive numbers. If the numbers were not squared, they would by default always sum to 0.

The variance, produced by this formula, V, is of limited value because it is difficult to understand. However, its square root, the standard deviation, is the number you are really looking for. The standard deviation is derived by first finding the variance and then taking its square root:

$$std = \sqrt{\frac{1}{N} \sum_{i=1}^{N} (D_i - M)^2}$$

where N is the number of elements in the sample and M is the sample mean.

As an example, for the following sample

11 20 40 30 99 30 50

you compute the variance as follows:

	D	D−M	(D−M)^2
	11	−29	841
	20	−20	400
	40	0	0
	30	−10	100
	99	59	3481
	30	−10	100
	50	10	100
sum	280	0	5022
mean(M)	40	0	717.42

Here the average of the squared differences is 717.42. To derive the standard deviation, you simply take the square root of that number; the result is approximately 26.78. To interpret the standard deviation, remember that it is the *average distance that the elements are from the mean of the sample.*

The standard deviation tells you how nearly the mean represents the entire sample. For example, if you owned a candy bar factory and your plant foreman reported that daily output averaged 2500 bars last month but that the standard deviation was 2000, you would know that the production line needed better supervision!

If your sample follows a standard normal distribution, then about 68% of the sample will be within one standard deviation from the mean, and about 95% will be within two standard deviations.

The following function computes and returns the standard deviation of a given sample. Notice that **sqrt( )** requires a **double** type argument and returns **double** explicit type conversions. Although it would have been possible to use a cast instead, many C compilers do not evaluate a cast correctly in a function call, so the safer option was chosen.

```
float std_dev(data,num)
float *data;
int num;
{
        int t;
        float std,avg;
        double temp,sqrt();

        avg=mean(data,num);   /* get average */
        std=0;
        for(t=0;t<num;++t)
                std+=((data[t]-avg)*(data[t]-avg));

        std/=num;
        temp=std;      /* convert to double for sqrt() */
        temp=sqrt(temp);
        std=temp;
        return std;
}
```

Simple Plotting
On the Screen

The advantage of using graphs with statistics is that together they can convey the meaning clearly and accurately. A graph also shows at a glance how the sample was actually distributed and how variable the data is. This discussion is limited to two-dimensional graphs, which use the X-Y coordinate system. (Creating three-dimensional graphs is a discipline unto itself and beyond the scope of this book.)

There are two basic forms of two-dimensional graphs: the *bar graph* and the *scatter graph*. The bar graph uses solid bars to represent the magnitude of each element, while the scatter graph uses a single point per element, located at its X and Y coordinates. Figure 6-2 shows an example of each.

The bar chart is usually used with a relatively small set of information, such as the Gross National Product for the last ten years or the percentage output of a factory on a monthly basis. The scatter graph is generally used to display a large number of data points, such as the daily stock price of a

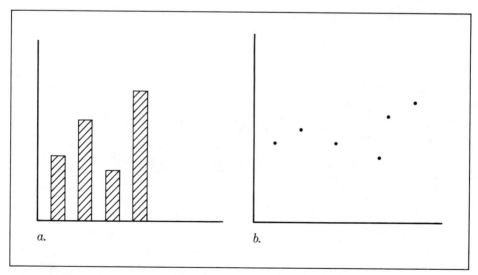

a.   b.

Figure 6-2.   Samples of a bar graph (*a*) and a scatter graph (*b*)

company over a year. Also, a modification of the scatter graph that connects the data points with a solid line is useful for plotting projections.

Here is a simple plotting function that creates a bar graph on the IBM PC. C library functions found in some form on most C compilers allow the function to use the built-in graphics capabilities of the IBM PC. The functions **line( )** and **mode( )** are supplied by the Aztec C compiler's graphics library; other compilers may call these by different names. If your compiler does not have functions like these, you can create them by interfacing to the operating system, as described in Chapter 5.

```
simple_plot(data,num)   /* bar chart of info */
float *data;
int num;
{
        int a,t;
        mode(6); /* 640x200 b&w graphics mode */

        scr_curs(24,0); printf("%d",0);
        scr_curs(0,0); printf("%d",200);
        scr_curs(24,76); printf("%d",580);
        for(t=0;t<num;++t) {
                a=data[t];
                if(a<0) a=0;
                line((t*10)+20,0,(t*10)+20,a);
        }
        getchar();   /* wait before returning to 25x80
                        character mode */

        mode(3);
}
```

On the IBM PC, the maximum-resolution graphics mode is mode 6, which offers a resolution of 640×200. The function **scr_curs( )** is a function supplied by the compiler's manufacturer to set the cursor to the desired X-Y position. The **line( )** function used in **simple_plot( )** has the general form

$$\textbf{line}(start\_X, start\_Y, end\_X, end\_Y);$$

where all values must be integers.

This simple plotting routine has a serious limitation—it assumes that all data will be between 0 and 199 because the only valid numbers that can be used to call **line( )** are within the range 0 to 199. This assumption is fine in the unlikely event that your data elements consistently fit in that range. To make the plotting routine handle arbitrary units, you must *normalize* the data before plotting it in order to scale the data values to fit the required range. The process of normalization involves finding a ratio between the actual range of the data and the physical range of the screen resolution. Each data element can be multiplied by this ratio to produce a number that fits the range of the screen. The formula to do this for the Y-axis on the PC is

$$Y' = Y * \frac{200}{(max-min)}$$

where Y' is the value used when calling the plotting function. The same function can be used to spread the scale when the data range is very small. This results in a graph that fills the screen as much as possible.

The following function **barplot( )** scales the X- and Y-axes and plots a bar graph of as many as 580 elements. The X-axis is assumed to be time and is in increments of 1 unit. Generally, the normalizing procedure finds the greatest value and the smallest value in the sample and then calculates their difference. This number, which represents the spread between the minimum and maximum, is used to divide the resolution of the screen. In the case of the IBM PC, the numbers are 200 for the Y-axis and 580 for the X-axis (to create a little room for the border). The ratio is then used to convert the sample data into the proper scale.

```
barplot(data,num)   /* bar chart of info */
float *data;
int num;
{
        int x,y,t,max,min,incr;
        float a, norm,spread;

        mode(6);  /* 640x200 b&w graphics mode */
        /* first find max value to enable normalization */
        max=getmax(data,num);
        min=getmin(data,num);
        if(min>0) min=0;
        spread=max-min;
        norm=200/spread;   /* absolute increment/spread */
        scr_curs(24,0); printf("%d",min);
        scr_curs(0,0); printf("%d",max);
        scr_curs(24,76); printf("%d",num);
        for(t=1;t<24;++t) {
                scr_curs(t,0);
                printf("-");
        }
        for(t=0;t<num;++t) {
                a=(data[t]-min)*norm;   /* normalize */
```

```
                   y=a; /* type conversion */
                   incr=580/num;
                   x=(t*incr)+20+incr;
                   line(x,0,x,y);
              }
         getchar();
         mode(3);
    }
```

This version also prints hash marks along the Y-axis that represent 1/24th of the difference between the minimum and maximum values. Figure 6-3 gives a sample of the output of **barplot( )** with 20 elements. By no means does **barplot( )** provide all the features you may desire, but it will do a good job of displaying a single sample.

Only a slight modification to **barplot( )** is required to make a function that plots a scatter graph. The major alteration changes **line( )** to a function

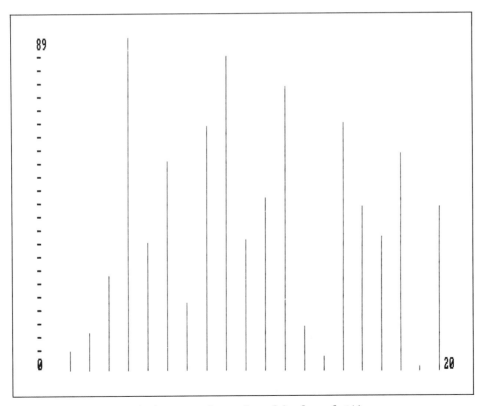

Figure 6-3. A sample bar graph produced by **barplot( )**

that plots only one point. In the Aztec C compiler's graphics library, this function is called **point( )**, but your compiler may call it something different. The general form of **point( )** is

point(*x,y*);

where *x* and *y* are integers. Here is the new function **scatterplot( )**:

```
scatterplot(data,num,ymin,ymax,xmax)
float *data;
int num,ymin,ymax,xmax;
{
        int x,y,t,incr;
        float norm,a,spread;

        /* first find max value to enable normalization */

        if(ymin>0) ymin=0;
        spread=ymax-ymin;
        norm=200/spread;   /* absolute increment/spread */
        scr_curs(24,0); printf("%d",ymin);
        scr_curs(0,0); printf("%d",ymax);
        scr_curs(24,76); printf("%d",xmax);
        for(t=1;t<24;++t) {
                scr_curs(t,0);
                printf("-");
        }
        incr=580/xmax;
        for(t=0;t<num;++t) {
                a=(data[t]-ymin)*norm;   /* normalize */
                y=a; /* type conversion */
                x=(t*incr)+20+incr;
                point(x,y);
        }
}
```

In **scatterplot( )** the minimum and maximum data values are passed into the function, instead of being computed by the function as they are in **barplot( )**. This allows you to plot multiple data sets on the same screen without changing the scale. Figure 6-4 shows a sample scatter graph of 30 data elements produced by this function.

Projections
And the Regression Equation

Statistical information is often used to make "informed guesses" about the future. Even though everyone knows that the past does not necessarily predict the future and that there are exceptions to every rule, historical data is still used in this way, because very often, past and present trends do continue into the future. When they do, you can try to determine specific values at future points in time. This process is called making a *projection* or *trend analysis*.

Figure 6-4.   Sample scatter graph produced by **scatterplot( )**

For example, consider a fictitious ten-year study of life spans, which collected the following data:

Year	Life Span
1970	69
1971	70
1972	72
1973	68
1974	73
1975	71
1976	75
1977	74
1978	78
1979	77

Figure 6-5.   Bar graph of life expectancy

You might first ask yourself whether there is a trend here at all. If there is, you may want to know which way it is going. Finally, if there is indeed a trend, you might wonder what life expectancy will be in, say, 1985.

First look at the bar graph of this data, as shown in Figure 6-5. By examining the graph you can conclude that life spans are getting longer in general. Also, if you placed a ruler on the graph to try to fit the data and drew a line that extended into 1985, you could project that that life span would be about 82 in 1985. However, while you may feel confident about your intuitive analysis, you would probably rather use a more formal and exact method of projecting life span.

Given a set of historical data, the best way to make projections is to find the *line of best fit* in relation to the data. This is what you did with the ruler. A line of best fit most closely represents each point of the data and its trend. Although some or even all of the actual data points may not be on the line, the line best represents them. The validity of the line is based on how close to the line the sample data points are.

A line in two-dimensional space has the basic equation

$$Y = a + bX$$

where X is the dependent variable, Y is the independent variable, a is the Y-intercept, and b is the slope of the line. Therefore, to find a line that best fits a sample, you must determine a and b.

Any number of methods can be used to determine the values of a and b, but the most common and generally best is called the *method of least squares*. It attempts to minimize the distance between the actual data points and the line. The method involves two steps: the first computes b, the slope of the line, and the second finds a, the Y-intercept. To find b, use the formula

$$b = \frac{\sum_{i=1}^{N} (X_i - M_x)(Y_i - M_y)}{\sum_{i=1}^{N} (X_i - M_x)^2}$$

where M_x is the mean of the X coordinate and M_y is the mean of the Y coordinate. The derivation of this formula is beyond the scope of this book, but having found b, you can use it to compute a, as shown here:

$$a = M_y - bM_x$$

After you have calculated a and b, you can plug in any number for X and find the value of Y. For example, if you use the life expectancy data, you find that the regression equation looks like

$$Y = 67.46 + 0.95 * X$$

Therefore, to find the life expectancy in 1985, which is 15 years from 1970, you have

$$Life\ Expectancy = 67.46 + 0.95 * 15$$

$$\cong 82$$

However, even with the line of best fit for the data, you may still want to know how well that line actually correlates with the data. If the line and data have only a slight correlation, then the regression line is of little use. However, if the line fits the data well, then it is a much more valid indicator. The most common way to determine and represent the correlation of the data to the regression line is to compute the *correlation coefficient*, which is a number between 0 and 1. The correlation coefficient is a percentage that is related to the distance of each data point in the sample from the line. If the correlation coefficient is 1, then the data corresponds perfectly to the line. A coefficient of 0 means that there is no correlation between the line and the points—in fact, any line would be as good (or as bad) as the one used. The formula to find the correlation coefficient is

$$Cor = \frac{\dfrac{1}{N} \displaystyle\sum_{i=1}^{N} (X_i - M_x)(Y_i - M_y)}{\sqrt{\dfrac{1}{N} \displaystyle\sum_{i=1}^{N} (X_i - M_x)^2} \ \sqrt{\dfrac{1}{N} \displaystyle\sum_{i=1}^{N} (Y_i - M_y)^2}}$$

where M_x is the mean of X and M_y is the mean of Y. Generally, a value of 0.81

is considered a strong correlation. It indicates that about 66% of the data fits the regression line. To convert any correlation coefficient into a percentage, you simply square it.

Here is the function **regress( )**. It uses the methods just described to find the regression equation and the coefficient of correlation, as well as to make a scatter plot of both the sample data and the line:

```
regress(data,num)
float *data;
int num;
{
        float a,b,x_avg,y_avg,temp,temp2;
        float data2[580],correlation(),cor;
        float std_dev();
        int t,min,max;
        char s[80];

        /* find mean of y */
        y_avg=0;
        for(t=0;t<num;++t)
                y_avg+=data[t];
        y_avg/=num;

        /* find mean of x */
        x_avg=0;
        for(t=1;t<=num;++t) /* because y is in time units*/
                x_avg+=t;
        x_avg/=num;


        /* now find b */
        temp=0; temp2=0;
        for(t=1;t<=num;++t) {
                temp+=(data[t-1]-y_avg)*(t-x_avg);
                temp2+=(t-x_avg) * (t-x_avg);
        }

        b=temp/temp2;

        /* now find a */
        a=y_avg-(b*x_avg);

        /* now compute coefficient of correlation */
        for(t=0;t<num;++t) data2[t]=t+1; /* load x axis */
        cor=temp/(num);
        cor=cor/(std_dev(data,num) * std_dev(data2,num));

        printf("regression equation is: Y = %f + %f * X\n",a,b);
        printf("Correlation Coefficient: %f\n",cor);
        printf("plot data points and regression line? (y/n) ");
        gets(s);
        if(toupper(*s)=='N') return;

        mode(6); /* 640x200 b&w graphics mode */
        /* now do scatter graph and regression line */
        for(t=0;t<num*2;++t)    /* create plot regression line */
```

```
                data2[t]=a+(b*(t+1));
        min=getmin(data,num)*2;
        max=getmax(data,num)*2;
        scatterplot(data,num,min,max,num*2);    /* plot the points */
        scatterplot(data2,num*2,min,max,num*2);
        gets(s);
        mode(3);
}
```

A scatter plot of both the sample life-expectancy data and the regression line is shown in Figure 6-6. The important point to remember while using projections like this is that the past does not necessarily predict the future — if it did, it wouldn't be fun!

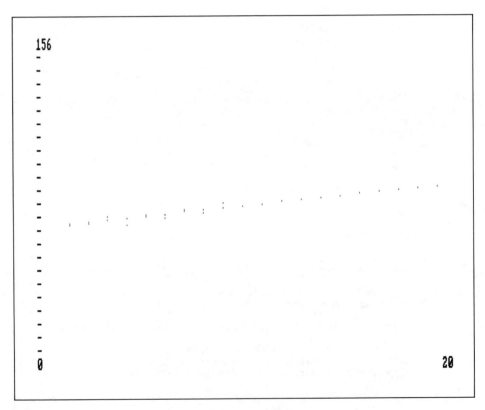

Figure 6-6. Regression line for life expectancy

Making a Complete Statistics Program

So far, this chapter has developed several functions that perform statistical calculations on single-variable populations. In this section you will put the functions together to form a complete program for analyzing data, printing bar charts or scatter plots, and making projections. Before you can design a complete program, you must define a data structure to hold the variable data information, as well as a few necessary support functions.

First you need an array to hold the sample information. You can use a single-dimension, floating-point array called **data** of size **MAX**. **MAX** is defined so that it fits the largest sample you will need, which in this case will be 100. The **main( )** function, along with the menu selection function **menu( )** and the support function **is_in( )**, is shown here:

```
#define MAX 100
#include "stdio.h"
float mean(),std_dev(),median(),find_mode();

main()   /* stats driver */
{

        char ch;
        float data[MAX];   /* this array will hold data */
        float a,m,md,std;
        int num; /* number of data items */
        num=0;

        for(;;) {
                ch=menu();
                switch(toupper(ch)) {
                    case 'E': num=enter_data(data);
                        break;
                    case 'B':a=mean(data,num);
                        std=std_dev(data,num);
                        m=median(data,num);
                        md=find_mode(data,num);
                        printf("Average: %f\n",a);
                        printf("Standard Deviation: %f\n",std);
                        printf("Median: %f\n",m);
                        printf("Mode: %f\n",md);
                        break;
                    case 'R': regress(data,num);
                        break;
                    case 'D': display(data,num);
                        break;
                    case 'L': num=load(data);
```

```
                                    break;
                    case 'S': save(data,num);
                            break;
                    case 'P': barplot(data,num);
                            break;
                    case 'Q': exit(0);
                    }
            }

    }

    menu()
    {
            char ch;
            do {
                    printf("\nEnter data\n");
                    printf("Basic statistics \n");
                    printf("Regression line and scatter plot\n");
                    printf("Plot a bar graph\n");
                    printf("Save\n");
                    printf("Load\n");
                    printf("Display data\n");
                    printf("Quit\n\n");
                    printf("choose one (E, B, R, P, S, L, D, Q): ");
                    ch=toupper(dos(1,0,0));
            } while(!is_in(ch,"BESLQDPR"));
            printf("\n");
            return ch;
    }

    is_in(ch,s)
    char ch,*s;
    {
            while(*s) {
                    if(ch==*s) return ch;
                    else s++;
            }
            return 0;
    }
```

The function **is—in( )** returns TRUE if the character is in the string and
FALSE if it is not.

Besides the statistical functions developed already, you also will need routines to save and load data. The **save( )** routine must also store the number of
data elements, and the **load( )** must read back that number.

```
save(data,num)
float *data;
int num;
{
        FILE *fp;
        int t;
        char s[80];

        printf("enter filename: ");
        gets(s);
```

```
        if((fp=fopen(s,"w"))==0) {
                printf("cannot open file\n");
                exit(1);
        }
        putw(num,fp);  /* write out count */

        for(t=0;t<num;++t) fprintf(fp,"%f ",data[t]);

        fclose(fp);
}

load(data)
float *data;
{
        FILE *fp;
        int t,num;
        char s[80];

        printf("enter filename: ");
        gets(s);
        if((fp=fopen(s,"r"))==0) {
                printf("cannot open file\n");
                exit(1);
        }

        num=getw(fp);
        for(t=0;t<num;++t) fscanf(fp,"%f",&data[t]);

        fclose(fp);
        return num;
}
```

For your convenience, here is the entire program:

```
#define MAX 100
#include "stdio.h"
float mean(),std_dev(),median(),find_mode();

main()  /* stats driver */
{
        char ch;
        float data[MAX];  /* this array will hold data */
        float a,m,md,std;
        int num; /* number of data items */
        num=0;

        for(;;) {
                ch=menu();
                switch(ch) {
                    case 'E': num=enter_data(data);
                        break;
                    case 'B':a=mean(data,num);
                        std=std_dev(data,num);
                        m=median(data,num);
                        md=find_mode(data,num);
                        printf("Average: %f\n",a);
                        printf("Standard Deviation: %f\n",std);
```

```
                              printf("Median: %f\n",m);
                              printf("Mode: %f\n",md);
                              break;
                      case 'R': regress(data,num);
                          break;
                      case 'D': display(data,num);
                          break;
                      case 'L': num=load(data);
                          break;
                      case 'S': save(data,num);
                          break;
                      case 'P': barplot(data,num);
                          break;
                      case 'Q': exit(0);
                  }
          }

}

menu()
{
        char ch;
        do {
                printf("\nEnter data\n");
                printf("Basic statistics \n");
                printf("Regression line and scatter plot\n");
                printf("Plot a bar graph\n");
                printf("Save\n");
                printf("Load\n");
                printf("Display data\n");
                printf("Quit\n\n");
                printf("choose one (E, B, R, P, S, L, D, Q): ");
                ch=toupper(dos(1,0,0));
        } while(!is_in(ch,"BESLQDPR"));
        printf("\n");
        return ch;
}

is_in(ch,s)
char ch,*s;
{
        while(*s) {
                if(ch==*s) return ch;
                else s++;
        }
        return 0;
}

display(data,num)
float *data;
int num;
{
        int t;

        for(t=0;t<num;++t)
                printf("item %d; %f\n",t+1,data[t]);

        printf("\n");
}
```

```
enter_data(data)
float *data;
{
        int t,num;

        printf("number of items?: ");
        num=get_num();

        for(t=0;t<num;++t) {
                printf("enter item %d: ",t+1);
                scanf("%f",&data[t]);
        }
        return num;
}

float mean(data,num)
float *data;
int num;
{
        int t;
        float avg;

        avg=0;
        for(t=0;t<num;++t)
                avg+=data[t];

        avg/=num;

        return avg;
}

float std_dev(data,num)
float *data;
int num;
{
        register int t;
        float std,avg;
        double temp,sqrt();

        avg=mean(data,num);   /* get average */
        std=0;
        for(t=0;t<num;++t)
        {
                std+=((data[t]-avg)*(data[t]-avg));
        }
        std/=num;
        temp=std;
        temp=sqrt(temp);
        std=temp;
        return std;
}

float median(data,num)
float *data;
int num;
{
        register int t;
```

```
        float dtemp[MAX];

        for(t=0;t<num;++t) dtemp[t]=data[t]; /* copy data to sort */
        quick(dtemp,num);  /* sort data into ascending order */
        return dtemp[num/2];
}

float find_mode(data,num)
float *data;
int num;
{
        register int t,w;
        float md,oldmode;
        int count,oldcount;

        oldmode=0; oldcount=0;
        for(t=0;t<num;++t) {
                md=data[t];
                count=1;
                for(w=t+1;w<num;++w)
                        if(md==data[w]) count++;
                if(count>oldcount) {
                        oldmode=md;
                        oldcount=count;
                }
        }
        return oldmode;
}

regress(data,num)
float *data;
int num;
{
        float a,b,x_avg,y_avg,temp,temp2;
        float data2[580],cor;
        float std_dev();
        int t,min,max;
        char s[80];

        /* find mean of y */
        y_avg=0;
        for(t=0;t<num;++t)
                y_avg+=data[t];
        y_avg/=num;

        /* find mean of x */
        x_avg=0;
        for(t=1;t<=num;++t) /* because y is time */
                x_avg+=t;
        x_avg/=num;


        /* now find b */
        temp=0; temp2=0;
        for(t=1;t<=num;++t) {
                temp+=(data[t-1]-y_avg)*(t-x_avg);
                temp2+=(t-x_avg) * (t-x_avg);
        }
        b=temp/temp2;
```

```
        /* now find a */
        a=y_avg-(b*x_avg);

        /* now compute coefficient of correlation */
        for(t=0;t<num;++t) data2[t]=t+1; /* load x axis */
        cor=temp/(num);
        cor=cor/(std_dev(data,num) * std_dev(data2,num));

        printf("regression equation is: Y = %f + %f * X\n",a,b);
        printf("Correlation Coefficient: %f\n",cor);
        printf("plot data points and regression line? (y/n) ");
        gets(s);
        if(toupper(*s)=='N') return;
        mode(6); /* 640x200 b&w graphics mode */
        /* now do scatter graph and regression line */
        for(t=0;t<num*2;++t)    /* create plot regression line */
                data2[t]=a+(b*(t+1));
        min=getmin(data,num)*2;
        max=getmax(data,num)*2;
        scatterplot(data,num,min,max,num*2);   /* plot the points */
        scatterplot(data2,num*2,min,max,num*2);
        gets(s);
        mode(3);
}


barplot(data,num)   /* bar chart of info */
float *data;
int num;
{
        int y,t,max,min,incr;
        float a, norm,spread;
        char s[80];

        mode(6); /* 640x200 b&w graphics mode */
        /* first find max value to enable normalization */
        max=getmax(data,num);
        min=getmin(data,num);
        if(min>0) min=0;
        spread=max-min;
        norm=200/spread;   /* absolute increment/spread */
        scr_curs(24,0); printf("%d",min);
        scr_curs(0,0); printf("%d",max);
        scr_curs(24,76); printf("%d",num);
        for(t=1;t<24;++t) {
                scr_curs(t,0);
                printf("-");
        }
        for(t=0;t<num;++t) {
                a=data[t];
                a=a-min;
                a*=norm; /* normalize */
                y=a; /* type conversion */
                incr=580/num;
                line((t*incr)+20+incr,0,(t*incr)+20+incr,y);
        }
        gets(s);
        mode(3);
}
```

```
scatterplot(data,num,ymin,ymax,xmax)
float *data;
int num,ymin,ymax,xmax;
{
        int y,t,incr;
        float norm,a,spread;

        /* first find max value to enable normalization */
        if(ymin>0) ymin=0;
        spread=ymax-ymin;
        norm=200/spread;  /* absolute increment/spread */
        scr_curs(24,0); printf("%d",ymin);
        scr_curs(0,0); printf("%d",ymax);
        scr_curs(24,76); printf("%d",xmax);
        for(t=1;t<24;++t) {
                scr_curs(t,0);
                printf("-");
        }
        incr=580/xmax;
        for(t=0;t<num;++t) {
                a=data[t];
                a=a-ymin;
                a*=norm; /* normalize */
                y=a; /* type conversion */
                point((t*incr)+20+incr,y);
        }

}

getmax(data,num)
float *data;
int num;
{
        int t,max;

        for(max=data[0],t=1;t<num;++t)
                if(data[t]>max) max=data[t];
        return max;
}

getmin(data,num)                                              }
float *data;
int num;
{
        int t,min;

        for(min=data[0],t=1;t<num;++t)
                if(data[t]<min) min=data[t];
        return min;
}

save(data,num)
float *data;
int num;
{
        FILE *fp;
        int t;
        char s[80];
```

```
                    printf("enter filename: ");
                    gets(s);

                    if((fp=fopen(s,"w"))==0) {
                        printf("cannot open file\n");
                        exit(1);
                    }
                    putw(num,fp);   /* write out count */

                    for(t=0;t<num;++t) fprintf(fp,"%f ",data[t]);

                    fclose(fp);
}

load(data)
float *data;
{
            FILE *fp;
            int t,num;
            char s[80];

            printf("enter filename: ");
            gets(s);
            if((fp=fopen(s,"r"))==0) {
                    printf("cannot open file\n");
                    exit(1);
            }

            num=getw(fp);
            for(t=0;t<num;++t) fscanf(fp,"%f",&data[t]);

            fclose(fp);
            return num;
}

get_num()
{
            char s[80];
            gets(s);
            return(atoi(s));
}
quick(item,count)   /* quick sort */
float *item;
int count;
{

            qs(item,0,count-1);

}

qs(item,left,right)   /* quick sort */
float *item;
int left,right;
{

            register int i,j;
            float x,y;
```

```
i=left; j=right;

x=item[(left+right)/2];

do {
        while(item[i]<x && i<right) i++;
        while(x<item[j] && j>left) j--;

        if(i<=j) {
                y=item[i];
                item[i]=item[j];
                item[j]=y;
                i++; j--;
        }
} while(i<=j);

if(left<j)  qs(item,left,j);
if(i<right) qs(item,i,right);
}
```

Using the Statistics
Program

To give you an idea of how you can use the statistics program developed in this chapter, here is an example of a simple stock-market analysis for Widget, Incorporated. As an investor, you will be trying to decide if it is a good time to invest in Widget by buying stock; if you should sell "short" (the process of selling shares you do not have and hoping for a rapid price drop so that you can buy them later at a cheaper price); or if you should invest elsewhere.

For the past 24 months, Widget's stock price has been as follows:

Month	Stock Price ($)
1	10
2	10
3	11
4	9
5	8
6	8
7	9
8	10
9	10
10	13
11	11
12	11
13	11
14	11
15	12
16	13
17	14
18	16
19	17
20	15
21	15
22	16
23	14
24	16

You should first find out if Widget's stock price has established a trend. After entering the figures, you find the following basic statistics:

Mean: 12.08
Standard deviation: 2.68
Median: 11
Mode: 11

Next you should plot a bar graph of the stock price, as shown in Figure 6-7.

The bar graph looks as if there might be a trend, but it is best to perform a formal regression analysis. The regression equation is

$$Y = 7.90 + 0.33 * X$$

with a correlation coefficient of 0.86, or about 74%. This is quite good—in fact, a definite trend is clear. Printing a scatter graph, as shown in Figure 6-8, makes this strong growth readily apparent. Such results could cause an investor to throw caution to the wind and buy 1000 shares as quickly as possible!

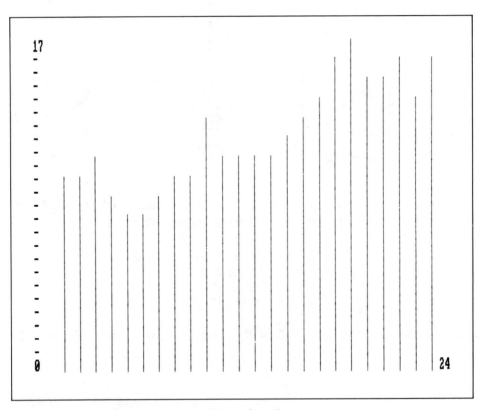

Figure 6-7. Bar chart of Widget's stock price

Final Thoughts

The correct use of statistical analysis requires a general understanding of how the results are derived and what they really mean. As with the Widget example, it is easy to forget that past events cannot account for circumstances that can radically affect the final outcome. Blind reliance on statistical evidence can cause some very disturbing results.

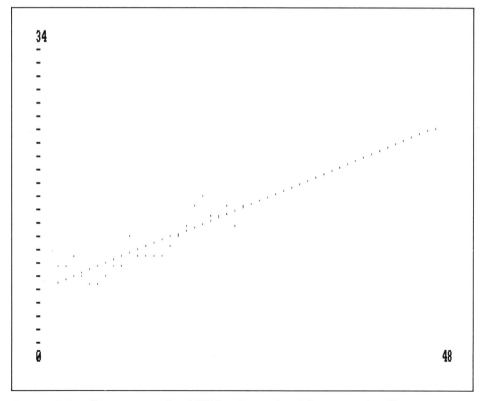

Figure 6-8. Scatter graph of Widget's stock with regression line

Encryption
and
Data Compression

C H A P T E R   7

People who like computers and programming often like to play with codes and ciphers. Perhaps the reason for this is that all codes involve algorithms, just as programs do. Or perhaps these people simply have an affinity for cryptic things that most people cannot understand. All programmers seem to receive a great deal of satisfaction when a nonprogrammer looks at a program listing and says something like, "My God, that sure looks complicated!" After all, the act of writing a program is called "coding."

Closely associated with the topic of cryptography is *data compression*. Data compression is the compacting of information into a smaller space than is usually used. Because data compression can play a role in encryption and uses many of the same principles, it is included in this chapter.

Computer-based cryptography is important for two primary reasons. The most obvious is the need to keep sensitive data on shared systems secure. Although password protection is adequate for many situations, important, confidential files are routinely coded to provide a higher level of protection. The second reason is that computer-based codes are used in data transmission. Not only are codes used for such things as secret government information, but they are starting to be used by broadcasters to protect their sky-to-earth station transmissions. Because these types of coding procedures are so complex, they are usually done by computer.

Data compression is commonly used to increase the storage capacity of various storage devices. Although the cost of storage devices has fallen sharply in the past few years, there can still be a need to fit more information into smaller areas.

A Short History Of Cryptography

Although no one knows when secret writing began, one of the earliest examples is a cuneiform tablet made around 1500 B.C. It contains a coded formula for making pottery glaze. The Greeks and Spartans used codes as early as 475 B.C., and the upper class in Rome frequently used simple ciphers during the reign of Julius Caesar. During the Dark Ages, interest in cryptography (as well as many other intellectual pursuits) decreased except among monks, who used it occasionally. With the birth of the Italian Renaissance, the art of cryptography again flourished. By the time of Louis XIV of France, a code based on 587 randomly selected keys was used for government messages.

In the 1800s, two factors helped move cryptography forward. The first was Edgar Allan Poe's stories, such as "The Gold Bug," which featured coded messages and excited the imagination of many readers. The second was the invention of the telegraph and Morse code. Morse code was the first binary representation (dots and dashes) of the alphabet that received wide use.

By World War I, several nations had constructed mechanical "code machines" that permitted easy encoding and decoding of text by using sophisticated, complex ciphers. The story of cryptography changes slightly at this point, to the story of code-breaking. Before the use of mechanical devices to encode and decode messages, complex ciphers were used infrequently because of the time and effort required both for encoding and decoding. Hence, most codes could be broken within a relatively short period of time.

However, the art of code-breaking became much more difficult when the code machines were used. Although modern computers would have made even those codes fairly easy to break, even computers cannot dwarf the incredible talent of Herbert Yardley, still considered the master code-breaker of all time. He not only broke the U.S. diplomatic code in 1915 in his spare time, but he also broke the Japanese diplomatic code in 1922—even though he did not know Japanese! He accomplished this by using frequency tables of the Japanese language.

By World War II, the major method used to break codes was to steal the enemy's code machine, thereby foregoing the tedious (if intellectually satisfying) process of code-breaking. In fact, the Allies' possession of a German code machine (unknown to the Germans) contributed greatly to the outcome of the war.

With the advent of computers—especially multiuser computers—secure and unbreakable codes have become even more important. Not only do computer files occasionally need to be kept secret, but access to the computer itself must also be managed and regulated. Numerous methods of encrypting data files have been developed, and the DES (Data Encryption Standard) algorithm, accepted by the National Bureau of Standards, is generally considered to be secure from code-breaking efforts. However, DES is very difficult to implement and may not be suitable for all situations.

Types of Ciphers

Of the more traditional coding methods, there are two basic types: *substitution* and *transposition*. A substitution cipher replaces one character with another, but leaves the message in the proper order. A transposition cipher essentially scrambles the characters of a message according to some rule. These types of codes can be used at whatever level of complexity is desired and can even be intermixed. The digital computer adds a third basic encryption technique, called *bit manipulation*, which alters the computerized representation of data by some algorithm.

All three methods may make use of a *key*. A key is a string of characters that is needed to decode a message. Do not confuse the key with the method, however, because the key itself is never sufficient to decode—the encryption algorithm must also be known. The key "personalizes" a coded message so that only those people that know the key can decode it, even though the method used to encode the message may be accessible.

Two terms that you should become familiar with are *plaintext* and *ciphertext*. The plaintext of a message is text you can read; the ciphertext is the encoded version.

This chapter presents computerized methods that use each of the three basic methods to code text files. You will see several short programs that encode and decode text files. With one exception, all of these programs have both a **code( )** and a **decode( )** function: the **decode( )** function always reverses the **code( )** process used to create the ciphertext.

Substitution Ciphers

One of the simplest substitution ciphers involves offsetting the alphabet by a specified amount. For example, if each letter were offset by three, then

abcdefghijklmnopqrstuvwxyz

would become

defghijklmnopqrstuvwxyzabc

Notice that the letters *abc* shifted off the front were added to the end. To encode a message using this method, you simply substitute the shifted alphabet for the real one. For example, the message

meet me at sunset

becomes

phhw ph dw vxqvhw

The program shown here enables you to code any text message using any offset after you specify which letter of the alphabet to begin with.

```c
#include "ctype.h"
#include "stdio.h"
main(argc,argv)  /* simple substitution cipher */
int argc;
char *argv[];
{
        if(argc!=5) {
            printf("usage: input output encode/decode offset\n");
            exit();
        }
        if(!isalpha(*argv[4])){
            printf("start letter must be alphabetical character\n");
            exit();
        }

        if(toupper(*argv[3])=='E') code(argv[1],argv[2],*argv[4]);
        else decode(argv[1],argv[2],*argv[4]);
}

code(input,output,start)
char *input,*output;
char start;
{
        int ch;
        FILE *fp1,*fp2;

        if((fp1=fopen(input,"r"))==0) {
                printf("cannot open input file\n");
                exit();
        }

        if((fp2=fopen(output,"w"))==0) {
                printf("cannot open output file\n");
                exit();
        }

        start=tolower(start);
        start=start-'a';
        do {
                ch=tolower(getc(fp1));
                if(ch==EOF) break;
                if(isalpha(ch)) {
                        ch+=start;
                        if(ch>'z') ch-=26;
                }
                putc(ch,fp2);
        } while(1);
        fclose(fp1); fclose(fp2);
decode(input,output,start)
char *input,*output;
char start;
{
        int ch;
        FILE *fp1,*fp2;

        if((fp1=fopen(input,"r"))==0) {
                printf("cannot open input file\n");
                exit();
        }
```

```
if((fp2=fopen(output,"w"))==0) {
        printf("cannot open output file\n");
        exit();
}

start=tolower(start);
start=start-'a';
do {
        ch=tolower(getc(fp1));
        if(ch==EOF) break;
        if(isalpha(ch)) {
                ch-=start;
                if(ch<'a') ch+=26;
        }
        putc(ch,fp2);
} while(1);
fclose(fp1); fclose(fp2);
}
```

As an example, you could use this program to code a file called "message," to put the coded version into a file called "cmess," and to offset the alphabet by two places. You would first type from the command line

```
>code message cmess encode c
```

To decode, you would then type

```
>code cmess message decode c
```

Although a substitution cipher based on a constant offset will generally fool grade-schoolers, it is not suitable for most purposes because it is too easy to crack. After all, there are only 26 possible offsets, and it is easy to try all of them within a short period of time. An improvement on the substitution cipher is to use a scrambled alphabet instead of a simple offset.

A second failing of the simple substitution cipher is that it preserves the spaces between words, which makes it doubly easy for a code-breaker to crack. Another improvement would be to encode spaces. (Actually, all punctuation should be encoded, but for simplicity, the examples will not do this.) For example, you could map this random string containing every letter of the alphabet and a space

abcdefghijklmnopqrstuvwxyz<space>

into this string:

qazwsxedcrfvtgbyhnujm ikolp

You may wonder if there is a significant improvement in the security of a message encoded by using a randomized version of the alphabet compared to using a simple offset version. The answer is *yes*—there are 26 factorial (26!) ways to arrange the alphabet; with the space, that number becomes 27 factorial (27!) ways. The factorial of a number is that number times every whole number smaller than it, down to 1. For example, 6! is 6*5*4*3*2*1 = 720. Therefore, 26! is a very large number.

The program shown here is an improved substitution cipher that uses the randomized alphabet shown earlier. If you encoded the message

meet me at sunset

by using the improved substitution cipher program, it would look like

tssjptspqjpumgusj

which is definitely a harder code to break.

```
#include "ctype.h"
#include "stdio.h"

char sub[28]=      "qazwsxedcrfvtgbyhnujm ikoip";
char alphabet[28]="abcdefghijklmnopqrstuvwxyz ";

main(argc,argv)  /* improved substitution cipher */
int argc;
char *argv[];
{
        if(argc!=4) {
                printf("usage: input output encode/decode\n");
                exit();
        }
        if(toupper(*argv[3])=='E') code(argv[1],argv[2]);
        else decode(argv[1],argv[2]);
}

code(input,output)
char *input,*output;
{
        int ch;
        FILE *fp1,*fp2;

        if((fp1=fopen(input,"r"))==0) {
                printf("cannot open input file\n");
                exit();
        }

        if((fp2=fopen(output,"w"))==0) {
                printf("cannot open output file\n");
                exit();
        }
```

```
            do {
                    ch=tolower(getc(fp1));
                    if(ch==EOF) break;
                    if(isalpha(ch) || ch==' ') {
                            ch=sub[find(alphabet,ch)];
                    }
                    putc(ch,fp2);
            } while(1);
            fclose(fp1); fclose(fp2);
    }
    decode(input,output)
    char *input,*output;
    {
            int ch;
            FILE *fp1,*fp2;

            if((fp1=fopen(input,"r"))==0) {
                    printf("cannot open input file\n");
                    exit();
            }

            if((fp2=fopen(output,"w"))==0) {
                    printf("cannot open output file\n");
                    exit();
            }

            do {
                    ch=tolower(getc(fp1));
                    if(ch==EOF) break;
                    if(isalpha(ch) || ch==' ') {
                            ch=alphabet[find(sub,ch)];
                    }
                    putc(ch,fp2);
            } while(1);
            fclose(fp1); fclose(fp2);
    }

    find(s,ch)
    char *s;
    char ch;
    {
            register int t;

            for(t=0;t<28;t++) if(ch==s[t]) return t;
    }
```

Although code-breaking is examined later in this chapter, you should know that even this improved substitution code can still be broken easily by using a frequency table of the English language, in which the statistical information of the use of each letter of the alphabet is recorded. By looking at the coded message of the example, you can probably deduce that "s" represents "e," the most common letter in the English language, and that "p" represents the space. You can probably decode the rest. (You use the same process to solve the "cryptogram," which is next to the crossword puzzle in your newspaper.) Furthermore, the larger the coded message is, the easier it is to crack with a frequency table.

To impede the progress of a code-breaker who applies frequency tables to a coded message, you can use a *multiple substitution cipher* in which the same letter in the plaintext message would not necessarily have the same letter in the coded form. You can do this by adding a second randomized alphabet, and switching between it and the first alphabet each time a letter is repeated. For example, the program can be rewritten to use this second string:

poi uytrewqasdfghjklmnbvcxz

The multiple substitution cipher shown here will work only with letters of the alphabet, switching randomized alphabets after a letter is repeated twice. It requires that all messages be only one line long.

```
#include "ctype.h"
#include "stdio.h"
char sub[28]=      "qazwsxedcrfvtgbyhnujm ikolp";
char sub2[28]=     "poi uytrewqasdfghjklmnbvcxz";
char alphabet[28]="abcdefghijklmnopqrstuvwxyz ";
char count[27];
main(argc,argv)  /* multiple substitution cipher */
int argc;
char *argv[];
{
        register int t;

        for(t=0;t<27;++t) count[t]=0;
        if(argc!=4) {
                printf("usage: input output encode/decode\n");
                exit();
        }
        if(toupper(*argv[3])=='E') code(argv[1],argv[2]);
        else decode(argv[1],argv[2]);
}

code(input,output)
char *input,*output;
{
        int ch,change,t;
        FILE *fp1,*fp2;

        if((fp1=fopen(input,"r"))==0) {
                printf("cannot open input file\n");
                exit();
        }

        if((fp2=fopen(output,"w"))==0) {
                printf("cannot open output file\n");
                exit();
```

```
        }

        change=1;
        do {
                ch=tolower(getc(fp1));
                if(ch==EOF) break;
                t=index(ch);
                count[t]++;
                if(isalpha(ch) || ch==' ') {
                    if(change)
                            ch=sub[find(alphabet,ch)];
                    else {
                            ch=sub2[find(alphabet,ch)];
                    }
                }
                putc(ch,fp2);
                if(count[t]==2) {
                    change=!change;
                    count[t]=0;
                }
        } while(1);
        fclose(fp1); fclose(fp2);
}
decode(input,output)
char *input,*output;
{
        int ch,change;
        FILE *fp1,*fp2;

        if((fp1=fopen(input,"r"))==0) {
                printf("cannot open input file\n");
                exit();
        }

        if((fp2=fopen(output,"w"))==0) {
                printf("cannot open output file\n");
                exit();
        }
        change=1;
        do {
                ch=getc(fp1);
                if(ch==EOF) break;
                if(isalpha(ch) || ch==' ') {
                    if(change) {
                        ch=alphabet[find(sub,ch)];
                        count[index(ch)]++;
                    }
                    else {
                        ch=alphabet[find(sub2,ch)];
                        count[index(ch)]++;
                    }
                }
                putc(ch,fp2);
                if(count[index(ch)]==2)  {
                        change=!change;
                        count[index(ch)]=0;
                }
        } while(1);
        fclose(fp1); fclose(fp2);
}
```

```
find(s,ch)
char *s;
char ch;
{
        register int t;

        for(t=0;t<28;t++) if(ch==s[t]) return t;
}

index(ch)
char ch;
{
        ch=tolower(ch);
        if(isalpha(ch)) return ch-'a';
        else return 26;
}
```

For example, after you use the program on the message

meet me at sunset

it appears as

tsslzsspplpumguuj

To see how this works, examine the ordered alphabet and the two random-ized alphabets (called R1 and R2) set up over one another:

alphabet	acdefghijklmnopqrstuvwxyz<space>
R1	qazwsxedcrfvtgbyhnujm ikolp
R2	poi uytrewqasdfghjklmnbvcxz

Here is how the program operates: at the start, R1 is used. The first letter in the message is "m," which corresponds to "t" in R1. The "m" position in the array **count** is incremented to 1. The next letter is "e," which becomes "s," and the "e" position in the **count** array is incremented to 1. When the second "e" is encountered, because R1 is still used to translate it, it too becomes "s," and the "e" position in **count** is incremented to 2. This causes the program to change to the R2 alphabet and to zero the "e" position in the **count** array. The "t" then becomes "l" and the space becomes "z." After the "m" of "me" is translated to "s," the R1 alphabet is used again because a repeated letter has been encountered. The process of alternating alphabets continues until the message ends.

Using a multiple substitution cipher makes it much harder to break a code by using frequency tables. It would be possible to use several different randomized alphabets and a more complex switching routine to have all letters in the coded text occur equally. In this case, a frequency table would be useless in breaking the code.

Transposition Ciphers

One of the earliest known transposition codes was designed by the Spartans around 475 B.C. It used a device called a *skytale*. A skytale is basically a strap that is wrapped around a cylinder upon which a message is written crossways. The strap is then unwound and delivered to the recipient of the message, who also has a cylinder of equal size. Theoretically, it is impossible to read the strap without the cylinder, because the letters are out of order. In actual practice, however, this method leaves something to be desired because many different cylinder sizes can be tried until the message begins to make sense.

You can create a computerized version of a skytale by placing your message into an array a certain way and writing it out a different way. For example, if the following **union**

```
union message {
        char s[100];
        char s2[20][5];
} skytale;
```

is initialized to nulls, and if you then placed the message

meet me at sunset

into array **skytale.s** but viewed it as the two-dimensional array **skytale.s2**, it would look like this.

m	e	e	t	
m	e		a	t
	s	u	n	s
e	t	0	0	0
0	0	0	0	0

⋮

If you then wrote the array out by column, the message would look like this:

mm e...eest...e u...tan... ts...

where the periods indicate the null padding. To decode the message, columns
are fed into **skytale.s2**. Then the array **skytale.s** can be displayed in normal
order. The **skytale.s** array can be printed as a string because the message
will be null-terminated. The Skytale Cipher program uses this method to
code and decode messages.

```
#include "ctype.h"
#include "stdio.h"
union message {
        char s[100];
        char s2[20][5];
} skytale;

main(argc,argv)  /* skytale cypher */
int argc;
char *argv[];
{
        int t;

        for(t=0;t<100;++t) skytale.s[t]=0; /* load array */

        if(argc!=4) {
                printf("usage: input output encode/decode\n");
                exit();
        }
```

```
            if(toupper(*argv[3])=='E') code(argv[1],argv[2]);
            else decode(argv[1],argv[2]);
    }

code(input,output)
char *input,*output;
{
            int t,t2;
            FILE *fp1,*fp2;

            if((fp1=fopen(input,"r"))==0) {
                    printf("cannot open input file\n");
                    exit();
            }

            if((fp2=fopen(output,"w"))==0) {
                    printf("cannot open output file\n");
                    exit();
            }
            for(t=0;t<100;++t) {
                    skytale.s[t]=getc(fp1);
                    if(skytale.s[t]==EOF) {
                            skytale.s[t]=0;
                            break;
                    }
            }
            for(t=0;t<5;++t)
                for(t2=0;t2<20;++t2)
                    putc(skytale.s2[t2][t],fp2);

            fclose(fp1); fclose(fp2);
    }

decode(input,output)
char *input,*output;
{
            int t,t2;
            FILE *fp1,*fp2;

            if((fp1=fopen(input,"r"))==0) {
                    printf("cannot open input file\n");
                    exit();
            }

            if((fp2=fopen(output,"w"))==0) {
                    printf("cannot open output file\n");
                    exit();
            }
            for(t=0;t<5;++t)
                for(t2=0;t2<20;++t2)
                    if((skytale.s2[t2][t]=getc(fp1))==EOF) break;

            for(t=0;t<100;++t)
                        putc(skytale.s[t],fp2);

            fclose(fp1); fclose(fp2);
    }
```

Naturally, there are other methods of obtaining transposed messages. One method particularly suited for computer use swaps letters within the message as defined by some algorithm. For example, here is a program that transposes letters up to a user-specified distance, starting from the front of the array and alternating its exchange with the end of the array:

```
#include "ctype.h"
#include "stdio.h"
main(argc,argv)  /* transposition cipher */
int argc;
char *argv[];
{
        int dist;

        if(argc!=5) {
            printf("usage: input output encode/decode distance\n");
            exit();
        }

        dist=atoi(argv[4]);
        if(toupper(*argv[3])=='E') code(argv[1],argv[2],dist);
        else decode(argv[1],argv[2],dist);
}

code(input,output,dist)
char *input,*output;
int dist;
{
        char done,temp;
        int t;
        char s[256];
        FILE *fp1,*fp2;

        if((fp1=fopen(input,"r"))==0) {
                printf("cannot open input file\n");
                exit();
        }

        if((fp2=fopen(output,"w"))==0) {
                printf("cannot open output file\n");
                exit();
        }

        done=0;
        do {
            for(t=0;t<(dist*2);++t) {
                s[t]=getc(fp1);
                if(s[t]==EOF) {
                        s[t]=0; /* if eof then null */
                        done=1;
                }
            }
            for(t=0;t<dist;t++) {
                temp=s[t];
```

```
                        s[t]=s[t+dist];
                        s[t+dist]=temp;
                        t++;
                        temp=s[t];
                        s[t]=s[dist*2-t];
                        s[dist*2-t]=temp;
                }
                for(t=0;t<dist*2;t++) putc(s[t],fp2);
        } while(!done);
        fclose(fp1); fclose(fp2);
}
decode(input,output,dist)
char *input,*output;
int dist;
{
        char done,temp;
        int t;
        char s[256];
        FILE *fp1,*fp2;

        if((fp1=fopen(input,"r"))==0) {
                printf("cannot open input file\n");
                exit();
        }

        if((fp2=fopen(output,"w"))==0) {
                printf("cannot open output file\n");
                exit();
        }

        done=0;
        do {
            for(t=0;t<(dist*2);++t) {
                s[t]=getc(fp1);
                if(s[t]==EOF) {
                        s[t]=0; /* if eof then null */
                        done=1;
                }
            }
            for(t=0;t<dist;t++) {
                t++;
                temp=s[t];
                s[t]=s[dist*2-t];
                s[dist*2-t]=temp;
                t--;
                temp=s[t];
                s[t]=s[t+dist];
                s[t+dist]=temp;
                t++;
            }
            for(t=0;t<dist*2;t++) putc(s[t],fp2);
        } while(!done);
        fclose(fp1); fclose(fp2);
}
```

If you use this method with a distance of 10, the message

> meet me at sunset

will look something like this:

> <space>usetn smte metae

Used by themselves, transposition ciphers can accidentally create "clues" in the transposition process. In the sample text just given, the partial words "set" and "me" are suspiciously suggestive.

Bit-Manipulation Ciphers

The digital computer has given rise to a new method of encoding: manipulating the bits that compose the actual characters of the plaintext. Although the real purist would claim that *bit manipulation* (or *alteration*, as it is sometimes called) is really just a variation on the substitution cipher, the concepts, methods, and options differ so significantly that it must be considered a cipher method in its own right.

Bit-manipulation ciphers are well-suited for computer use because they employ operations easily performed by the system. Also, the ciphertext tends to look completely unintelligible, which adds to security by making the data look like unused or crashed files and thereby confusing anyone who tries to gain access to the file.

Generally, bit-manipulation ciphers are applicable only to computer-based files and cannot be used to create hardcopy messages because the bit manipulations tend to produce nonprinting characters. For this reason, you should assume that any file coded by bit-manipulation methods will remain in a computer file.

Bit-manipulation ciphers convert plaintext into ciphertext by altering the actual bit pattern of each character through the use of one or more of the following logical operators:

AND
OR
NOT
XOR
1's complement

C is perhaps the best language for creating bit-manipulation ciphers because it supports the following bitwise operators:

Operator	Meaning
|	OR
&	AND
^	XOR
~	1's complement

The simplest and least secure bit-manipulation cipher uses only ~, the 1's complement operator. (Remember that the ~ operator causes each bit within a byte to be inverted: 1 becomes 0, and 0 becomes 1.) Therefore, a byte complemented twice is the same as the original. The 1's Complement Cipher program presented here codes any text file.

```
#include "stdio.h"
main(argc,argv)  /* 1's complement cipher */
int argc;
char *argv[];
{
        if(argc!=4) {
                printf("usage: input output encode/decode\n");
                exit();
        }
        if(toupper(*argv[3])=='E') code(argv[1],argv[2]);
        else decode(argv[1],argv[2]);
}

code(input,output)
char *input,*output;
{
        int ch;
        FILE *fp1,*fp2;

        if((fp1=fopen(input,"r"))==0) {
                printf("cannot open input file\n");
                exit();
        }
```

```
            if((fp2=fopen(output,"w"))==0) {
                    printf("cannot open output file\n");
                    exit();
            }

            do {
                    ch=getc(fp1);
                    if(ch==EOF) break;
                    ch=~ch;
                    if(ch==EOF) ch++;
                    putc(ch,fp2);
            } while(1);
            fclose(fp1); fclose(fp2);
    }
    decode(input,output)
    char *input,*output;
    {
            int ch;
            FILE *fp1,*fp2;

            if((fp1=fopen(input,"r"))==0) {
                    printf("cannot open input file\n");
                    exit();
            }

            if((fp2=fopen(output,"w"))==0) {
                    printf("cannot open output file\n");
                    exit();
            }

            do {
                    ch=getc(fp1);
                    if(ch==EOF) break;
                    ch=~ch;
                    if(ch==EOF) ch--;
                    putc(ch,fp2);
            } while(1);
            fclose(fp1); fclose(fp2);
    }
```

Notice that the EOF character has been given special care so that it will
not confuse the disk-file routines. If an EOF is created with the encryption
process, you must alter it so that it will become another character. Although
this creates a double mapping in some cases, it is usually not possible to
create an EOF by inverting the bits of a text file; the extra code is just a
precaution. Also, it assumes that EOF is -1, which is the case for most C
compilers; however, if EOF is not -1, you should consult your user manual
and make appropriate changes. If you think that a double mapping could
occur, you should find some other method of handling this problem.

It is not possible to show what the ciphertext of a message would look like,
because the bit manipulation used here generally creates nonprinting characters. Try it on your computer and examine the file — it will look quite cryptic, indeed!

There are two problems with this simple coding scheme. First, the encryption program does not use a key to decode, so anyone with access to the program can decode an encoded file. Second, and perhaps more important, this method would be easily spotted by any experienced computer programmer.

An improved method of bit-manipulation coding uses the XOR operator. The XOR operator has the following truth table:

XOR	0	1
0	0	1
1	1	0

The outcome of the XOR operation is TRUE if and only if one operand is TRUE and the other is FALSE. This gives the XOR a unique property: if you XOR a byte with another byte called the *key*, and then take the outcome of that operation and XOR it again with the key, the result will be the original byte, as shown here.

```
       1 1 0 1    1 0 0 1   ┐
XOR    0 1 0 1    0 0 1 1 (key)  │
       ───────    ───────       │
       1 0 0 0    1 0 1 0       ├─same
       1 0 0 0    1 0 1 0       │
XOR    0 1 0 1    0 0 1 1 (key)  │
       ───────    ───────       │
       1 1 0 1    1 0 0 1   ┘
```

When used to code a file, this process solves the two inherent problems of the method that uses 1's complement. First of all, because it uses a key, the encryption program alone cannot decode a file; second, because using a key makes each file unique, what has been done to the file is not obvious to someone schooled only in computer science.

The key does not have to be just one byte long. For example, you could use a key of several characters and alternate the characters through the file. However, a single-character key is used here to keep the program uncluttered.

```c
#include "stdio.h"
main(argc,argv) /* XOR cipher with key */
int argc;
char *argv[];
{
        if(argc!=5) {
                printf("usage: input output decode/encode key\n");
                exit();
        }
        if(toupper(*argv[3])=='E')
                code(argv[1],argv[2],*argv[4]);
        else
                decode(argv[1],argv[2],*argv[4]);

}

code(input,output,key)
char *input,*output;
char key;
{
        int ch;
        FILE *fp1,*fp2;

        if((fp1=fopen(input,"r"))==0) {
                printf("cannot open input file\n");
                exit();
        }

        if((fp2=fopen(output,"w"))==0) {
                printf("cannot open output file\n");
                exit();
        }

        do {
                ch=getc(fp1);
                if(ch==EOF) break;
                ch=ch^key;
                if(ch==EOF) ch++;
                putc(ch,fp2);
        } while(1);
        fclose(fp1); fclose(fp2);
}

decode(input,output,key)
char *input,*output;
char key;
{
        int ch;
        FILE *fp1,*fp2;

        if((fp1=fopen(input,"r"))==0) {
                printf("cannot open input file\n");
                exit();
        }

        if((fp2=fopen(output,"w"))==0) {
                printf("cannot open output file\n");
```

```
                exit();
        }

        do {
                ch=getc(fp1);
                if(ch==EOF) break;
                ch=ch^key;
                if(ch==EOF+1) ch--;
                putc(ch,fp2);
        } while(1);
        fclose(fp1); fclose(fp2);
}
```

Data Compression

Data-compression techniques essentially squeeze a given amount of information into a smaller area. Data compression is often used in computer systems to increase the storage (by reducing the storage needs of the computer user) to save transfer time (especially over phone lines), and to provide a level of security. Although there are many data-compression schemes available, this chapter will examine only two of them. The first is *bit compression*, where more than one character is stored in a single byte, and the second is *character deletion*, in which actual characters from the file are deleted.

Eight Into Seven

Most modern computers use byte sizes that are even powers of two because of the binary representation of data in the machine. The uppercase and lower-case letters and the punctuation only require about 63 different codes needing only 6 bits to represent a byte. (A 6-bit byte could have values of 0 through 63.) However, most computers use an 8-bit byte; thus, 25% of the byte's storage is wasted in simple text files. You could, therefore, actually compact 4 characters into 3 bytes if you could use the last 2 bits in each byte. The only problem is the way in which ASCII codes are organized—there are more than 63 different ASCII character codes, and the uppercase and lower-case alphabet falls more or less in the middle. This means that some of the characters will require at least 7 bits. It is possible to use a non-ASCII representation (which, on rare occasions, is done), but it is not generally advisable. An easier option is to compact 8 characters into 7 bytes, exploiting the fact that no letter or common punctuation mark uses the 8th bit of a byte. Therefore, you can use the 8th bit of each of the 7 bytes to store the eighth character. However, you should realize that many computers—including the IBM PC—do use 8-bit characters to represent special characters or graphics characters. Also, some word processors use the eighth bit to indicate text-processing instructions. Therefore, the use of this type of data compaction will only work on "straight" ASCII files that do not use the 8th bit for anything.

To visualize how this works, consider the following 8 characters represented as 8-bit bytes:

byte 1	0 1 1 1		0 1 0 1
byte 2	0 1 1 1		1 1 0 1
byte 3	0 0 1 0		0 0 1 1
byte 4	0 1 0 1		0 1 1 0
byte 5	0 0 0 1		0 0 0 0
byte 6	0 1 1 0		1 1 0 1
byte 7	0 0 1 0		1 0 1 0
byte 8	0 1 1 1		1 0 0 1

As you can see, the eighth bit is always 0. This is always the case unless the eighth bit is used for parity checking. The easiest way to compress 8 characters into 7 bytes is to distribute the 7 significant bits of byte 1 into the 7 unused eighth-bit positions of bytes 2 through 8. The 7 remaining bytes then appear as follows:

byte 1—read down

byte 2	1	1	1	1	1	1	0	1
byte 3	1	0	1	0	0	0	1	1
byte 4	1	1	0	1	0	1	1	0
byte 5	0	0	0	1	0	0	0	0
byte 6	1	1	1	0	1	1	0	1
byte 7	0	0	1	0	1	0	1	0
byte 8	1	1	1	1	1	0	0	1

To reconstruct byte 1, you just put it back together again by taking the eighth bit off of each of the 7 bytes.

This compression technique compresses any text file by 1/8, or 12.5%. This is quite a substantial savings. For example, if you were transmitting the source code for your favorite program to a friend over long-distance phone lines, you would be saving 12.5% of the expense of transmission. (Remember, the object code, or executable version of the program, needs the full 8 bits.)

The following program compresses a text file using the method just described:

```
#include "stdio.h"
main(argc,argv) /* Bit Comparison */
int argc;
char *argv[];
{
        if(argc!=4) {
                printf("usage: input output compress/decompress\n");
                exit();
        }
        if(toupper(*argv[3])=='C')
                compress(argv[1],argv[2]);
        else
                decompress(argv[1],argv[2]);

}

compress(input,output)
char *input,*output;
{
        char ch,ch2,t,done;
        FILE *fp1,*fp2;

        if((fp1=fopen(input,"r"))==0) {
                printf("cannot open input file\n");
                exit();
        }

        if((fp2=fopen(output,"w"))==0) {
                printf("cannot open output file\n");
                exit();
        }

        done=0;
        do {
            ch=getc(fp1);
            if(ch==EOF) break;
            ch=ch << 1;
            for(t=0;t<7;++t) {
                    ch2=getc(fp1);
                    if(ch2==EOF) {
                            ch2=0;
                            done=1;
```

```
                      }
                      ch2=ch2 & 127;  /* turn off top bit */
                      ch2=ch2 | ((ch<<t) & 128);
                      putc(ch2,fp2);
                   }
            } while(!done);
            fclose(fp1); fclose(fp2);
      }

      decompress(input,output)
      char *input,*output;

      {
            unsigned char ch,ch2,t,done;
            char s[7],temp;
            FILE *fp1,*fp2;

            if((fp1=fopen(input,"r"))==0) {
                   printf("cannot open input file\n");
                   exit();
            }

            if((fp2=fopen(output,"w"))==0) {
                   printf("cannot open output file\n");
                   exit();
            }

            done=0;
            do {
                   ch=0;
                   for(t=0;t<7;++t) {
                      temp=getc(fp1);
                      if(temp==EOF) break;
                      ch2=temp; /* type conversion */
                      s[t]=ch2 & 127; /* turn off top bit */
                      ch2=ch2 & 128;  /* turn off all but top bit */
                      ch2=ch2 >> t+1;
                      ch=ch | ch2;
                   }
                   putc(ch,fp2);
                   for(t=0;t<7;++t) putc(s[t],fp2);
            } while(temp!=EOF);
            fclose(fp1); fclose(fp2);
      }
```

This program's code is fairly complex because various bits must be shifted around. Keep in mind that some C compilers handle signed characters differently than unsigned characters. (The compiler used here—Aztec C for the IBM PC—required that unsigned characters be used for bit shifts, but that a signed character be used to detect EOF, thereby requiring the type conversions you see in the routines.)

The 16-Character Language

Although unsuitable for most situations, an interesting method of data compression deletes unnecessary letters from words, in essence making most words into abbreviations. Data compression is accomplished because the unused characters are not stored. The use of abbreviations to save space is very common: for example, "Mr." is commonly used instead of "Mister." Instead of using actual abbreviations, the method presented in this section automatically removes certain letters from a message. To do this, a *minimal alphabet* will be needed. A minimal alphabet is one in which several seldom-used letters have been removed, leaving only those necessary to form most words or avoid ambiguity. Therefore, any character not in the minimal alphabet will be extracted from any word in which it appears. Exactly how many characters there are in a minimal alphabet is a matter of choice. However, this section uses the 14 most common letters, plus spaces and newlines.

Automating the abbreviation process requires that you know what letters in the alphabet are used most frequently so that you can create a minimal alphabet. In theory, you could count the letters in each word in a dictionary; however, different writers use a different frequency mix than others, so a frequency chart based just on the words that make up the English language may not reflect the actual usage frequency of letters. (It would also take a *long* time to count the letters!) As an alternative, you can count the frequency of the letters in this chapter and use them as a basis for our minimal alphabet. To do this, you could use this simple program. The program skips all punctuation except periods, commas, and spaces.

```
#include "stdio.h"
#include "ctype.h"

main(argc,argv) /* character frequency program */
int argc;
char *argv[];
{
        FILE *fp1;
        int alpha[26],t;
        int space=0,period=0,comma=0;
        char ch;

        if(argc!=2) {
                printf("Please specify text file.\n");
                exit(0);
        }

        if((fp1=fopen(argv[1],"r"))==0) {
                printf("cannot open input file\n");
                exit();
        }

        for(t=0;t<26;t++) alpha[t]=0;
```

```
do {
        ch=getc(fp1);
        if(isalpha(ch))
                alpha[toupper(ch)-'A']++;
        else switch(ch) {
                case ' ': space++;
                        break;
                case '.': period++;
                        break;
                case ',': comma++;
                        break;
        }
} while(ch!=EOF);

for(t=0;t<26;++t)
        printf("%c: %d\n",'A'+t,alpha[t]);

printf("period: %d\n",period);
printf("space: %d\n",space);
printf("comma: %d\n",comma);
fclose(fp1);
}
```

By running the program on the text of this chapter, you get the following frequency:

A	2525
B	532
C	838
D	1145
E	3326
F	828
G	529
H	1086
I	2242
J	39
K	94
L	1103
M	1140
N	2164
O	1767
P	697
Q	62
R	1656
S	1672
T	3082
U	869
V	376
W	370
X	178
Y	356
Z	20
Space	5710
Period	234
Comma	513

The frequency of letters in this chapter compares well with the standard English mix and is offset only by the repeated use of the C keywords in the programs.

To achieve significant data compression, you need to cut the alphabet substantially by removing the letters used least frequently. Although there are many different ideas about exactly what a workable minimum alphabet is, the 14 most common letters and the space account for about 85% of all the characters used in this chapter. Because the newline character is also necessary to preserve word breaks, it must also be included. Therefore, the minimal alphabet used in this section consists of 14 characters, a space, and a newline.

A C D E H I L M N O R S T U <space> <newline>

Here is a program that removes all characters except the 16 selected.

```
#include "stdio.h"
main(argc,argv)   /*  Character deletion compression program */
int argc;
char *argv[];
{
        if(argc!=3) {
                printf("usage: input output\n");
                exit();
        }
        comp2(argv[1],argv[2]);
}

comp2(input,output)
char *input,*output;
{
        char ch;
        FILE *fp1,*fp2;

        if((fp1=fopen(input,"r"))==0) {
                printf("cannot open input file\n");
                exit();
        }

        if((fp2=fopen(output,"w"))==0) {
                printf("cannot open output file\n");
                exit();
        }

        do {
                ch=getc(fp1);
                if(ch==EOF) break;
                if(is_in(toupper(ch),"ACDEJILMNORSTU '\n'")) {
                        if(ch=='\n') putc('\r',fp2);
                        putc(ch,fp2);
                }
        } while(1);
```

```
        fclose(fp1); fclose(fp2);
}

is_in(ch,s)
char ch,*s;
{
        while(*s) {
                if(ch==*s) return 1;
                s++;
        }
        return 0;
}
```

If you use this program on the message

> Attention High Command:
>
>> Attack successful. Please send additional supplies
>> and fresh troops. This is essential to maintain our
>> foothold.
>
>> General Frashier

the compressed message would look like this:

> Attention i Command
>
>> Attac successul lease send additional sulies
>> and res troos Tis is essential to maintain our
>> ootold
>
>> eneral rasier

As you can see, the message is largely readable, although some ambiguity is present. Ambiguity is the chief drawback of this method of data compression. However, if you are familiar with the vocabulary of the writer of the message, you could probably select a better minimal alphabet that would remove some of this ambiguity. In spite of the potential for ambiguity, quite a bit of space was saved. The original message was 168 bytes long and the compacted message was 142 bytes long—a savings of about 16%.

If both character deletion and bit compression were applied to the message, then about 28% less storage space would have been needed, which could be important. For example, if you were a submarine captain and wanted to send a message to headquarters but did not want to give away your position, you might want to compress the message by using both methods so that it would be as short as possible.

Both the bit-compression and character-deletion methods of data compression have uses in encryption. Bit compression further encrypts the information and makes decoding more difficult. If used before encryption, the character-deletion method has one wonderful advantage: it disguises the character frequency of the source language.

Code-Breaking

No chapter on encryption is complete without a brief look at code-breaking. The art of code-breaking is essentially one of trial and error. With the use of digital computers, relatively simple ciphers can easily be broken through exhaustive trial and error. However, the more complex codes either cannot be broken or require techniques and resources not commonly available. For simplicity, this section focuses on breaking the more straightforward codes.

If you wish to break a message that was ciphered using a simple substitution method and only an offset alphabet, then all you need to do is try all 26 possible offsets to see which one fits. A program to do this is shown here.

```
#include "ctype.h"
#include "stdio.h"
main(argc,argv)  /* code breaker for simple substitution
                    cipher */
int argc;
char *argv[];
{
        if(argc!=2) {
                printf("usage: input\n");
                exit();
        }
        bc(argv[1]);
}

bc(input)
char *input;
{
        register int t,t2;
        char ch,s[1000],q[10];
        FILE *fp1;

        if((fp1=fopen(input,"r"))==0) {
                printf("cannot open input file\n");
                exit();
        }

        for(t=0;t<1000;++t) {
                s[t]=getc(fp1);
                if(s[t]==EOF) break;
        }
        s[t]='\0';
```

```
        fclose(fp1);
        for(t=0;t<26;++t) {
                for(t2=0;s[t2];t2++) {
                        ch=s[t2];
                        if(isalpha(ch)) {
                                ch=tolower(ch)+t;
                                if(ch>'z') ch-=26;
                        }
                        printf("%c",ch);
                }
                printf("\n");
                printf("decoded? (y/n): ");
                gets(q);
                if(*q=='y') break;
        }
        printf("\noffset is: %d",t);

}
```

With only a slight variation, you could use the same program to break
ciphers that use a random alphabet. In this case, substitute manually entered
alphabets, as shown in this program:

```
#include "ctype.h"
#include "stdio.h"
char sub[28];
char alphabet[28]="abcdefghijklmnopqrstuvwxyz ";
main(argc,argv)  /* code-breaker for random substitution */
int argc;
char *argv[];
{
        char s[80];

        if(argc!=2) {
                printf("usage: input");
                exit();
        }

        do {
                printf("enter test alphabet:\n");
                gets(sub);
                bc2(argv[1]);
                printf("\nIs this right?: (y/n) ");
                gets(s);
        } while(tolower(*s)!='y');

}

bc2(input)
char *input;
{
        char ch;
        FILE *fp1,*fp2;

        if((fp1=fopen(input,"r"))==0) {
                printf("cannot open input file\n");
                exit();
```

```
        }
        do {
                ch=getc(fp1);
                if(ch==EOF) break;
                if(isalpha(ch) || ch==' ') {
                        putchar(alphabet[find(sub,ch)]);
                }
        } while(1);
        fclose(fp1); fclose(fp2);
}

find(s,ch)
char *s;
char ch;
{
        register int t;
        for(t=0;t<28;t++) if(ch==s[t]) return t;
}
```

Unlike substitution ciphers, transposition and bit-manipulation ciphers are harder to break using the trial-and-error methods. If you have to break such complex codes, good luck!

Oh, and by the way—hsaovbno wlymljapvu pz haahpuhisl, pa vjjbyz vusf hz hu hjjpklua.

Random Number Generators And Simulations

C H A P T E R   8

Random number sequences are used in a variety of programming situations that range from simulations, which are the most common, to games and other recreational software. Unlike other programming languages, C does not contain a built-in function that generates random numbers. Although many C compilers have some sort of random number generator in their standard libraries, many do not. Also, the quality of many random number generators is not sufficient for some demanding situations, and at times it is important to have control over the way random numbers are produced.

In this chapter you will study the way various random number generating functions are written and learn how to evaluate them. You will also look at two interesting simulations that use the random number generators developed in the chapter. The first is a grocery store check-out simulation and the second is a random-walk stock portfolio manager.

Random Number Generators

Technically, the term *random number generator* is absurd; numbers, in and of themselves, are not random. For example, is 100 a random number? Is 25? Of course not. What is really meant by "random number generator" is something that creates a *sequence* of numbers that appear to be in random order. This raises a more complex question: What is a random sequence of numbers? The only correct answer is that a random sequence of numbers is one in which all elements are completely unrelated. This definition leads to the paradox that any sequence can be both nonrandom and random, depending on the way the sequence was obtained. For example, this following list of numbers:

$$1\ 2\ 3\ 4\ 5\ 6\ 7\ 8\ 9\ 0$$

was created by typing the top row of keys on the keyboard in order, so the sequence certainly cannot be construed as random. But what if you happened to pull out exactly that sequence from a barrel full of ping-pong balls that had numbers written on them? Then it *would* be a random sequence. This discussion shows that the randomness of a sequence depends on *how it was generated*, not on what the actual sequence is.

Keep in mind that sequences of numbers generated by a computer are *deterministic:* each number other than the first depends on the number that precedes it. Technically, this means that only a *quasi-random* sequence of numbers can be created by a computer. However, this is sufficient for most problems, and for the purposes of this book, the sequences will simply be called random.

Generally, it is best if the numbers in a random sequence are *uniformly distributed.* (Do not confuse this with the normal distribution, or bell-shaped curve.) In a uniform distribution, all events are equally probable, so that a graph of a uniform distribution tends to be a flat line rather than a curve.

Before the widespread use of computers, whenever random numbers were needed they were produced by either throwing dice or pulling numbered balls from a jar. In 1955, the RAND Corporation published a table of 1 million random digits obtained with the help of a computer-like machine. In the early days of computer science, although many methods were devised to generate random numbers, most were discarded.

One particularly interesting method that almost worked was developed by John von Neumann—the father of the modern computer. Often referred to as the *middle-square method*, it squares the previous random number, and then extracts its middle digits. For example, if you were creating three-digit numbers and the previous value was 121, then you would square 121 to make 14641. Extracting the middle three digits would give you 464 as the next number. The problem with this method is that it tends to lead to a very short repeating pattern called a *cycle*, especially after a zero has entered the pattern. For this reason the method is not presently used.

Today, the most common way to generate random numbers is by using the following equation:

$$R_{n+1} = (aR_n + c) \bmod m$$

where

$$R >= 0$$
$$a >= 0$$
$$c >= 0$$
$$m > R, a, \text{ and } c$$

This method is sometimes referred to as the *linear congruential method*. Looking at the equation, you probably think that random number generation seems simple. There is a catch, though—how well this equation performs depends heavily on the values of a, c, and m. Choosing these values is sometimes more of an art than a science. There are complex rules that can help you choose those values; however, this discussion will cover only a few simple rules and experiments.

The modulus (m) should be fairly large because it determines the range of the random numbers. The modulus operation yields the remainder of a division that uses the same operands. Hence,

$$10 \ \% \ 4 = 2$$

because 4 goes into 10 twice with a remainder of 2. Therefore, if the modulus is 12, then only the numbers 0 through 11 can be produced by the randomizing equation, whereas if the modulus is 21,425, the numbers 0 through 21,424 can be produced. Remember, a small modulus does not actually affect randomness, only range. The choice of the multiplier, a, and the increment, c, is much harder. Usually the multiple can be fairly large and the increment fairly small. A lot of testing is necessary to confirm that a good generator has been created.

As a first example, here is a common random number generator. The equation shown in **ran1( )** has been used as the basis for the random number generator in a number of popular languages.

```
float ran1()
{
        static long int a=100001;

        a = (a*125) % 2796203;
        return (float) a/2796203;
}
```

This function has three important features. First, the random number is actually an integer —**long int** in this case—even though the function returns a **float**. The integers are necessary for the linear congruential method, but random number generators, by convention, are expected to return a number between 0 and 1, which means it is a floating point.

Second, the *seed,* or starting value, is hard-coded into the function by using the **static long int a.** This method provides a seed value to the next call. Although this feature is fine for most situations, it is possible to let the user specify the initial value to try to make the sequence more random. If a user-specified seed value is used, the function is as follows:

```
float ran1(seed)
float seed;
{
        static long int a;
        static char once=1;

        if(once){
                a=seed*1000;    /* get a first value */
                once=0;
        }

        a = (a*125) % 2796203;
        return (float) a/2796203;
}
```

However, for the rest of this chapter, the seed will be hard-coded into the functions for the sake of simplicity.

Third, the random number is divided by the modulus prior to the return. This obtains a number between 0 and 1. If you study this, you will see that the value of **a** prior to the return line must be between 0 and 2796202. Therefore, when **a** is divided by 2796203, a number equal to or greater than 0 but less than 1 is obtained.

Many random number generators are not useful because they produce nonuniform distributions or have short, repeating sequences. Even when they are very slight, these problems can produce biased results if the same random number generator is used over and over again. The solution is to create several different generators and use them either individually or jointly to obtain more random numbers. Therefore, the code for two other random number generators are presented here. The following generator, called **ran2( )**, produces a good distribution:

```
float ran2()
{
        static long int a=1;

        a = (a * 32719+3) % 32749;
        return (float) a/32749;
}
```

The generator called **ran3( )** uses fairly small numbers.

```
float ran3()
{
        static long int a=203;

        a = (a *10001 + 3) % 1717;
        return (float) a/1717;
}
```

Each of these random number generators produces a good sequence of random numbers. Yet the questions remain: How "random" are the numbers? How good are these generators?

Determining the Quality Of a Generator

You can use several tests to determine the randomness of a number sequence. None of these tests will tell you if a sequence is random, but they will tell you if it is not. The tests can identify a nonrandom sequence, but just because a test does not find a problem does not mean that a given sequence is indeed random. The test does, however, raise your confidence in the random number generator that produced the sequence. For the purposes of this chapter most of these tests are either too complicated or time-consuming in their most rigorous forms. Therefore, you will look briefly at some of the ways a sequence can be tested and how it can fail.

To begin, here is the way to find out how closely the distribution of the numbers in a sequence conforms to what you would expect a random distribution to be. For example, say that you are attempting to generate random sequences of the digits 0 through 9. Therefore, the probability of each digit occurring is 1/10, because there are 10 possibilities for each number in the sequence, all of which are equally possible. Assume that the sequence

$$9\ 1\ 8\ 2\ 4\ 6\ 3\ 7\ 5\ 8\ 2\ 9\ 0\ 4\ 2\ 4\ 7\ 8\ 6\ 2$$

was actually generated. If you count the number of times each digit occurs, the result is

Digit	Occurrences
0	1
1	1
2	4
3	1
4	3
5	1
6	2
7	2
8	3
9	2

The question you should ask next is if this distribution is sufficiently similar to the expected distribution.

Remember: If a random number generator is good, it generates sequences randomly; in a truly random state, all sequences are possible. This seems to imply that any sequence generated should qualify as a valid random sequence. So how can you tell if this sequence is random? In fact, how could any sequence of the ten digits be nonrandom, since any sequence is possible? The answer is that some sequences are *less likely* to be random than others. You can determine the *probability* of a given sequence's randomness by using the *chi-square test*. The chi-square test basically subtracts the expected number of occurrences from the observed number of occurrences for all possible outcomes to produce a number, generally called V. You can then look up this number in a table of chi-square values to find the likelihood that the sequence is random in distribution. A small chi-square table is given in Figure 8-1; you can find complete tables in most books on statistics.

The formula to obtain V is

$$V = \sum_{1 \leq i \leq N} \frac{(O_i - E_i)^2}{E_i}$$

where O_i is the number of observed occurrences, E_i is the number of expected occurrences, and N is the number of discrete elements. The value for E_i is determined by multiplying the probability of that element occurring by the number of observations. In this case, because each digit is expected to

	p=99%	p=95%	p=75%	p=50%	p=25%	p=5%
n=5	0.5543	1.1455	2.675	4.351	6.626	11.07
n=10	2.558	3.940	6.737	9.342	12.55	18.31
n=15	5.229	7.261	11.04	14.34	18.25	25.00
n=20	8.260	10.85	15.45	19.34	23.83	31.41
n=30	14.95	18.49	24.48	29.34	34.80	43.77

Figure 8-1. Selected chi-square values

occur one-tenth of the time, if 20 samples are taken, the value for E will be 2 for all digits. N is 10 because there are 10 possible elements, the digits 0 through 9. Therefore,

$$V = \frac{(1-2)^2}{2} + \frac{(1-2)^2}{2} + \frac{(4-2)^2}{2} + \frac{(1-2)^2}{2} + \frac{(3-2)^2}{2} + \frac{(1-2)^2}{2} +$$

$$\frac{(2-2)^2}{2} + \frac{(2-2)^2}{2} + \frac{(3-2)^2}{2} + \frac{(2-2)^2}{2} = 5$$

To determine the likelihood that the sequence is not random, find the row in the table in Figure 8-1 that equals the number of observations; in this case, it is 20. Then read across until you find a number that is greater than V. In this case, it is column 1. This means that there is a 99% likelihood that a sample of 20 elements will have a V greater than 8.260. Therefore, there is only a 1% probability that the sequence is random. To "pass" the chi-square test, the probability of V must fall between 25% and 75%. (This range is derived from mathematics beyond the scope of this book.)

You might, however, counter this conclusion with the following question: Since all sequences are possible, how can this sequence have only a 1% chance of being legitimate? The answer is that it is just a probability—the chi-square test is actually not a test at all, only a confidence builder. In fact, if you use the chi-square test, you should obtain several different sequences and average the results to avoid rejecting a good random number generator. Any single sequence might be rejected, but averaging several sequences together should provide a good test.

On the other hand, a sequence can pass the chi-square test and still not be random. For example,

1 3 5 7 9 2 4 6 8

would pass the chi-square test but does not appear very random. In this case, a *run* has been generated. A run is simply a sequence of strictly ascending or descending numbers that are at evenly spaced intervals. Each group of four digits is in strictly ascending order and as such (assuming it continued) would not be a random sequence. Runs can be separated by "noise" digits as well: the digits that comprise the run can be interspersed throughout an otherwise random sequence. It is possible to design tests to detect these situations, but they are beyond the scope of this book.

Another feature to test for is the length of the *period;* that is, how many numbers can be generated before the sequence begins to repeat — or worse, degenerate into a short cycle. All computer-based random number generators eventually repeat a sequence. The longer the period, the better the generator. Even though the frequency of the numbers within the period is uniformly distributed, the numbers do not constitute a random series, because a truly random series will not repeat itself consistently. Generally, a period of several thousand numbers is sufficient for most applications. (Again, a test for this can be performed, but it is beyond the scope of this book.)

Several other tests can be applied to determine the quality of a random number generator. In fact, there probably has been more code written to test random number generators than has been written to construct them. Here is yet another test that allows you to test random number generators "visually" by using a graph to show how the sequence is generated.

Ideally, the graph should be based on the frequency of each number. However, since a random number generator can produce thousands of different numbers, this is impractical. Instead, you will create a graph grouped by the tenths digit of each number; for example, since all random numbers produced are between 0 and 1, the number 0.9365783 is grouped under 9 and 0.34523445 is grouped under 3. This means that the graph of the output of the Random Number Generator Display program has 10 lines, with each line representing the number of times a particular number in the group occurred. The program also prints the mean of each sequence, which can be used to detect a bias in the numbers. Like the other graphics programs in this chapter, this program runs only on an IBM PC that is equipped with a color-graphics display adapter.

```
int freq1[10]={0,0,0,0,0,0,0,0,0,0};
int freq2[10]={0,0,0,0,0,0,0,0,0,0};
int freq3[10]={0,0,0,0,0,0,0,0,0,0};

main()   /* random number generator display program */
{
        int x,y;
        float ran1(),ran2(),ran3();
        float f,f2,f3,r,r2,r3;
        char s[80];

        mode(4);
        ground(0);
        palette(1);
        color('R');
        f=0;f2=0;f3=0;
```

```
        scr_curs(0,6);
        printf("Comparison of Random Number");
        scr_curs(2,15);
        printf("Generators");
        line(0,20,90,20);
        line(110,20,200,20);
        line(220,20,310,20);
        scr_curs(23,3);
        printf("ran1()        ran2()        ran3()");

        for(x=0;x<1000;++x) {
                r=ran1();
                f+=r;
                y=r*10;
                freq1[y]++;

                r2=ran2();
                f2+=r2;
                y=r2*10;
                freq2[y]++;

                r3=ran3();
                f3+=r3;
                y=r3*10;
                freq3[y]++;

                display();
        }
        gets(s);
        mode(3);
        printf("mean of random number function 1: %f\n",f/1000);
        printf("mean of random number function 2: %f\n",f2/1000);
        printf("mean of random number function 3: %f\n",f3/1000);
}

display()
{
        register int t;
        for(t=0;t<10;++t) {
                line(t*10,20,t*10,freq1[t]+20);
                line(t*10+110,20,t*10+110,freq2[t]+20);
                line(t*10+220,20,t*10+220,freq3[t]+20);
        }
}

float ran1()
{
        static long int a=100001;

        a = (a*125) % 2796203;
        return (float) a/2796203;
}

float ran2()
{
        static long int a=1;

        a = (a * 32719+3) % 32749;
```

```
        return (float) a/32749;
}

float ran3()
{
        static long int a=203;

        a = (a *10001 + 3) % 1717;
        return (float) a/1717;
}
```

In this program, the functions **ran1( )**, **ran2( )**, and **ran3( )** have been included to do a side-by-side comparison. Each function generates 1000 numbers, and based on the digit in the tenths position, the appropriate frequency array is updated. The function **display( )** plots all three frequency arrays on the screen after each random number is generated, so you can watch the display grow. Figure 8-2 shows the output from each random

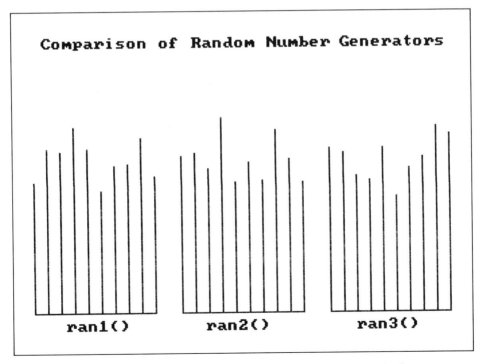

Figure 8-2. Output from the Random Number Generator Display program

number generator at the end of the thousand numbers. The mean is 0.496960 for **ran1( )**, 0.490550 for **ran2( )**, and 0.512488 for **ran3( )**. These are acceptable results.

To use the display program effectively, you should watch both the shape of the graph and the way that it grows to check for any short, repeating cycles. This "test" is, of course, not conclusive, but it does give you insight into the way a generator produces its numbers, and it can speed up the testing process by allowing obviously poor generating functions to be rejected quickly. (It also makes a great program to run when someone asks you to show them your computer!)

Using Multiple Generators

One simple technique that improves the randomness of sequences produced by the three generators is to combine them under the control of one master function. This function selects between two of them, based on the result of the third. With this method you can obtain very long periods and diminish the effects of any cycle. The function called **random( )** shown here combines **ran1( )**, **ran2( )**, and **ran3( )**.

```
float random()  /* random selection of generators */
{
        float f;

        f=ran3();

        if(f>.5) return ran1();
        else return ran2();
}
```

The result of **ran3( )** is used to decide whether **ran1( )** or **ran2( )** becomes the value of the master function **random( )**. Feel free to alter the mix between them by changing the constant in the **if** to obtain the exact distribution you require.

Here is a program to display the graph of **random( )** and its mean.

```
int freq1[10]={0,0,0,0,0,0,0,0,0,0};
float random(),ran1(),ran2(),ran3();

main()    /* using random numbers to further randomize */
{         /* the output from random number generators  */

        int x,y;
        float f,f2,f3,r,r2,r3;
        char s[80];

        mode(4);
        ground(0);
        palette(1);
        color('R');
        f=0;f2=0;f3=0;
        scr_curs(0,6);
        printf("Output Obtained by Combining");
        scr_curs(2,5);
        printf("Three Random Number Generators");
        for(x=0;x<1000;++x) {
                r=random();
                f+=r;
                y=r*10;
                freq1[y]++;
                display();
        }
        gets(s);
        mode(3);
        printf("mean of random number function 1: %f\n",f/1000);

}

display()
{
        register int t;
        for(t=0;t<10;++t)
                line(t*10+110,20,t*10+110,freq1[t]+20);
}

float random()   /* random selection of generators */
{
        float f;

        f=ran3();

        if(f>.5) return ran1();
        else return ran2();
}
```

```
float ran1()
{
        static long int a=100001;

        a = (a*125) % 2796203;
        return (float) a/2796203;
}

float ran2()
{
        static long int a=1;

        a = (a * 32719+3) % 32749;
        return (float) a/32749;
}

float ran3()
{

        static long int a=203;

        a = (a *10001 + 3) % 1717;
        return (float) a/1717;
}
```

The mean of **random( )** is 0.494316.

Figure 8-3 shows the final graph after 1000 random numbers have been computed.

Simulations

For the remainder of this chapter, the application of random number generators will be examined for computer *simulations*. A *simulation* is a computerized model of a real-world situation. Anything can be simulated, and the success of the simulation is based primarily upon how well the programmer understands the event being simulated. Because real-world situations often have thousands of variables, many things are difficult to simulate effectively. However, there are several events that lend themselves very well to simulation. Simulations are important for two reasons. First, they let you alter the parameters of a situation to test and observe the possible results, even though in real life such experimentation might be either too costly or dangerous. For example, a simulation of a nuclear power plant can be used to test the effects of certain types of failures without danger. Second, simulation allows you to create situations that cannot occur in the real world. For example, a psychologist might want to study the effects of gradually increasing the intelligence of a mouse to that of a human to find out at what point the mouse runs a maze the fastest. Although this cannot be done in real life, a simulation may provide insight into the nature of intelligence versus instinct. Here is the first of two examples of simulations that use random number generators.

Simulating a Check-out Line

The first example simulates a check-out line in a grocery store. Assume that the store is open for ten hours a day, with peak hours from 12 to 1 P.M. and from 5 to 6 P.M. The 12 to 1 P.M. slot is twice as busy as normal, and the 5 to 6 P.M. slot is three times as busy. As the simulation runs, one random number

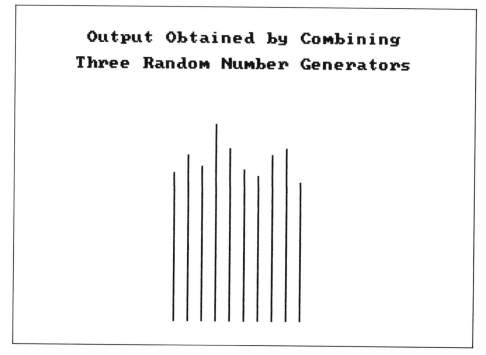

Figure 8-3.   The final graph of **random( )**

generator "creates" customers, another generator determines how long it will take one customer to check out, and a third generator decides which of the open lines the customers will go to. The goal of the simulation is to help management find the optimal number of check-out lines that need to be available on a typical shopping day, while limiting the number of people in line at any time to ten or less and not having cashiers waiting for customers to serve.

The key to this type of simulation is to create multiple processes. Although C does not support simultaneity directly, you can simulate multi-processing by having each function inside of a main program loop do some work and return—in essence, time-slicing the functions. For example, the function that simulated the check-out only checks out a part of each order each time it is called. In this way, each function inside the main loop continues to execute. The **main( )** function to the Check-out program is shown here with its global data.

```
float ran1(), ran2(), ran3();

char queues[10];
char open[10];
int  cust;
int time=0;

main()
{
        int x,y;
        char s[80];

        mode(4);
        ground(0);
        palette(1);
        color('R');
        for(x=0;x<10;++x) {
                queues[x]=0;
                open[x]=0;  /* all closed at start of day */
        }
        scr_curs(24,20); printf("1          10");
        scr_curs(24,0); printf("Check-out lines:");
        open[0]=1; /* open up number 1 */
        do {
                add_cust();
                add_queue();
                display();
                check_out();
```

```
display();
if(time>30 && time<50) add_cust();
if(time>70 && time < 80) {
        add_cust();
        add_cust();
}
time++;
} while (time<100);
gets(s);
mode(3);
}
```

The **mode( )**, **ground( )**, **color( )**, and **palette( )** functions are in the Aztec
C standard library; they are used to set the screen into 200×320 color
graphics mode with the foreground in red and the background in black. Try
to set your screen in the same way with the functions provided by your compiler. As in earlier chapters, the **scr—curs( )** function moves the cursor to
the specified X,Y screen position.

The body of the main loop used to drive the simulation is shown here.

```
add_cust();
add_queue();
display();
check_out();
display();
if(time>30 && time<50) add_cust();
if(time>70 && time < 80) {
        add_cust();
        add_cust();
}
time++;
```

The function **add—cust( )** uses either **ran1( )** or **ran3( )** to generate the
number of customers arriving at the check-out lines at each request. The
add—queue( ) is used to place the customers into an open check-out line
according to the results of **ran2( )**, and it also opens a new line if all of the
currently open lines are full. The **display( )** shows a graphics representation
of the simulation. The **check—out( )** uses **ran2( )** to assign each customer a
check-out count, and each call decrements that count by 1. When a customer's count is 0, the customer leaves the check-out line.

The variable **time** alters the rate at which customers are generated in
order to match the peak hours of the store. In essence, each pass through the
loop is one-tenth of an hour.

Figures 8-4, 8-5, and 8-6 show the state of the check-out lines when **time** = 28, **time** = 60, and **time** = 88, corresponding to normal time, the end of first peak, and the end of the second peak, respectively. Notice that at the end of the second peak, a maximum of six check-out lines is needed. This means that if the simulation was completed properly, the grocery store does not need to operate the remaining four lines.

You can directly control several variables in the program. First, you can alter the way customers arrive and the number of customers that arrive. You can also change **add—cust( )** to return gradually more or fewer customers

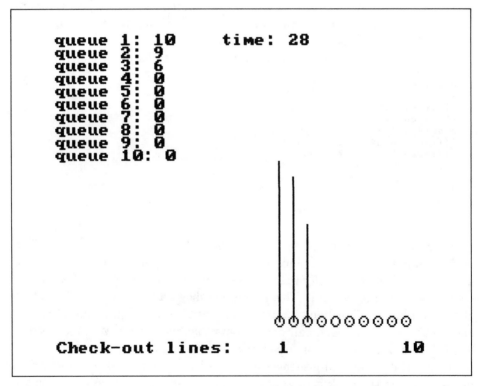

Figure 8-4. The status of the check-out line when **time** = 28

as the peak hours approach or wane. The program assumes that customers will randomly choose which line to stand in. Although this may be true of some customers, others will obviously choose the shortest line. You can account for this by altering the **add—queue( )** function to put customers into the shortest line at some times and to place customers randomly at other times. The simulation does not account for the occasional accident—such as a dropped ketchup bottle—or for an unruly customer at the check-out counter, both of which would cause a line to stall temporarily.

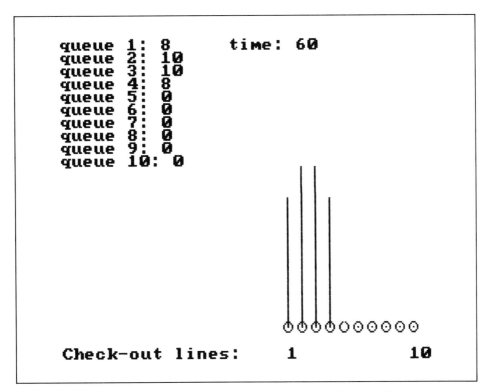

Figure 8-5. The status of the check-out line when **time** = 60

The entire program is shown here.

```
float ran1(), ran2(), ran3();

char queues[10];
char open[10];
int  cust; /* total number of customers */
int time=0;

main()  /* check-out line simulation */
{
        int x,y;
        char s[80];

        mode(4);
        ground(0);
        palette(1);
        color('R');
        for(x=0;x<10;++x) {
                queues[x]=0;
```

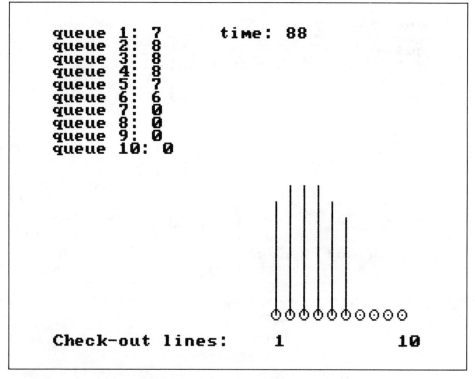

Figure 8-6. The status of the check-out line when **time** = 88

```
                        open[x]=0;  /* all closed at start of day */
                }
        scr_curs(24,20); printf("1              10");
        scr_curs(24,0); printf("Check-out lines:");
        open[0]=1; /* open up number 1 */
        do {
                add_cust();
                add_queue();
                display();
                check_out();
                display();
                if(time>30 && time<50) add_cust();
                if(time>70 && time < 80) {
                        add_cust();
                        add_cust();
                }
                time++;
        } while (!bdos(11,0,0) && time<100);
        gets(s);
        mode(3);
}

add_cust()
{

        float f,r;
        static char swap=0;

        if(swap) f=ran1();  /* get a random number */
        else f=ran3();  /* use two different number generators */
        swap=!swap;

        if(f<.5) return;  /* no customers */
        else if(f<.6) {
                cust++;  /* add one customer */
                return;
        }
        else if(f<.7) {
                cust+=2;  /* add two customers */
                return;
        }
        else if(f<.8) {
                cust+=3;
                return;
        }
        else cust+=4;
}

check_out()
{
        static char count[10]={0,0,0,0,0,0,0,0,0,0};
        register int t;

        for(t=0;t<10;++t) {
                if(queues[t]) {
                        /* get check out time */
                        while(count[t]==0) count[t]=ran2()*5;
                        count[t]--;
                        if(count[t]==0) queues[t]--;
                }
```

```
                                if(!queues[t]) open[t]=0;   /* close the line */
                }
        }

        add_queue()
        {
                register int t;
                int line;

                while(cust) {
                        if(allfull())
                                for(t=0;t<10;t++) if(!open[t]) {
                                        open[t]=1;
                                        break;
                                }
                        line=ran3()*10;
                        if(open[line] && queues[line]<10) {
                                queues[line]++;
                                cust--;
                        }
                        if(t==10) return;   /* all queues full */
                }
        }


        allfull()
        {
                register int t;

                for(t=0;t<10;t++) if(queues[t]<10 && open[t]) return 0;
                return 1;
        }

        display()
        {
                register int t;

                scr_curs(0,15);
                printf("time: %d",time);
                for(t=0;t<10;++t) {
                        color(12);
                        line((t*10)+160,20,(t*10)+160,120);
                        color('R');
                        circle((t*10)+160,20,3);
                        line((t*10)+160,20,(t*10)+160,queues[t]*10+20);
                        scr_curs(0+t,0); printf("queue %d: %d  ",t+1,queues[t]);
                }
        }

        float ran1()
        {
                static long int a=100001;

                a = (a*125) % 2796203;
                return (float) a/2796203;
        }

        float ran2()
        {
                static long int a=1;
```

```
        a = (a * 32719+3) % 32749;
        return (float) a/32749;
}

float ran3()
{

        static long int a=203;

        a = (a *10001 + 3) % 1717;
        return (float) a/1717;

}
```

Random-Walk
Portfolio Management

The art of stock portfolio management is generally based on various theories
and assumptions about many factors, some of which cannot be easily known
unless you are an insider. There are buy/sell strategies based on statistical
analyses of stock prices and PE ratios; there are correlations with the price
of gold, the GNP, and even the cycles of the moon. The computer scientist's
revenge is to use the computer to simulate the free marketplace — the stock
exchange — without all of the theoretical worry.

You may think that the stock exchange is simply too hard to simulate; that
it has too many variables and too many unknowns; and that it swings wildly
at times and coasts smoothly at others. However, the problem itself is the
solution: because the marketplace is so complex, it can be thought of as
being composed of *randomly occurring events*. This means that you can simulate the stock exchange as a series of disconnected, random occurrences. This
simulation is affectionately referred to as the *random-walk method* of portfolio management. The term is derived from the classic experiment that
involves a drunk wandering a street, randomly weaving from lamppost to
lamppost. With the random-walk theory, you let chance be your guide
because it is as good as any other method.

Before you continue, be warned: the random-walk method is generally
discredited by professional money managers; it is presented here for your
enjoyment, not for actual investing.

To implement the random-walk method, first select ten companies from
the *Wall Street Journal* by some chance method, such as throwing darts at it
and using the companies whose names you hit. After you have selected ten

companies, feed their names into the Random-Walk Simulation program so that it can tell you what to do with them.

Basically, the program can tell you five things to do with the stock of each company:

- Sell

- Buy

- Sell short

- Buy on margin

- Hold (do nothing).

The operations of selling, buying, and holding stock are obvious. When you *sell short*, you sell stock that you do not own in the hopes that soon you can buy it cheaper and deliver it to the person you sold it to. Selling short is a way to make money when the market is going down. When you *buy on margin*, you use, for a small fee, the money of the brokerage house to finance part of the cost of the stock that you purchased. The idea behind buying on margin is that if the stock increases enough, you make more money than you could if you had bought a smaller amount of stock with cash. This makes money only in a bull (rising) market.

The Random-Walk Simulation program is shown here. The **bdos(7)** call checks for keyboard status and waits for a key-press. This allows you to use the sequence produced by the random number generator at a random point — in essence, creating a random seed value. This prevents the program from always producing the same advice.

```
char stock[10][30];  /* company names */
float ran3();

main()  /* random-walk simulation */
{
        register int t;
        char ch,s[80],*action();

        printf("Wait awhile, then strike a key.\n");
        do {  /* start at random place in number generator */
                ran3();
        } while(!bdos(11,0,0));
        bdos(7,0,0);

        printf("enter new stock names? ");
        gets(s);
        if(toupper(*s)=='Y') enter();
```

```
        do {
                for(t=0;t<10;++t)
                    printf("%30s: %s\n",stock[t],action());
                printf("\nagain? (y/n)");
                gets(s);
        } while(toupper(*s)=='Y' || *s==0);
}

enter()
{
        register int t;

        for(t=0;t<10;t++) {
                printf("enter company name: ");
                gets(stock[t]);
        }
}

char *action()
{
        register int x;
        float f;

        f=ran3();
        x=f*10;

        switch(x) {
                case 0: return "sell";
                case 1: return "buy";
                case 3: return "sell short";
                case 4: return "buy on margin";
                default: return "hold";
        }
}

float ran1()
{
        static long int a=100001;

        a = (a*125) % 2796203;
        return (float) a/2796203;
}

float ran2()
{
        static long int a=1;

        a = (a * 32719+3) % 32749;
        return (float) a/32749;
}

float ran3()
{
        static long int a=203;

        a = (a *10001 + 3) % 1717;
        return (float) a/1717;
}
```

The program requires that you interpret the instructions in the following way:

Instruction	Interpretation
Buy	Buy as much of the specified stock as you can afford without borrowing.
Sell	Sell all of the stock if any is owned. Then randomly select a new company for reinvesting your money.
Sell short	Sell 100 shares of the specified company, even though you don't own it, in the hopes that you can buy it cheaper in the future.
Buy on margin	Borrow money to buy shares of the specified stock.
Hold	Do nothing.

For example, if you were to run this program using the fictitious company names of Com1 through Com10, the first day's advice would look like this:

Com1:	sell
Com2:	buy
Com3:	buy on margin
Com4:	sell short
Com5:	hold
Com6:	hold
Com7:	hold
Com8:	buy
Com9:	hold
Com10:	sell short

The second day's advice might be

Com1:	hold
Com2:	hold
Com3:	sell
Com4:	sell short
Com5:	hold
Com6:	hold
Com7:	buy
Com8:	buy on margin
Com9:	hold
Com10:	sell

If you prefer, you can run the program weekly instead of daily.

Feel free to alter the program in any way. For example, you could change the program to give you amounts of stock to buy and sell, depending on your available investment dollars. Again, remember that this program is only for fun and is not recommended as a way to make actual investments in the market. However, it is interesting to create a portfolio on paper and to track its performance.

Expression Parsing and Evaluation

CHAPTER 9

How do you write a program that will take as input a string containing a numeric expression, for example 10−5*3, and return the answer, in this case −5? If a "high priesthood" still exists among programmers, then it must be made up of those few who know how to do this. Almost everyone who uses a computer is mystified by the way high-level language compilers, spreadsheet programs, and database managers convert complex expressions, such as 10*3−(4+c)/12, into instructions that a computer can execute. This conversion process is called *expression parsing*. It forms the backbone of all language compilers and interpreters, spreadsheet programs, and anything else that converts those numeric expressions understood by humans into forms that a computer can use. Few programmers know how to write an expression parser; this realm of programming is generally thought of as "off-limits," except by the enlightened few.

However, this is not the case. Expression parsing is actually very straightforward and is similar to other programming tasks. In some ways it is easier, because it works with the strict rules of algebra. This chapter develops what is commonly referred to as a *recursive descent parser,* as well as all of the necessary support routines to enable you to evaluate complex numeric expressions. All of these routines will be placed in one file that you can use whenever you need it. After you have mastered the parser, you can enhance and modify it to suit your needs—and join the "high priesthood" yourself.

Expressions

Although expressions can be made up of all types of information, you will be studying only one type: *numeric expressions.* For the purposes of this chapter, assume that numeric expressions can be made up of the following:

- Numbers
- The operators +, −, /, *, ^, %, and =
- Parentheses
- Variables.

The ^ symbol indicates exponentiation, as in BASIC, and the = symbol represents the assignment operator. All of these items follow the rules of algebra with which you are familiar. Some examples of expressions are

```
10−8
(100−5) * 14/6
a+b−c
10^5
a=10−b
```

Assume the following precedence for each operator:

```
highest: ^
         * / %
         + −
lowest:  =
```

Operators of equal precedence evaluate from left to right.

For the examples in this chapter, the following assumptions will be made: All variables are single letters, which means that 26 variables—the letters A through Z—are available for use. All numbers are integers, although you could easily write the routines to handle floating-point numbers. Finally, only a minimal amount of error checking is included in the routines to keep the logic clear and uncluttered.

Take a look at the sample expression

$$10-2*3$$

This expression has a value of 4. Although you could easily create a program that would compute that specific expression, you may wonder how to create a computer program that will give you the correct answer for any arbitrary expression of this type. At first you might think that you could use a routine like this:

```
a = get first operand
while(operands present) {
        op = get operator
        b  = get second operand
        a  = a op b
}
```

According to this routine, you could get the first operand, the operator, and the second operand; perform the operation; then get the next operator and operand, if any; perform that operation; and so on. If you use this basic method, the expression $10-2*3$ evaluates to 24 (that is, $8*3$) instead of the correct answer, 4, because the procedure neglects the precedence of the operators. You cannot take the operands and operators in order from left to right, because the multiplication must be done before the subtraction. A beginner may think that this problem could be easily overcome—and sometimes, in very restrictive cases, it can—but the problem only gets worse when parentheses, exponentiation, variables, function calls, and the like are added in.

Although there are a few ways to write functions that evaluate expressions of this sort, you will study the one that is most easily written and is also the most common. (Some other methods used to write parsers employ complex tables that almost require another computer program to generate them. These are sometimes called *table-driven parsers*.) The method that you will examine is called a recursive descent parser, and you will see how it got its name in the course of this chapter.

Dissecting an Expression

Before you can develop a parser to evaluate expressions, you must get pieces of the expression easily. For example, given the expression

$$A*B-(W+10)$$

you must be able to get the operands A, B, and W, the parentheses, and the operators $*$, $+$, and $-$. In general, you need a routine that returns each item in the expression individually. The routine also needs to be able to skip over spaces and tabs, and it must know when the end of the expression has been reached.

Formally, each piece of an expression is called a *token*. Therefore, the function that returns the next token in the expression is called **get_token( )**. A global character pointer is needed to hold the expression string. This pointer is called **prog**. The variable **prog** is global because it must maintain its value between calls to **get_token( )** and it must allow other functions to use it. You also need to know what *type* of token you are getting. For the parser developed in this chapter, you only need three types: VARIABLE, NUMBER, and DELIMITER, where DELIMITER is used for both operators and parentheses. Here is **get_token( )** with its necessary globals, **#define** statements, and support functions.

```
#define DELIMITER       1
#define VARIABLE        2
#define NUMBER          3

extern char *prog;   /* holds expression to be analyzed */
char token[80];
char tok_type;


get_token()
{

        register char *temp;

        tok_type=0;
        temp=token;

        while(iswhite(*prog)) ++prog;  /* skip over white space */

        if(is_in(*prog,"+-*/%^=()")){
                tok_type=DELIMITER;
                *temp++=*prog++;
                /* advance to next position */
        }
        else if(isalpha(*prog)) {
                while(!isdelim(*prog)) *temp++=*prog++;
```

```
                tok_type=VARIABLE;
        }
        else if(isdigit(*prog)) {
                while(!isdelim(*prog)) *temp++=*prog++;
                tok_type=NUMBER;
        }

        *temp=0;

}

iswhite(c)
char c;
{
        /* look for spaces and tabs */
        if(c==' ' || c==9) return 1;
        return 0;
}

isdelim(c)
char c;
{
        if(is_in(c," +-/*%^=()") || c==9 || c=='\r' || c==0)
                return 1;
        return 0;
}

is_in(ch,s)
char ch,*s;
{
        while(*s) if(*s++==ch) return 1;
        return 0;
}
```

This function's first step is to check for the null terminator, which indicates the end of the expression string. Because C uses null-terminated strings, if a null is reached, you know that the expression has ended and a null token is returned. Although spaces are added into expressions to add clarity, these spaces only confuse the parser and you must skip over them.

After the spaces have been skipped, **prog** will be pointing to either a number, a variable, an operator, or a null, if trailing spaces end the expression. If the next character is an operator, that character is returned as a string in the global variable **token**, and the type of DELIMITER is placed in **tok_type**. If the next character is a letter instead, it will be assumed to be one of the variables and will be returned as a string in **token**; **tok_type** will be assigned the value VARIABLE. If the next character is a number, then the integer is returned as a string in **token** with a type of NUMBER. Finally, if the next character is none of these, you can then assume that the end of the expression has been reached and that **token** is null.

As stated earlier, to keep the code clean in this function, a certain amount of error checking has been omitted and some assumptions have been made. For example, any unrecognized character may end an expression. Also, in this version, variables may be any length, but only the first letter is significant. However, you can fill in these and other details according to your specific application. You can modify or enhance **get_token( )** easily to enable character strings, floating-point numbers, or whatever you want to be returned from an input-string token.

To understand how **get_token( )** works, study what it returns for each token from the expression A+100−(B*C)/2:

Token	Token Type
A	VARIABLE
+	DELIMITER
100	NUMBER
−	DELIMITER
(	DELIMITER
B	VARIABLE
*	DELIMITER
C	VARIABLE
)	DELIMITER
/	DELIMITER
2	NUMBER
null	null

Don't forget that **token( )** always holds a null-terminated string, even if that string is just a single character.

Expression Parsing

Remember that there are several ways to parse and evaluate an expression. For the purposes of this chapter, think of expressions as *recursive data structures* that are defined in terms of themselves. If, for the moment, you restrict expressions to using only +, −, *, /, and parentheses, you could say that all expressions can be defined by using these rules:

$$Expression => Term\ [+\ Term]\ [-\ Term]$$
$$Term => Factor\ [*\ Factor]\ [/\ Factor]$$
$$Factor => Variable,\ Number,\ or\ (Expression)$$

where any part can be null. The square brackets mean optional, and the $=>$ means "produces." In fact, the rules are called the *production rules* of the expression. Therefore, you would read the second rule as "Term produces factor times factor, or factor divided by factor." The precedence of the operators is implicit in the way an expression is defined.

The expression

$$10+5*B$$

has two terms: 10 and $5*B$. However, it has three factors: 10, 5, and B. These factors consist of two numbers and one variable.

On the other hand, the expression

$$14*(7-C)$$

has two terms, 14 and $(7-C)$, which is one number and one parenthesized expression. The parenthesized expression evaluates to one number and one variable.

This process forms the basis for a recursive descent parser, which is basically a set of mutually recursive routines that work in a chain-like fashion. At each appropriate step, the parser can perform the specified operations in the algebraically correct sequence. To see how this process works, follow the parsing of the input expression

$$10/3-(100+56)$$

and perform the arithmetic operations at the right time:

Step 1. Get first term: 10/3.

Step 2. Get each factor and divide integers. That value is 3.

Step 3. Get the second term: (100+56). At this point, you must analyze the second expression recursively.

Step 4. Get each factor and add. The result is 156.

Step 5. Return from the recursive call and subtract 156 from 3, which yields an answer of −153.

If you are a little confused at this point, don't worry. This is a complex concept that takes getting used to. There are two things to remember about this recursive view of expressions: first, the precedence of the operators is *implicit* in the way the production rules are defined; second, this method of parsing and evaluating expressions is similar to the way you would parse and evaluate without a computer.

A Simple Expression
Parser

In the remainder of this chapter, two parsers are developed. The first one parses and evaluates only constant expressions—that is, expressions with no variables. This is the parser in its simplest form. The second parser includes the 26 user variables A through Z.

Here is the entire simple version of the recursive descent parser for integer expressions.

```
/* simple recursive descent parser for integer expressions
                - no user variables -                      */

#define DELIMITER     1
#define VARIABLE      2
#define NUMBER        3

extern char *prog;   /* holds expression to be analyzed */
char token[80];
char tok_type;

get_exp(result)
int *result;
{
        get_token();
        if(!*token) {
                serror(2);
                return;
        }
        level2(result);
        return result;
}
```

```
level2(result)
int *result;
{
        register char    op;
        int hold;

        level3(result);
        while((op = *token) == '+' || op == '-') {
                get_token();
                level3(&hold);
                arith(op,result,&hold);
        }
}

level3(result)
int *result;
{
        register char    op;
        int hold;

        level4(result);
        while((op = *token) == '*' || op == '/' || op == '%') {
                get_token();
                level4(&hold);
                arith(op,result,&hold);
        }
}

level4(result)
int *result;
{
        int hold;

        level5(result);
        if(*token== '^') {
                get_token();
                level4(&hold);
                arith('^',result,&hold);
        }
}

level5(result)
int *result;
{
        register char    op;

        op = 0;
        if((tok_type == DELIMITER) && *token=='+' ||  *token == '-')
                op = *token;
                get_token();
        }
        level6(result);
        if(op)
                unary(op,result);
}

level6(result)
int *result;
{
        if((*token == '(') && (tok_type == DELIMITER)) {
                get_token();
```

```
                    level2(result);
                    if(*token != ')')
                            serror(1);
                    get_token();
            }
            else
                    primitive(result);
}

primitive(result)
int *result;
{
        register int i;

        if(tok_type==NUMBER) {
                *result=atoi(token);
                return  get_token();
        }
        serror(0);  /* otherwise syntax error in expression */
}

arith(o,r,h)
char o;
int *r,*h;
{
        register int t,ex;

        switch(o) {
                case '-':
                        *r=*r-*h;
                        break;
                case '+':
                        *r=*r+*h;
                        break;
                case '*':
                        *r=*r * *h;
                        break;
                case '/':
                        *r=(*r)/(*h);
                        break;
                case '%':
                        t=(*r)/(*h);
                        *r=*r-(t*(*h));
                        break;
                case '^':
                        ex=*r;
                        if(*h==0) {
                                *r=1;
                                break;
                        }
                        for(t=*h-1;t>0;--t) *r=(*r) * ex;
                        break;
        }
}

unary(o,r)
char o;
int *r;
{
        if(o=='-') *r=-(*r);
}
```

```
putback() /* return a token to its resting place */
{

        char *t;

        t=token;
        for(;*t;t++) prog--;

}


serror(error)
int error;
{

        static char *e[]= {
                        "syntax error",
                        "unbalanced parentheses",
                        "no expression present"
                };
        printf("%s\n",e[error]);
}

get_token()
{

        register char *temp;

        tok_type=0;
        temp=token;

        while(iswhite(*prog)) ++prog;   /* skip over white space */

        if(is_in(*prog,"+-*/^%()")){
                tok_type=DELIMITER;
                *temp++=*prog++;
                /* advance to next position */
        }
        else if(isalpha(*prog))
                serror(0); /* not a number - abort */

        else if(isdigit(*prog)) {
                while(!isdelim(*prog)) *temp++=*prog++;
                tok_type=NUMBER;
        }

        *temp=0;

}

iswhite(c)
char c;
{
        /* look for spaces and tabs */
        if(c==' ' || c==9) return 1;
        return 0;
}

isdelim(c)
char c;
{
```

```
            if(is_in(c," +-/*^%()") || c==9 || c=='\r' || c==0)
                    return 1;
            return 0;
    }

    is_in(ch,s)
    char ch,*s;
    {
            while(*s) if(*s++==ch) return 1;
            return 0;
    }
```

The parser as shown can accept the operators $+$, $-$, $*$, $/$, and $\%$, as well as exponentiation ($\char94$), the unary minus, and parentheses. It has six levels and the **primitive( )** function, which returns the value of an integer number. Also included are the routines **arith( )** and **unary( )** for performing the various arithmetic operations, as well as **get_token( )**. As discussed previously, the two globals **token** and **tok_type** return the next token and its type from the expression string. The **extern prog** is a pointer to the expression string, which is assumed to be loaded by another part of the program.

A simple **main( )** function that demonstrates the use of the parser is shown here.

```
    char *prog;   /* holds expression to be parsed */

    main()   /* Parser driver program */
    {
            int answer;
            char *p;

            p=malloc(100);
            if(!p) {
                    printf("allocation failure\n");
                    exit();
            }

            do {
                    prog=p;
                    printf("enter expression: ");
                    gets(prog);

                    get_exp(&answer);

                    printf("answer is: %d\n",answer);
            } while(*p);
    }
```

To understand exactly how the parser evaluates an expression, work through the following expression, which you can assume is contained in **prog**.

$$10-3*2$$

When **get‗exp( )** (the entry routine into the parser) is called, it gets the first token, and if that token is null, it prints the message **no expression present** and returns. If a token is present, then **level2( )** is called. (A **level1( )** will be added to the parser momentarily when the assignment operator is added, but it is not needed here.)

Now the token contains the number 10. The **level2( )** function calls **level3( )**, and **level3( )** calls **level4( )**, which in turn calls **level5( )**. The **level5( )** function checks to see if the token is a unary $+$ or $-$; in this case it is not, so **level6( )** is called. The **level6( )** function either recursively calls **level2( )** in the case of a parenthesized expression, or calls **primitive( )** to find the value of the integer.

Finally, when **primitive( )** is executed and **result** contains the integer 10, **get‗token** obtains another token, and the functions begin to return up the chain. The token is now the operator $-$ and the functions return up to **level2( )**.

The next step is very important. Because the token is $-$, it is saved, **get‗token** obtains new token 3, and the descent down the chain begins again. Again, **primitive( )** is entered, the integer 3 is returned in **result**, and the token ∗ is read. This causes a return back up the chain to **level3( )**, where the final token 2 is read. At this point, the first arithmetic operation occurs with the multiplication of 2 and 3. This result is then returned to **level2( )** and the subtraction is performed to yield an answer of 4. Although the process may seem complicated at first, you should work through some other examples to verify for yourself that it functions correctly every time.

You could use this parser as a desktop calculator, as illustrated by the sample driver program. You could also use it in a database or a simple spreadsheet application. Before it could be used in a language or a sophisticated calculator, the parser would have to be able to handle variables, which is the subject of the next section.

Adding Variables to the Parser

All programming languages and many calculators and spreadsheets use variables to store values for later use. The simple parser in the preceding section must be expanded to include variables before you can use it for this purpose. First you need the variables themselves. Since the parser is restricted to integer expressions only, you can use integer variables. The parser will only recognize the variables A through Z, although you could expand it if you wanted. Each variable uses one array location in a 26-element array. Therefore, you should add the following:

```
int vars[26]= {              /* 26 user variables, A-Z */
        0,0,0,0,0,0,0,0,0,0,0,0,0,0,0,0,0,0,0,0,0,0,0,0,0,0
        };
```

As you can see, the variables are initialized to zero as a courtesy to the user.

You also need a routine to look up the value of a given variable. Because you are using the letters A through Z as variable names, you can easily index the array **vars** based on its name. Here is the function **find__var( )**.

```
find_var(s)
char *s;
{
        if(!isalpha(*s)){
                serror(1);
                return 0;
        }
        return vars[toupper(*token)-'A'];
}
```

As written, this function actually accepts long variable names, but only the first letter is significant. You can modify this feature to fit your needs.

You must also modify the **primitive( )** function to treat both numbers and variables as primitives, as shown here.

```
primitive(result)
 int *result;
{
        register int i;

        switch(tok_type) {
        case VARIABLE:
                *result=find_var(token);
                return get_token();
        case NUMBER:
                *result=atoi(token);
                return get_token();
        default:
                serror(0);
        }
}
```

Technically, this is all you need for the parser to use variables correctly; however, there is no way for these variables to be assigned values. Often you can assign variables outside the parser, but since it is possible to treat the = as an assignment operator, there are many ways to make it part of the parser. One method is to add a **level1( )** to the parser, as shown here.

```
level1(result)
 int *result;
{
        int hold;
        int slot,ttok_type;
        char temp_token[80];

        if(tok_type==VARIABLE) {
                /* save old token */
                strcpy(temp_token,token);
                ttok_type=tok_type;

                slot=toupper(*token)-'A';
                get_token();
                if(*token != '=') {
                        putback(); /* return current token */
                        /* restore old token - not assignment */
                        strcpy(token,temp_token);
                        tok_type=ttok_type;
                }
                else {
                        get_token(); /* get next part of exp */
                        level2(result);
                        vars[slot]=*result;
                        return;
                }
        }

        level2(result);

}
```

As you can see, you must look ahead to determine whether an assignment is actually being made; in this situation you need to save the state of the parser so that it can be restored if it is not an assignment.

Here is the entire enhanced parser.

```
/* recursive descent parser for integer expressions
   that may include variables                        */

#define DELIMITER    1
#define VARIABLE     2
#define NUMBER       3

extern char *prog;  /* holds expression to be analyzed */
char token[80];
char tok_type;

int vars[26]= {          /* 26 user variables, A-Z */
       0,0,0,0,0,0,0,0,0,0,0,0,0,0,0,0,0,0,0,0,0,0,0,0,0,0
       };

get_exp(result)
```

```
 int *result;
{
        get_token();
        if(!*token) {
                serror(2);
                return;
        }
        level1(result);
        return result;
}

level1(result)
 int *result;
{
        int hold;
        int slot,ttok_type;
        char temp_token[80];

        if(tok_type==VARIABLE) {
                /* save old token */
                strcpy(temp_token,token);
                ttok_type=tok_type;

                slot=toupper(*token)-'A';
                get_token();
                if(*token != '=') {
                        putback(); /* return current token */
                        /* restore old token - not assignment */
                        strcpy(token,temp_token);
                        tok_type=ttok_type;
                }
                else {
                        get_token(); /* get next part of exp */
                        level2(result);
                        vars[slot]=*result;
                        return;
                }

        }

        level2(result);

}

level2(result)
 int *result;
{
        register char   op;
        int hold;

        level3(result);
        while((op = *token) == '+' || op == '-') {
                get_token();
                level3(&hold);
                arith(op,result,&hold);
        }
}

level3(result)
 int *result;
{
```

```
           register char    op;
           int hold;

           level4(result);
           while((op = *token) == '*' || op == '/' || op == '%') {
                   get_token();
                   level4(&hold);
                   arith(op,result,&hold);
           }
}

level4(result)
 int *result;
{
           int hold;

           level5(result);
           if(*token== '^') {
                   get_token();
                   level4(&hold);
                   arith('^',result,&hold);
           }
}

level5(result)
 int *result;
{
           register char    op;

           op = 0;
           if((tok_type==DELIMITER) && *token=='+' || *token=='-') {
                   op = *token;
                   get_token();
           }
           level6(result);
           if(op)
                   unary(op,result);
}

level6(result)
 int *result;
{
           if((*token == '(') && (tok_type == DELIMITER)) {
                   get_token();
                   level1(result);
                   if(*token != ')')
                           serror(1);
                   get_token();
           }
           else
                   primitive(result);
}

primitive(result)
 int *result;
{
           register int i;

           switch(tok_type) {
           case VARIABLE:
                   *result=find_var(token);
```

```
                       return get_token();
            case NUMBER:
                    *result=atoi(token);
                    return  get_token();
            default:
                    serror(0);
            }
}


arith(o,r,h)
char o;
int *r,*h;
{
        register int t,ex;

        switch(o) {
                case '-':
                        *r=*r-*h;
                        break;
                case '+':
                        *r=*r+*h;
                        break;
                case '*':
                        *r=*r * *h;
                        break;
                case '/':
                        *r=(*r)/(*h);
                        break;
                case '%':
                        t=(*r)/(*h);
                        *r=*r-(t*(*h));
                        break;
                case '^':
                        ex=*r;
                        if(*h==0) {
                                *r=1;
                                break;
                        }
                        for(t=*h-1;t>0;--t) *r=(*r) * ex;
                        break;
                }
}

unary(o,r)
char o;
int *r;
{
        if(o=='-') *r=-(*r);
}

putback() /* return a token to its resting place */
{

        char *t;

        t=token;
        for(;*t;t++) prog--;

}
```

```
find_var(s)
char *s;
{

        if(!isalpha(*s)){
                serror(1);
                return 0;
        }
        return vars[toupper(*token)-'A'];
}

serror(error)
int error;
{
        static char *e[]= {
                        "syntax error",
                        "unbalanced parentheses",
                        "no expression present"
                    };
        printf("%s\n",e[error]);

}

get_token()
{

        register char *temp;

        tok_type=0;
        temp=token;

        while(iswhite(*prog)) ++prog;  /* skip over white space */

        if(is_in(*prog,"+-*/%^=()")){
                tok_type=DELIMITER;
                *temp++=*prog++;
                /* advance to next position */
        }
        else if(isalpha(*prog)) {
                while(!isdelim(*prog)) *temp++=*prog++;
                tok_type=VARIABLE;
        }
        else if(isdigit(*prog)) {
                while(!isdelim(*prog)) *temp++=*prog++;
                tok_type=NUMBER;
        }

        *temp=0;

}

iswhite(c)
char c;
{
        /* look for spaces and tabs */
        if(c==' ' || c==9) return 1;
        return 0;
}

isdelim(c)
char c;
```

```
{
        if(is_in(c," +-/*%^=()") || c==9 || c=='\r' || c==0)
                return 1;
        return 0;
}

is_in(ch,s)
char ch,*s;
{
        while(*s) if(*s++==ch) return 1;
        return 0;
}
```

To see how this version of the parser functions, you can use the same **main( )** function you used for the simple parser. With the enhanced parser you can now enter expressions such as

$$A=10/4$$
$$A-B$$
$$C=A*(F-21)$$

Syntax Checking
In a Recursive Descent Parser

In expression parsing, a *syntax error* is a situation in which the input expression does not conform to the strict rules required by the parser. Usually this is caused by human error—most commonly, by typing mistakes. For example, the following expressions will not be parsed correctly by the parsers in this chapter:

$$10**8$$
$$(10-5)*9$$
$$/8$$

The first expression has two operators in a row; the second has unbalanced parentheses; and the last has a division sign starting an expression. None of these conditions are allowed by the parsers. Because syntax errors can cause the parser to give erroneous results, it is necessary to guard against them.

As you have studied the code to the parsers, you have probably noticed the function **serror( )**, which is called in certain situations. Unlike many other parsers, the recursive descent method makes syntax checking easy because, for the most part, syntax errors occur in either **primitive( )**, **find_var( )**, or **level6( )**, where parentheses are checked. The syntax checking as it now stands has only one problem: the entire parser is not aborted on syntax error. This can cause multiple error messages to be generated.

The best way to implement **serror( )** is to have it execute a **reset( )** routine. Many compilers come with a pair of companion functions called, for example, **set_exit( )** and **reset( )**. Together, these two functions allow a program branch to a *different* function. Therefore, in **serror( )**, you would execute a **reset( )** to some safe point in your program outside the parser.

If your compiler does not have this type of routine pair or if you are trying to write portable code, your only other option is to add a global variable that is checked at each level. The variable would initially be FALSE, and any call to **serror( )** would make it TRUE, causing the parser to abort one function at a time.

If you leave the code the way it is, all that will happen is that multiple syntax error messages may be issued. This could be an annoyance in some situations but a blessing in others because multiple errors will be caught. Generally, however, you will want to enhance the syntax checking before using it in commercial programs.

Converting Pascal And BASIC to C

C H A P T E R   1 0

Most programmers spend much of their time converting programs from one language into another. This is called *translating*. You may find the process either easy or difficult, depending on the methods you use to translate and how well you know the source and destination languages. This chapter presents some topics and techniques to help you convert Pascal and BASIC programs into C.

Why would anyone want to translate a program written in one language into another? One reason is *maintainability:* a program written in an unstructured language like BASIC is difficult to maintain or enhance. Another reason is *speed and efficiency:* C as a language is very efficient, and some demanding tasks have been translated into C for better performance. A third reason is *practicality:* a user may see a useful program listed in one language but may own or use a compiler in a different language. You will probably find that you want to translate a program into C for one or more of these reasons.

Pascal and BASIC were chosen from the field of nearly a hundred computer languages because they are popular languages among microcomputer users and because they represent opposite ends of the programming-language spectrum. Pascal is a structured language that has many similarities to C, whereas BASIC is a nonstructured language and has virtually no similarities to C. Although this chapter cannot cover each language in every detail, it will examine several of the most important problems that you will confront. It is assumed that you are familiar with either Pascal or BASIC; no attempt will be made to teach either language.

Converting Pascal To C

Pascal and C have many similarities, especially in their control structures and their use of stand-alone subroutines with local variables. This makes it possible to do lots of *one-to-one translations:* you can often simply substitute the C equivalent keyword or function. With one-to-one translating you can use the computer to assist you with the translation process. A simple translation program will be developed later in the chapter.

Although Pascal and C are similar, there are three differences between them. The first is that Pascal is more restrictive and in some ways more limited than C. For example, standard Pascal not only makes it difficult to write system code (since memory addresses cannot be directly loaded into pointers, as in C), it also will not perform type conversions for you. A second and more important difference is that Pascal is formally block structured, whereas C is not. The term *block structured* refers to a language's ability to create logically connected units of code that can be referenced together. The term also means that procedures can have other procedures nested inside them, known only to the outer procedure. Although C is commonly called a block-structured language because it allows the easy creation of blocks of code, it does not allow functions to be defined inside other functions. For example, the following Pascal code is valid:

```
procedure A;
var
    x:integer;

    procedure B;
```

```
      begin
         WriteLn('inside proc b');
      end;

   begin
      WriteLn('starting A');
      B;
   end;
```

Here, **procedure B** is defined inside of **procedure A**. This means that **procedure B** is known only to **procedure A** and may only be used by **procedure A**. Outside of **procedure A**, another **procedure B** could be defined without conflict. The same code translated into C, however, would need to have two functions:

```
A()
{
        printf("starting A\n");
        B();
}

B()
{
        printf("inside function B\n");
}
```

In addition, you would have to make sure that there were no other functions called B anywhere else in the program.

The second difference between Pascal and C is that all Pascal variables, functions, and procedures must be declared before they are used. In standard Pascal, this means that forward references are not allowed without the **forward** statement. In C, all variables must be declared before they are used, but forward references to functions are not restricted—in fact, they are very common.

A third difference is that standard Pascal does not support separate compilation, whereas separate compilation is encouraged in C.

A Comparison of Pascal and C

Figure 10-1 compares Pascal keywords with C keywords and operators. As you can see, many Pascal keywords have no C equivalent because Pascal uses keywords in places where C uses operators to accomplish the same steps. At times, Pascal is simply "wordier" than C.

In addition to the keywords, Pascal has several built-in *standard identifi-*

ers that can be used directly in a program. These identifiers may be functions (like **writeln**) or global variables (like **MaxInt**) that hold information

Pascal	C
and	&&
array	
begin	{
case	switch
const	#define
div	/ (using integers)
do	
downto	
else	else
end	}
file	
forward	extern (on occasion)
for	for
function	
goto	goto
if	if
in	
label	
mod	%
nil	(sometimes \0)
not	!
of	
or	||
packed	
procedure	
program	
record	struct
repeat	do
set	
then	
type	
to	
until	while (as in do/while)
var	
while	while
with	

Figure 10-1. Pascal keywords compared with C keywords and operators

Pascal	C
Pascal	**C**
Boolean	char or integer
byte	char
char	char
EOF	EOF (in stdio library)
false	0
flush	flush( ) (in stdio library)
integer	integer
read	scanf( ) and others
real	float
true	any nonzero value
write	printf( )

Figure 10-2. Some standard Pascal identifiers and their C equivalents

about the state of the system. Also, Pascal uses standard identifiers to specify such data types as **real**, **integer**, **Boolean**, and **character**. Figure 10-2 shows several standard Pascal identifiers and their C equivalents. In addition to those in the figure, many of Pascal's built-in functions have equivalents in C that are found in the standard library; however, they may vary from compiler to compiler.

Pascal also differs from C in its operators. Figure 10-3 shows the Pascal operators and their C equivalents.

Converting Pascal Loops Into C loops

Because program control loops are fundamental to most programs, you should compare Pascal's loops with C's loops. Pascal has three built-in loops: **for**, **while**, and **repeat-until**. C has a corresponding loop for each.

The Pascal **for** has the general form

for *initial value* **to** *target value* **do** statement;

The Pascal **for** is much more limited than the C **for** because it does not allow increments other than 1 (or −1 if the **downto** is used), and because the loop condition is rigidly tied to the counting mechanism, unlike C's more flexible design. However, these differences do not affect the process of translating

Pascal	C	Meaning
+	+	Addition
−	−	Subtraction
*	*	Multiplication
/	/	Division
div	/	Integer division
mod	%	Modulus
^		Exponentiation
:=	=	Assignment
=	==	Equals as a condition
<	<	Less than
>	>	Greater than
>=	>=	Greater than or equal to
<=	<=	Less than or equal to
<>	!=	Not equal

Figure 10-3. Pascal operators and their C equivalents

from Pascal into C, because the Pascal **for** can be viewed simply as a C subset. For example, the Pascal statement

```
for x:=10 to 100 do writeln(x);
```

can be translated into C as

```
for(x=10;x<=100;++x) printf("%d\n",x);
```

The Pascal **while** and the C **while** are virtually the same. However, Pascal's **repeat-until** and C's **do-while** require that you use different keywords and "reverse" the loop-test condition. The reason is that the Pascal **repeat-until** implies that a loop runs *until* something *becomes* true, whereas the C **do-while** loops *while* the loop condition *is* true. A sample translation of both these types of loops is shown here.

```
Pascal                    C
while x<5 do              while(x<5)
begin                     {
    writeln(x);               printf("%d \n",x);
    read(x);                  x=getnum( );
end;                      }

repeat                    do {
    read(x);                  x=getnum( );
    writeln(x);               printf("%d \n",x);
until x>5;                } while(x<=5);
```

Watch out for the translation of **repeat-until** into **do-while**: you must reverse the sense of the test condition.

A Sample Translation

For a taste of the translation process, follow the steps of converting a Pascal program into C. Here is a simple Pascal program.

```
program test (input,output);
var qwerty: real;

procedure tom (x: integer);
begin
     writeln(x*2);
end;

function ken (w: real): real;
begin
     ken:=w/3.1415;
     qwerty:=23.34
end;

begin
     qwerty:=0;
     writeln(qwerty);
     writeln('hello there');
     tom(25);
     writeln(ken(10));
     writeln(qwerty:2:4);
end.
```

This Pascal program has one function and one procedure declared. Since functions and procedures are the same in C, you do not need to worry about the difference, except to return the value properly. Therefore, **procedure tom** becomes

```
tom(x)
int x;
{
        printf("%d", x*2);
}
```

and **function ken** becomes

```
float ken(w)
float w;
{
        qwerty=23.34;
        return w/3.1415;
}
```

Because **ken( )** returns a **float**, you must explicitly declare it by placing the type declaration **float** in front of the name **ken**.

Next, the **program** code (which starts with the first **begin** that is not inside another function or procedure) must be converted into the **main( )** function. It becomes

```
main()
{
        qwerty=0;
        printf("%f",qwerty);
        printf("hello there\n");
        tom(25);
        printf("%f\n",ken(10));
        printf("%2.4f\n",qwerty):
}
```

Finally, you must declare the global variable **qwerty** as a **float**. After you do this and put the pieces together, the C translation of the Pascal program looks like this:

```
float qwerty;

main()
{
        qwerty=0;
        printf("%f",qwerty);
        printf("hello there\n");
        tom(25);
        printf("%f\n",ken(10));
        printf("%2.4f\n",qwerty):
}

tom(x)
int x;
{
        printf("%d", x*2);
}

float ken(w)
float w;
{
        qwerty=23.34;
        return w/3.1415;
}
```

Using the Computer to Help Convert Pascal to C

It is possible to construct a computer program that accepts source code in one language and outputs it in another. The best way to do this is to implement an actual language parser for the source language—but instead of generating code, it will output the destination language. You can occasionally find advertisements for such products in computer magazines, and their high prices reflect the complexity of the task.

A less ambitious approach is to construct a simple program to assist your program-conversion efforts by performing some of the simpler translation tasks. This "computer assist" can make conversion jobs much easier.

A computer-assist translator accepts as input a program in the source language and performs all one-to-one conversions into the destination language automatically, leaving the harder conversions up to you. For example, to assign **count** the value of 10 in Pascal you would write

```
count:=10;
```

In C, the statement is the same, except that there is no colon. Therefore, the computer-assist program can change the := assignment statement in Pascal to the = in C. However, the ways Pascal and C programs access disk files are different, and there is no straightforward way to perform such a conversion automatically. The translator leaves these types of translations for you to perform.

First, the translator needs a function that returns one token at a time from the Pascal program. The function **get_token( )**, developed in Chapter 9, can be modified for this use as shown here.

```
get_token()
{
        register char *temp;

        tok_type=0; tok=0;
        temp=token;

        if(*prog=='\r') {
                *temp++='\r';
                *temp++='\n';
                *temp='\0';
```

```
                prog+=2;
                return;
        }

        if(*prog=='\0') {
                *temp='\0';
                return;
        }
        while(iswhite(*prog)) ++prog;   /* skip over white space */

        /* relational equals */
        if(*prog=='=') {
                prog++;
                strcpy(token,"==");
                return;
        }

        /* assignment */
        if(*prog==':') {
                prog++;
                if(*prog=='=')
                {
                        *temp++ = '=';
                        prog++;
                }
                else *temp++=':';

                *temp='\0';
                return;
        }

        /* strings */
        if(is_in(*prog,"'")) {
                *temp++='"';   prog++;
                while(!is_in(*prog,"'")) *temp++=*prog++;
                *temp='"'; temp++; *temp='\0'; prog++;
                return;
        }

        /* operators - if needed */
        if(is_in(*prog,"+-*;.,/^%()")){
                tok_type=OP;
                *temp=*prog;
                prog++; /* advance to next position */
                if(*temp=='.') *temp=' ';
                temp++;
                *temp=0;
                return;
        }

        /* variables */
        if(isalpha(*prog)) {
                while(isalpha(*prog)) *temp++=*prog++;
                *temp='\0';
                translate(token);
                return;
        }

        /* numbers */
        if(isdigit(*prog)) {
```

```
          while(!isdelim(*prog)) *temp++=*prog++;
          tok_type=NUMBER;
          *temp=0;
          return;
     }
     prog++;   /* unknown character */
}
```

In **get_token( )**, the Pascal assignment := is converted into C as =, and = is converted into its C equivalent, ==. While this is sufficient for a simple translation program, a more complete translation program would have probably done this conversion in a larger operator-conversion routine.

The second important routine translates Pascal keywords and some functions into their C counterparts. Again, the function **translate( )** shown here is not the best way to code such a routine, but it is sufficient for the program's purposes.

```
translate(s)
char *s;
{
     if (!strcmp(s,"and")) strcpy(s,"&&");
     else if (!strcmp(s,"begin")) strcpy(s,"{");
     else if (!strcmp(s,"case")) strcpy(s,"switch");
     else if (!strcmp(s,"div")) strcpy(s,"/");
     else if (!strcmp(s,"do")) strcpy(s,"do");
     else if (!strcmp(s,"else")) strcpy(s,"else");
     else if (!strcmp(s,"end")) strcpy(s,"}");
     else if (!strcmp(s,"forward")) strcpy(s,"extern");
     else if (!strcmp(s,"for")) strcpy(s,"for");
     else if (!strcmp(s,"function")) strcpy(s,"\n");
     else if (!strcmp(s,"goto")) strcpy(s,"goto");
     else if (!strcmp(s,"if")) strcpy(s,"if");
     else if (!strcmp(s,"mod")) strcpy(s,"%");
     else if (!strcmp(s,"nil")) strcpy(s,"'\0'");
     else if (!strcmp(s,"not")) strcpy(s,"!");
     else if (!strcmp(s,"procedure")) strcpy(s,"\n");
     else if (!strcmp(s,"record")) strcpy(s,"struct");
     else if (!strcmp(s,"repeat")) strcpy(s,"do");
     else if (!strcmp(s,"until")) strcpy(s,"while");
     else if (!strcmp(s,"while")) strcpy(s,"while");
     else if (!strcmp(s,"writeln")) strcpy(s,"printf");
     else if (!strcmp(s,"write")) strcpy(s,"printf");
     else if (!strcmp(s,"real")) strcpy(s,"float");
     else if (!strcmp(s,"integer")) strcpy(s,"int");
     else if (!strcmp(s,"char")) strcpy(s,"char");
}
```

An improved version of this function would use a binary search on an array that holds the Pascal keywords, thereby eliminating the number of **strcmp( )** statements that could make this routine very slow if the list were expanded. Some words (such as **program**) have no equivalent in C, and in this case, a newline is substituted. A null string is not used, because it is reserved to indicate the end of the file.

Here is the entire translation program.

```
#include "stdio.h"
#include "ctype.h"

#define OP      1
#define KEYWORD 2
#define VAR     3
#define NUMBER  4

char token[80];
int tok_type;
int tok;

char s[10000];  /* holds source file */
char *prog;

main(argc,argv) /* computer assisted Pascal to C converter */
int argc;
char *argv[];
{
        FILE *fp1, *fp2;
        char *p;

        prog = s;

        if((fp1=fopen(argv[1],"r"))==0) {
                printf("cannot open input file\n");
                exit(0);
        }

        if((fp2=fopen(argv[2],"w"))==0) {
                printf("cannot open output file\n");
                exit(0);
        }

        while((*prog=getc(fp1))!=EOF)
                prog++; /* read in source */

        *prog='\0';
        prog=s;

        for(;;) {
                get_token();
                if(!*token) break;  /* end of input file */
                p=token;
                while(*p) putc(*p++,fp2);
                putc(' ',fp2);
        }
        fclose(fp1); fclose(fp2);
}

get_token()
{
```

```
register char *temp;

tok_type=0; tok=0;
temp=token;

if(*prog=='\r') {
        *temp++='\r';
        *temp++='\n';
        *temp='\0';
        prog+=2;
        return;
}

if(*prog=='\0') {
        *temp='\0';
        return;
}
while(iswhite(*prog)) ++prog;  /* skip over white space */

/* relational equals */
if(*prog=='=') {
        prog++;
        strcpy(token,"==");
        return;
}

/* assignment */
if(*prog==':') {
        prog++;
        if(*prog=='=')
        {
                *temp++ = '=';
                prog++;
        }
        else *temp++=':';

        *temp='\0';
        return;
}

/* strings */
if(is_in(*prog,"'")) {
        *temp++='"';  prog++;
        while(!is_in(*prog,"'")) *temp++=*prog++;
        *temp='"'; temp++; *temp='\0'; prog++;
        return;
}

/* operators - if needed */
if(is_in(*prog,"+-*;.,/^%()")){
        tok_type=OP;
        *temp=*prog;
        prog++; /* advance to next position */
        if(*temp=='.') *temp=' ';
        temp++;
        *temp=0;
        return;
}

/* variables */
```

```
                    if(isalpha(*prog)) {
                            while(isalpha(*prog)) *temp++=*prog++;
                            *temp='\0';
                            translate(token);
                            return;
                    }

                    /* numbers */
                    if(isdigit(*prog)) {
                            while(!isdelim(*prog)) *temp++=*prog++;
                            tok_type=NUMBER;
                            *temp=0;
                            return;
                    }
                    prog++;  /* unknown character */
        }

        iswhite(c)

        char c;
        {
                    /* look for spaces and tabs */
                    if(c==' ' || c==9) return 1;
                    return 0;
        }

        isdelim(c)
        char c;
        {
                    if(is_in(c," +-/*^%()") || c==9 || c=='\r' || c==0)
                            return 1;
                    return 0;
        }

        is_in(ch,s)
        char ch,*s;
        {
                    while(*s) if(*s++==ch) return 1;
                    return 0;
        }

        translate(s)
        char *s;
        {
                if (!strcmp(s,"and")) strcpy(s,"&&");
                else if (!strcmp(s,"begin")) strcpy(s,"{");
                else if (!strcmp(s,"case")) strcpy(s,"switch");
                else if (!strcmp(s,"div")) strcpy(s,"/");
                else if (!strcmp(s,"do")) strcpy(s,"do");
                else if (!strcmp(s,"else")) strcpy(s,"else");
                else if (!strcmp(s,"end")) strcpy(s,"}");
                else if (!strcmp(s,"forward")) strcpy(s,"extern");
                else if (!strcmp(s,"for")) strcpy(s,"for");
                else if (!strcmp(s,"function")) strcpy(s,"\n");
                else if (!strcmp(s,"goto")) strcpy(s,"goto");
                else if (!strcmp(s,"if")) strcpy(s,"if");
                else if (!strcmp(s,"mod")) strcpy(s,"%");
                else if (!strcmp(s,"nil")) strcpy(s,"'\0'");
                else if (!strcmp(s,"not")) strcpy(s,"!");
                else if (!strcmp(s,"procedure")) strcpy(s,"\n");
                else if (!strcmp(s,"record")) strcpy(s,"struct");
                else if (!strcmp(s,"repeat")) strcpy(s,"do");
```

```
      else if (!strcmp(s,"until")) strcpy(s,"while");
      else if (!strcmp(s,"while")) strcpy(s,"while");
      else if (!strcmp(s,"writeln")) strcpy(s,"printf");
      else if (!strcmp(s,"write")) strcpy(s,"printf");
      else if (!strcmp(s,"real")) strcpy(s,"float");
      else if (!strcmp(s,"integer")) strcpy(s,"int");
      else if (!strcmp(s,"char")) strcpy(s,"char");
}
```

In essence, the Computer Assisted Pascal to C program reads in the entire source code of the Pascal program, takes a token at a time from it, performs any translations it can, and writes out a C version. Except for a few operator changes, the standard function **strcmp( )** detects a translatable token, and **strcpy( )** converts it to the proper C token. To see how this simple program can make translating from Pascal to C easier, run this Pascal program through the translator program:

```
program test (input,output);
procedure tom (x: integer);
begin
     writeln(x*2);
end;

function ken (w: real): real;
begin
     if w=100 writeln('w is 100 inside ken');
     ken:= w/3.1415;
end;

begin
     writeln('hello there');
     tom(25);
     writeln(ken(10));
end.
```

The pseudo-C output is

```
test ( input , output ) ;
tom ( x : int ) ;
{
printf ( x * 2 ) ;
} ;


  ken ( w : float ) : float ;
{
if w == 100 printf ( " w is 100 inside ken " ) ;
ken = w / 3.1415;
} ;


{
printf ( " hello there " ) ;
tom ( 25 ) ;
printf ( ken ( 10 ) ) ;
}
```

As you can see, this is not C code, but you have saved a lot of typing. All you need do is edit this a line at a time to correct the differences.

Converting BASIC
To C

The task of converting BASIC to C is much more difficult than that of converting Pascal to C. BASIC is not a structured language, and it bears little similarity to C, which means that not only does it not have a complete set of control structures but, more importantly, it does not have stand-alone subroutines with local variables. The translation task is very tricky. Generally, it requires extensive knowledge of both BASIC and C, and an understanding of the program, because in essence you will be rewriting the program in C and using the BASIC version as a guide. Because of the complexity of the task, this section will look at some of the more troublesome translations and offer suggestions.

Converting BASIC Loops
Into C Loops

The **FOR/NEXT** loop is the only form of loop control in many versions of BASIC. The overall form of the **FOR/NEXT** loop in BASIC and the **for** loop in C is generally the same; there is initialization, test condition, and increment. The C **for** loop is much more sophisticated and flexible than the BASIC **FOR/NEXT**, but when you translate from BASIC to C, this does not matter. For example, the BASIC **FOR/NEXT** loop

```
10 FOR X=1 TO 100
20    PRINT X
30 NEXT
```

translates into C as

```
for(x=1; x<=100; ++x) printf("%d\n",x);
```

As you can see, the conversion is essentially a one-to-one substitution. The real trick in converting the **FOR/NEXT** loop is making sure that the loop control variable is not modified inside the loop. For example, in

```
10 FOR COUNT=10 TO 0 STEP -1
20    INPUT A
30    PRINT A*COUNT
40    IF A=100 THEN COUNT = 0
50 NEXT
```

the **IF/THEN** statement in line 40 could cause the loop to exit early. To translate this properly into C code, you must allow for this contingency as well:

```
for(count=10; count>0; --count) {
        a=getnum();
        printf("%d\n",a*count);
        if(a==100) break;
}
```

Some forms of BASIC have a **WHILE/WEND** loop available. In such a case, you would use a C **while** loop and your translation would be straightforward. If the BASIC you are using does not have the **WHILE/WEND** loop or if you choose not to use it, your job will be harder because you must recognize a *constructed loop* using **GOTO** statements. This will also be the case if a **do/while** type of loop is needed in BASIC. These types of translations become nightmarish because you must actually understand how the code works in order to recognize the loop and translate it into one of C's built-in loop control structures.

After finding the loop, there is an easy way to tell whether a constructed loop in BASIC should be translated into a C **while** or **do/while**. Recall that a **do/while** loop *always executes at least once* because the loop condition is checked at the bottom of the loop, whereas a **while** loop may or may not execute because its condition is checked at the top. Therefore, you must look carefully at each constructed loop in BASIC and determine where the loop test is applied. For example, the BASIC code

```
100 S=S+1
200 Q=S/3.1415
300 PRINT Q;
400 IF S <100 THEN GOTO 100
```

is actually a **do/while** loop in disguise because it will always execute at least once. After line 100 has been executed, lines 200 through 400 will execute as well. If **S** is less than 100, the program will loop back to line 100. In C, this code would be

```
do {
        s++;
        q=s/3.1415;
        printf("%f ",q);
} while(s<100);
```

In the following BASIC example, the loop test is performed at the start of the loop, so it requires the use of the **while** loop:

```
10 A=1
20 IF A>100 THEN GOTO 80
30 PRINT A
40 INPUT B
50 A=A+B
60 GOTO 20
80 PRINT "DONE"
```

The C equivalent is

```
a=1;
while(a<=100) {
        printf("%d\n",a);
        b=getnum();
        a=a+b;
}
printf("done");
```

Avoid placing any initialization inside the loop itself by accident. In this example, the statement **a=1** has to be outside the loop because it is a start-up condition and does not belong in the loop itself.

Converting the IF/THEN/ELSE Statement

Most forms of BASIC have only the single-line **IF/THEN/ELSE** statement. This means that when a block of statements must be executed based on the outcome of an **IF**, the **GOTO** or **GOSUB** must be used. You must recognize this situation, because you will want to structure the code into a proper C

if/else statement when you translate it. As an example, consider the following BASIC code fragment:

> **120 IF T<100 THEN GOTO 500**
> **130 Y=W**
> **140 T=10**
> **150 INPUT A\$**
> .
> .
> .
> **500 REM RESUME DISK READS**

To achieve an **IF** block in a BASIC program, the **IF** condition must be cast in the negative: it must not be the condition that you want to enter in the **IF** block, but rather the one that causes a jump around it. This is one of the worst problems in BASIC. Using **GOSUB** routines as the target of the **IF** or the **ELSE** does ease the problem slightly, but not entirely. If the BASIC code fragment were translated directly into C, it would look like this:

```
if(t<500) ;
else {
        y=w;
        t=10;
        gets(a);
}
/* resume disk reads */
```

You can now see the problem: the target of the **if** is really an empty statement. The only way to resolve this is to recode the **if** condition so that if it is true, the block of code is entered. The code fragment then becomes

```
if(t>=500) {
        y=w;
        t=10;
        gets(a);
}
/* resume disk reads */
```

Now the code, as written in C, makes sense.

The differences between the way the BASIC **IF/THEN** is used and the way the C **if** is used illustrate that the programming language often governs the approach to solving a problem. Most people find the positive form of the **if** more natural to use than the negative form.

Creating C Functions
From BASIC Programs

One reason that translating BASIC into C is difficult is that it does not support stand-alone subroutines with local variables. This means that a literal translation of a BASIC program into C would produce a large **main( )** and only a few other functions. A better translation would create a C program with a fairly small **main( )** and many other functions, but to do this requires knowledge of the program and a keen eye for reading code. However, here are a few rules to guide you.

First, make all **GOSUB** routines into functions. Also look for similar functions in which only the variables have changed, and collapse them into one function with parameters. For example, this BASIC code has two subroutines—one at 100 and the second at 200:

```
10  A=10
20  B=20
30  GOSUB 100
40  PRINT A,B
50  C=20
60  D=30
70  GOSUB 200
80  PRINT C,D
90  END
100 A=A*B
110 B=A/B
120 RETURN
200 C=C*D
210 D=C/D
220 RETURN
```

Both subroutines do exactly the same thing, except they operate on separate sets of variables. A proper translation of this program into C has only one function that uses parameters to avoid having two dedicated functions:

```
main()
{
        int a,b,c,d;

        a=10; b=20;
        f1(&a,&b);
        printf("%d %d\n",a,b);

        c=20; d=30;
        f1(&c,&d);
        printf("%d %d\n",c,d);
```

```
}

f1(x,y)
int *x,*y;
{

        *x=*x*(*y);
        *y=*x/*y;
}
```

This C translation approximates the meaning of the code to the reader more closely than does the BASIC version, which implies that there are actually two separate functions involved.

The second rule is to make all repeated code into a function. In a BASIC program, the same few lines of code may be repeated. A programmer often does this to make the code slightly faster. Because C is generally a compiled language, using functions, as opposed to using in-line code, has minimal effect; the increased clarity outweighs any gain in speed.

Getting Rid of Global Variables

In BASIC, all variables are global: they are known throughout the program and may be modified anywhere in the program. In the translation process, try to convert as many of these global variables as possible into local ones, because it makes the program more resilient and bug-free. The more global variables there are, the more likely it is that side effects will occur.

It is sometimes difficult to know when to make a variable local to a function. The easiest choices are the ones that control counters in short sections of code. For example, in this code

```
10 FOR X=1 TO 10
20    PRINT X
30 NEXT
```

X is used only to control the **FOR/NEXT** loop and can therefore be made into a local variable within a function.

Another type of variable that is a candidate for becoming local is a temporary variable. A temporary variable holds an intermediate result in a calculation. Temporary variables are often spread out in a program and can be hard to recognize. For example, the variable C12 shown here holds a temporary result in the calculation.

```
10 INPUT A,B
20 GOSUB 100
30 PRINT C12
40 END
100 C12=A*B
110 C12=C12/0.142
120 RETURN
```

The same code in C, with C12 as a local variable, would be

```
main()
{
        scanf("%f%f",a,b);
        printf("%f",f1(a,b));
}

float f1(a,b)
float a,b;
{
        float c12;

        c12=a*b;
        c12/=0.142;
        return c12;
}
```

Remember that it is always best to have as few global variables as possible, so it is important to find good candidates for local variables.

Final Thoughts on Translating

Although translating programs can be the most tedious of all programming tasks, it is also one of the most common. A good approach is to understand the way the program you are translating works, and to learn to use it. Once you know how it operates, the program is easier to recode; you know whether your new version is working correctly. Also, when you know the program you are translating, the job becomes more interesting because it is not just a simple symbol-substitution process.

The next chapter includes a specialized case of translating. In this situation, you will be translating a C program that you wrote with one compiler, into a program that will compile and run with a different C compiler. Although this sounds easy, it is often the hardest translating task of all.

Efficiency, Porting, And Debugging

CHAPTER 11

The ability to write programs that use system resources efficiently, are error-free, and are easily transported to other computers is the mark of a professional programmer. It is also this ability that transforms computer science into the "art of computer science," because so few formal techniques are available to ensure success. This chapter presents some of the methods by which efficiency, program debugging, and portability may be achieved.

Efficiency

When it pertains to a computer program, the term *efficiency* refers to the program's speed of execution, its use of system resources, or both. System resources include RAM, disk space, printer paper, and basically anything that can be allocated and used up. Whether or not a program is efficient is sometimes a subjective judgment—it depends on the situation. Consider a program that uses 47K of RAM to execute, 2 megabytes of disk space, and that has an average run time of 7 minutes. If this is a sort program running on an Apple II, then the program is probably not very efficient. However, if it is a weather-forecasting program running on a Cray computer, then the program is probably very efficient.

Another consideration when you are concerned with efficiency is that optimizing one aspect of a program will often degrade another. For example, making a program execute faster often means making it bigger if you use in-line code instead of function calls to speed up the calling sequence. Also, making more efficient use of disk space by compacting the data invariably makes disk access slower. These and other types of efficiency trade-offs can be frustrating—especially to the nonprogramming end-user, who cannot see why one thing should affect the other.

In light of these problems, you may wonder how efficiency can be discussed at all. Actually, there are some programming practices that are always efficient—or at least are more efficient than others. There are also a few techniques that make programs *both* faster and smaller.

The Increment and Decrement Operators

Discussions on the efficient use of C almost always start by considering the increment and decrement operators. Remember that the increment operator ++ increases its argument by one, and the decrement operator −− decreases its argument by one. The increment operator essentially replaces this type of assignment statement:

```
x = x + 1;
```

and the decrement operator replaces assignment statements of this type:

```
x = x - 1;
```

Besides the obvious advantage of reducing the number of keystrokes, the increment and decrement operators have another glorious advantage: they execute faster and need less RAM than their statement counterparts on most microcomputer C compilers. This is because of the way object code is generated by the compiler. For example, if you use a simple, imaginary assembly language that approximates the assembly language found on most microprocessors, the statement

```
x=x+1;
```

will generate this sequence of code:

```
move A,x   ; load value of x from memory into
           ;   accumulator
move B,1   ; put 1 into b register
add B      ; add b to the accumulator
store x    ; store new value back in x
```

However, if you use the increment operator, the following code will be produced:

```
move A,x   ; load value of x from memory into
           ;   accumulator
incr A     ; increase a (that is X) by 1
store x    ; store new value back in x
```

Here, one entire instruction has been eliminated, which means the code will execute faster and will be smaller.

Some C compilers automatically recognize such expressions as **x=x+1** and to produce better object code will output the code as if it had been written as **x++**. This process is called *optimizing*. However, you should not count on it very often, and if you have to port your code to a new computer using a different compiler, you should use the increment and decrement operators explicitly.

Pointers Versus Array Indexing

Another technique that almost always produces both smaller and faster code is substituting pointer arithmetic for array indexing. To help you understand why this could make a difference, take a look at the following two code fragments, which both do the same thing.

Pointer Arithmetic	*Array Indexing*
p=array;	
for(;;) {	for(;;) {
a=*(p++);	a=array[t++];
.	.
.	.
.	.
}	}

With the pointer method, after **p** has been loaded with the address of **array**, perhaps in an index register (such as SI on the 8086 processor), only an increment must be performed each time the loop repeats. However, the array-index version forces the program to compute the array index based on the value of **t** for every pass through the loop. The disparity between pointer arithmetic and array indexing grows as multiple indexes are used: pointer arithmetic can use simple addition, whereas each index requires its own sequence of instructions.

However, as a precaution, you may want to use array indexes when the index is derived through a complex formula and when the use of pointer arithmetic would obscure the meaning of the program. It is usually better to degrade performance slightly than to sacrifice clarity.

Use of Functions

Always remember that the use of stand-alone functions with local variables forms the basis of structured programming. Functions are the building blocks of C programs, and they are one of C's strongest assets. Do not let anything that is discussed in this section be construed otherwise. Now that you have been warned, you should know a few aspects of C functions and their effects on the size and speed of your code.

First and foremost, C is a *stack-oriented language:* all local variables and parameters to functions use the stack for temporary storage. When a function is called, the return address of the calling routine is placed on the stack as well. This allows the subroutine to return to the location from which it was called. When a function returns, this address—as well as all local variables and parameters—must be removed from the stack. The process of pushing this information onto the stack is generally referred to as the *calling sequence,* and the process of popping the information off of the stack is called the *returning sequence.* These sequences take time—sometimes quite a bit of time.

To understand how a function call can slow down your program, look at the two code examples shown here.

```
            Version 1                          Version 2
      for(x=1;x<100;++x) {              for(x=1;x<100;++x) {
          t=compute(x);                     t=abs(sin(q)/100/3.1416);
      }                                }

      float compute(q)
      int q;
      {
          float t;

          t=abs(sin(q)/100/3.1416);
          return t;
      }
```

Although each loop performs the same function, Version 2 is much faster because the overhead of the calling and returning sequences has been eliminated by using in-line code. To understand just how much time is taken up, study the following pseudo-assembly code, which shows the calling and returning sequences for the function **compute( )**. The actual code used depends on how the compiler is implemented and what processor is being used, but it generally follows the same pattern as this example.

```
; calling sequence
move A, x   ; put value of x into accumulator
push A
call compute  ; the call instruction places
              ; the return address on the stack

        .
        .
        .

; returning sequence
; the return value of the function must be placed
; into a register - we will use B
move B, stack-1   ; get value in temporary t
return   ; return to the calling routine
; calling routine then does the following
pop A    ; clear parameter use in the call
```

Using the **compute( )** function inside the loop causes the calling and returning sequences to be executed 100 times. If you really want to write fast code, then using **compute( )** inside a loop is not the right idea.

By now you may think that you should write a program that has just a few large functions so that it will run quickly. In the majority of cases, however, the slight time differential will not be meaningful, and the loss of structure will be acute. But there is another problem. Replacing functions that are used by several routines with in-line code will make your program very large, because the same code will be duplicated several times. Keep in mind that subroutines were invented primarily as a way to make efficient use of memory. A rule of thumb is that making a program faster means making it bigger, while making it smaller means making it slower.

Finally, it only makes sense to use in-line code instead of a function call when speed is of absolute priority. Otherwise, the liberal use of functions is definitely recommended.

Overdoing It

In some circles, C has gained a reputation for being a cryptic, hard-to-read language. This reputation is due entirely to overzealous programmers who always attempt to write very efficient programs. Because C allows very complex expressions to be written in one line, which can sometimes make the program run a little faster, some C programs are hard to decipher. An intensely optimized program is sometimes necessary, but in most cases it gains little and greatly reduces the program's maintainability. In all cases, you should have a very good reason when you reduce the readability of your code.

Porting Programs

It is common for a program written on one machine to be transported to another computer with a different processor, operating system, or both. This process is called *porting* and can be either very easy or extremely difficult, depending on the way the program was originally written. A program is *portable* if it can be easily ported. A program is not easily portable if it contains numerous *machine dependencies*—code fragments that will work only with one specific operating system or processor. C has been designed to allow portable code, but it still requires care, attention to detail, and often the sacrifice of maximum efficiency to actually achieve portable code. In this section you will examine a few specific problem areas and learn about some solutions.

Using #define

Perhaps the simplest way to make programs portable is to make *every* system- or processor-dependent "magic number" into a #**define** macro-substitution directive. These "magic numbers" include buffer sizes for disk accesses, special screen and keyboard commands, memory allocation information, and anything else that has even the slightest chance of changing when the program is ported. If you make the magic numbers into #**define** directives, these "defines" not only make the magic numbers obvious to the person doing the porting, but they also simplify editing; their values have to be changed only once instead of throughout the program.

For example, here are two functions that use **read( )** and **write( )** to access information in a disk file.

```
f1()
{
        write(fd
}
f2()
{
        read(fd,buf,128);
}
```

The problem is that the number **128** is hard-coded into both **read( )** and **write( )**. This might be acceptable for one operating system but less than optimal for another. A better way to code it is shown here.

```
#define buf_size 128

f1()
{
        write(fd,buf,buf_size);
}

f2()
{
        read(fd,buf,buf_size);
}
```

In this case, only the #**define** would have to change and all references to **buf_size** would be automatically corrected. This version not only is easier to change, but it also avoids many editing errors. Remember that there will probably be many references to **buf_size** in a real program, so the gain in portability is often substantial.

Operating-System Dependencies

Virtually all commercial programs have code in them that is specific to the operating system. For example, a spreadsheet program might make use of the IBM PC's video memory to allow fast switching between screens, or a graphics package may use special graphics commands that are only applicable to that operating system. Some operating-system dependencies are necessary for fast, commercially viable programs. However, there is no reason to hard-code any more dependencies than necessary.

As suggested earlier, disk-file functions can sometimes contain implicit machine dependencies. The **read( )** and **write( )** functions found in the standard library, for example, can work with various buffer sizes, but an operating system may require an even multiple of some number to operate most efficiently. Therefore, a buffer size of 128 might be fine for CP/M 2.2 but may not be acceptable for MS-DOS. In this case the buffer size should be defined, as discussed earlier.

When you must use system calls to access the operating system, it is best to do them all through one master function so that you only have to change it to accommodate a new operating system and can leave the rest of the code intact. For example, if system calls were needed to clear the screen and the end-of-line, and to locate the cursor at an X,Y coordinate, then you would create a master function like **op—sys—call( )**, shown here.

```
op_sys_call(op,x,y)
char op;
int x,y;
{
        switch(op) {
                case 1: clear_screen();
                        break;
                case 2: clear_eol();
                        break;
                case 3: goto_xy(x,y);
                        break;
        }
}
```

Only the code that forms the actual functions would have to change, leaving a common interface intact.

Debugging

To paraphrase Thomas Edison, programming is 10% inspiration and 90% debugging. Good programmers are usually good debuggers. Although you probably have good debugging skills, you should watch for certain types of bugs that can occur easily while you are using C.

Order of Process Errors

When the increment and decrement operators are used in programs written in C, the order in which the operations take place is affected by whether these operators precede or follow the variable. For example, the two statements

Version 1	*Version 2*
y=10;	y=10;
x=y++;	x=++y;

are not the same. The first one assigns the value of 10 to **x** and then increments **y**. The second increments **y** to 11 and then assigns the value 11 to **x**. Therefore, in Version 1, **x** contains 10; in Version 2, **x** contains 11. The rule is that increment and decrement operations occur before other operations if they precede the operand; otherwise, they occur afterwards.

An order-of-process error usually occurs when changes are made to an existing statement. For example, you may enter the statement

```
x = *p++;
```

which assigns the value pointed to by **p** to **x** and then increments the pointer **p**. However, say that you decide later that **x** really needs the value pointed to by **p** times the value pointed to by **p**. To do this, you might rewrite the statement to

```
x = *p++ * (*p);
```

However, this version doesn't work, because **p** has already been incremented. The proper solution is to write

```
x = *p * (*p++);
```

Errors like this can be hard to find. There may be clues, such as loops that don't run correctly or routines that are off by one. If you have any doubt about a statement, recode it in a way that you have confidence in.

Pointer Problems

A common error in C programs is the misuse of pointers. Pointer problems fall into two general categories: misunderstanding of indirection and the pointer operators, and the accidental use of invalid pointers. To solve the first type of problem, you must understand the C language; to solve the second, you must always verify the validity of a pointer before you use it.

The following program illustrates a typical pointer error that C programmers make:

```
main()  /* this program is WRONG */

{

        char *p;

        char *alloc();

        *p=alloc(100); /* this line is wrong */

        gets(p);

        printf(p);

}
```

This program will most likely crash, probably taking with it the operating system. It will crash because the address returned by **alloc( )** was *not* assigned to **p**, but to the memory location pointed to by **p**, which is completely unknown in this case. To correct this program, you must substitute

```
p=alloc(100); /* this is correct */
```

for the incorrect line.

The program has a second and more insidious error: there is no run-time check on the address returned by **alloc( )**. Remember, if memory is exhausted, **alloc( )** will return 0, which is never a valid pointer in C. The malfunction caused by this type of bug is difficult to find because it occurs rarely, only when an allocation request fails. Prevention is the best way to deal with this. Here is a corrected version of the program, which now includes a check for pointer validity.

```
main()   /* this program is now correct */

{

        char *p;

        char *alloc();

        p=alloc(100); /* this is correct */

        if(p==0) {

                printf("out of memory\n");

                exit(0);

        }

        gets(p);

        printf(p);

}
```

"Wild" pointers are extremely difficult to track down. If you are making assignments to a pointer variable that does not contain a valid pointer address, your program may appear to function correctly sometimes but crash at other times. Statistically, the smaller your program, the more likely it will run correctly even with a stray pointer, because very little memory is in use. As your program grows, failures become more common, but as you try to debug you will be thinking about recent additions or changes to your program, not about pointer errors. Hence, you will probably look in the wrong spot for the bug.

One indication of a pointer problem is that errors tend to be erratic. Your program may work right one time and wrong another. Sometimes other variables will contain garbage for no explainable reason. If these problems occur, check your pointers. As a matter of procedure, you should check all pointers when bugs begin to occur.

Although pointers can be troublesome, they are also one of the most powerful and useful aspects of the C language, and they are worth whatever trouble they may cause. Make the effort early on to learn to use them correctly.

One final point to remember about pointers is that you must initialize them before they are used. This seems simple enough, but many excellent C programmers still fall into this trap occasionally. For example, the following code fragment will be a disaster because you don't know where **x** is pointing:

```
int *x;

*x=100;
```

Assigning a value to that unknown location will probably destroy something of value—perhaps other code or data for your program.

Redefining Functions

You can—but should not—call your functions by the same names as those in the C standard library. Most compilers will use your function over the one in the library, causing direct and indirect problems.

Here is an example of a direct problem caused by redefining a library function.

```
main( )
{
        FILE *fp;
        char big[1000];
        init_array(big);
        if((fp=open("name","r"))==-1) {
                printf("cannot open file \n");
                exit(0);
        }
        .
        .
        .
init_array(p)
char *p;
{
        register int t;
        for(t=0;t<1000; t++,p++) {
```

```
                              *p=t;
                              if(t%100) open(p);
        }
        open(p)
        char *p;
        {
                *p='O';
        }
```

This program will either crash or do bizarre things. The standard function **open( )** has been redefined in the program to assign the character O to certain elements of an array. It has nothing to do with the **open( )** used in the same program to open a disk file.

An even worse version of the redefinition problem occurs when a standard library function is redefined, but the standard function is *not* used directly in the program—it is used indirectly by another standard function. Consider the following program:

```
        char text[1000];
        main( )
        {
                int x;
                scanf("%d",&x);
                .
                .
                .

        }
        getc(p) /* return char from array */
        {
                return text[p];
        }
        .
        .
        .
```

This program will not work with most compilers because **scanf( )**, a standard C function, will probably call **getc( )**, a standard C function that has been redefined in the program. The problem can be difficult to find, because you have no clue that you created a side effect. It will simply seem that **scanf( )** is not working correctly.

The only way to avoid such problems is never to give a function you have written the same name as one in the standard library. If you are not sure,

append your initials to the start of the name, as in **hs＿getc( )** instead of
getc( ).

Bizarre Syntax Errors

Occasionally you will see a syntax error that you cannot understand or even
recognize as an error. The C compiler itself may sometimes have a bug that
causes it to report false errors. The only solution is to redesign your code.
Other unusual errors simply require some backtracking to find.

One particularly unsettling error will occur when you try to compile this
code:

```
main( )
{
        char *p, *myfunc( ); /* myfunc( ) returns
        char pointer */
        .
        .
        .
}
myfunc( )
{
        .
        .
        .
}
```

Most compilers will issue an error message such as **function redefined**
and point to **myfunc( )**. How can this be? There are not two **myfunc( )**s. The
answer is that you have declared **myfunc( )** to be returning a character pointer inside **main( )**. This declaration causes a symbol-table entry to be made
with that information. When the compiler encounters **myfunc( )** later in the
program, there is no indication that **myfunc( )** will return anything other
than an integer, the default type. Hence, you have "redefined" the function.
The correct program would be as follows.

```
main( )
{
        char *p, *myfunc( ); /* myfunc( ) returns
```

```
                    char pointer */
                      .
                      .
                      .
      }
      char *myfunc( )
      {
                      .
                      .
                      .
      }
```

This code will generate another syntax error that is difficult to understand:

```
main() /* this program has a syntax error in it */
{
        func1();
}
func1();
{
        printf("this is func1 \n");
}
```

The error here is the semicolon after the declaration of **func1( )**. The compiler will see it as a statement outside of any function, which is an error; however, compilers will report this error in different ways. Many compilers will issue an error message such as **bad declaration syntax** while pointing at the first open brace after **func1( )**. Because you are used to seeing semicolons after statements, you may find it difficult to see where this error message is coming from.

"One Off" Errors

By now you know that all C indexes start at 0. A common error involves using a **for** loop to access the elements of an array. Consider the following program, which is supposed to initialize an array of 100 integers:

```
main()    /* this program will not work */
{
        int x, num[100];
        for(x=1; x<=100; ++x) num[x]=x;
}
```

The **for** loop in this program is wrong for two reasons. First, it does not initialize **num[0]**, the first element of array **num**. Second, it goes one past the end of the array; **num[99]** is the last element in the array and the loop runs to 100. The correct way to write this program is

```
main()    /* this is right */
{
        int x, num[100];
        for(x=0; x<100; ++x) num[x]=x;
}
```

Remember, an array of 100 has elements 0 through 99.

Boundary Errors

The C language and many standard library functions have very little or no run-time boundary checking. For example, it is possible to overwrite arrays, disk files, and (through pointer assignments) variables. These things usually do not occur, but when they do, it can be very difficult to link the symptom to its cause.

For example, this program is supposed to read a string from the keyboard and display it on the screen.

```
main()
{
        int var1;
        char s[10];
        int var2;
```

```
          var1=10;  var2=10;

          get_string(s);

          printf("%s %d %s",s,var1,var2);

    }

    get_string(string)

    char *string;

    {

          register int t;

          printf("enter twenty characters\n");

          for(t=0;t<20;++t) {

                *s++=getchar();

          }

    }
```

Here there are no direct coding errors. However, an indirect error arises when **get_string( )** is called with s. The s is declared to be 10 characters long, but **get_string( )** will read 20 characters, causing s to be overwritten.

The actual problem is that while s may display all 20 characters correctly, either **var1** or **var2** will not contain the correct value. All C compilers must allocate a region of memory—usually the stack region—for local variables. The variables **var1**, **var2**, and s will be located in memory as shown in Figure 11-1.

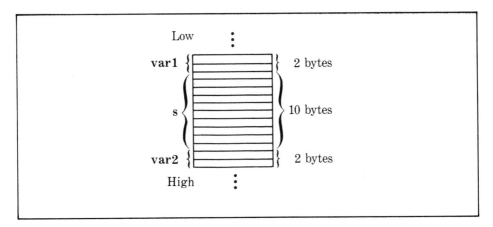

Figure 11-1. The variables **var1**, **var2**, and s in memory

Your C compiler may exchange the order of **var1** and **var2**, but they will still bracket **s**. When **s** is overwritten, the additional information is placed into the area that is reserved for **var2**, destroying any previous contents. Therefore, instead of printing the number 10 for both integer variables, the program will display something else for the one destroyed by the overrun of **s**. This will cause you to look for the problem in the wrong place.

Function Declaration Omissions

Any time a function returns a value type other than integer, the function must be declared to do this inside any other function that uses it. For example, this program multiplies two floating-point numbers together.

```
main() /* this is wrong */

{

        float x,y;

        scanf("%f%f",&x,&y);

        printf("%f",mul(x,y));

}

float mul(a,b)

float a,b;

{

        return a*b;

}
```

Although **main( )** expects an integer value from **mul( )**, **mul( )** returns a floating-point number. You will get meaningless answers, because **main( )** will only copy two bytes out of the eight needed for a **float**.

To correct this program, declare **mul( )** in **main( )** as shown:

```
main() /* this is correct */

{

        float x,y,mul();
```

```
        scanf("%f%f",&x,&y);

        printf("%f",mul(x,y));
}
float mul(a,b)
float a,b;
{
        return a*b;
}
```

Adding **mul( )** to the **float** declaration list tells **main( )** it should expect a floating-point value to be returned from **mul( )**.

Calling-Argument Errors

You must be sure to match whatever type of argument a function expects with the type you give it. For example, remember that **scanf( )** expects to receive the *address* of its arguments, not the value. This means that you must call **scanf( )** with arguments by using the & operator. The following code is wrong:

```
int x;
char string[10];
scanf("%d%s",x,string);
```

This code is correct:

```
scanf("%d%s",&x,string);
```

Remember, strings already pass their addresses to functions, so you should not use the & operator on them.

Another common error is to forget that C functions cannot modify their arguments. If it is necessary to modify an argument to a function, you must pass the address of the argument to the function and use pointer references to access the argument.

If a function's formal parameters are of type **float**, then you must pass floating-point variables to the function. For example, the following program will not function correctly:

```
main() /* this program is wrong */
{
        int x,y;
        scanf("%d%d",x,y);
        printf("%d",div(x,y));
}
float div(a,b)
float a,b;
{
        return a/b;
}
```

You cannot use a floating-point function such as **div( )** to return an integer value, and you cannot expect **div( )** to operate correctly — it expects floating-point numbers, not integers. You should remember that a cast can always be used to change one type to another if necessary.

General Debugging Theory

Everyone has a different approach to programming and debugging. However, some techniques have proved to be better than others. In the case of debugging, incremental testing is considered to be the least costly and most time-effective method, even though it can appear to slow the development process.

Incremental testing is simply the process of always having working code. As soon as it is possible to run a piece of your program, you should do so, testing that section completely. As you add to your program, continue to test the new sections as well as the way they connect to the established operational code. In this way you can be sure that any possible bugs are concentrated into a small area of code.

Incremental testing theory is generally based on probability and areas. As you know, *area* is a squared dimension. Each time you add length, you double area. Therefore, as your program grows, there is an n-squared area in which you must search for bugs. While debugging, you as a programmer want the smallest possible area to deal with. Through incremental testing you can subtract the area already tested from the total area, thereby reducing the region that may contain a bug.

Final Thoughts

Throughout this book, various algorithms and techniques have been discussed, some in considerable detail. Remember that computer science is both a theoretical and an empirical science. Although it is fairly easy to see why one algorithm is better than another, it is difficult to say what makes a successful program. When it comes to debugging, efficiency, and portability, experimenting will sometimes yield information more easily than would theoretical musing.

Programming is both a science and an art. It is a science because you must know logic and understand how and why algorithms work; it is an art because you create the total entity that is a program. As a programmer, you really have one of the best jobs on earth—you walk the line between art and science, and get the best of both.

The C Statement Summary

A P P E N D I X   A

This section contains a brief synopsis of important statements used in the C programming language.

break

A **break** is used to exit from a **do, for,** or **while** loop, thus bypassing the normal loop condition. It is also used to exit from a **switch** statement.

For example, here is **break** used in a loop:

```
while(x<100) {

        x=get_new_x();

        if(keystroke()) break;  /* key hit on

                                keyboard */

        process(x);

}
```

If a key is typed, the loop will terminate, regardless of the value of **x**.

A **break** always terminates the innermost **for, do, while,** or **switch** statement, no matter how they might be nested. In a **switch** statement, **break** effectively keeps program execution from "falling through" to the next **case**. (Refer to the **switch** statement for details.)

case

See the **switch** statement.

char

The data type **char** declares character variables. For example, to declare **ch** to be character type, you would write

```
char ch;
```

continue

The **continue** statement is used to bypass portions of code in a loop and to force the conditional test to be performed. For example, the following **while** loop simply reads characters from the keyboard until an **s** is typed:

```
while(ch=getchar) {
        if(ch!='s') continue;  /* read another char */
        process(ch);
}
```

The call to **process( )** does not occur until **ch** contains the character **s**.

default

A **default** is used in the **switch** statement to indicate that a default block of code should be executed if no matches are found in the **switch** (See **switch**).

do

The **do** loop is one of three loop constructs available in C. The general form of the **do** loop is

> **do** {
>   *statements block*
> } **while***(condition)* ;

If only one statement is repeated, the braces are not necessary, but they do add clarity.

The **do** loop is the only loop in C that always has at least one iteration because the condition is tested at the bottom of the loop.

The **do** loop is commonly used to read a disk file. This code reads a file until an EOF (end of disk file mark) is encountered:

```
do {
        ch=getc(fp);
        store(ch);
} while(ch!=EOF);
```

double

The data-type specifier **double** declares double-precision floating-point variables. To declare **d** to be of type **double**, you would write

```
double d;
```

else

See **if**.

entry

The **entry** is not currently implemented but is reserved for possible future use.

extern

The data-type modifier **extern** tells the compiler that a variable is declared elsewhere in the program. It is often used with separately compiled files that share the same global data and are linked together. In essence, it notifies the compiler of a variable and its type without declaring it again.

For example, if **first** were declared in another file as an integer, then the following declaration would be used in subsequent files.

```
extern int first;
```

float

A float is a data-type specifier that declares floating-point variables. To declare **f** to be of type **float**, you would write

```
float f;
```

for

The **for** loop allows automatic initialization and incrementation of a counter variable. The general form is

> **for**(*initialization*;*condition*;*increment*) {
>   *statement block*
> }

If the *statement block* is only one statement, the braces are not necessary.

Although **for** allows numerous variations, the *initialization* is generally used to set a counter variable to its starting value. The *condition* is usually a relational statement that checks the counter variable against a termination value, and the *increment* increments (or decrements) the counter value.

This code prints the message **hello** ten times:

```
for(t=0;t<10;t++) printf("hello\n");
```

The next example waits for a keystroke after printing **hello**.

```
for(t=0;t<10;t++) {
        printf("hello\n");
        getchar();
}
```

goto

The **goto** causes program execution to jump to the label specified in the **goto** statement. The general form of the **goto** is

goto label;

·
·
·

label:

All labels must end in a colon and must not conflict with keywords or function names. Furthermore, a **goto** can only branch within the current function, not from one function to another.

The following example prints the message **right** but not the message **wrong**:

```
goto lab1;
        printf("wrong");
lab1:
        printf("right");
```

if

The general form of the **if** statement is

```
if (condition) {
    statement block 1
}
else {
    statement block 2
}
```

If single statements are used, the braces are not needed. The **else** is optional.

The *condition* may be any expression. If that expression evaluates to any value other than 0, then *statement block 1* will be executed; otherwise, if it exists, *statement block 2* will be executed.

The following code can be used for keyboard input and to look for a **q**, which signifies "quit."

```
ch=getchar();
if(ch=='q') {
        printf("program terminated");
        exit(0);
}
else   proceed();
```

int

The type specifier **int** declares integer variables. To declare **count** as an integer, for example, you would write

```
int count;
```

long

The data-type modifier **long** declares double-length integer variables. For example, to declare **count** as a long integer, you would write

```
long int count;
```

register

A **register** is a declaration modifier that forces an integer or a character to be stored in a register of the CPU, instead of being placed in memory. The **register** can only be used on local variables. To declare **i** to be a register integer, you would write

```
register int i;
```

return

Using a **return** forces a return from a function and can transfer a value back to the calling routine. For example, the following function returns the product of its two integer arguments:

```
mul(a,b)

int a,b;

{

        return(a*b);

}
```

As soon as a **return** is encountered, the function returns, skipping any other code in the function.

short

The data-type modifier **short** declares integers that are one byte long. For example, to declare **sh** to be a short integer, you would write

```
short int sh;
```

sizeof

The compile-time operator **sizeof** returns the length of the variable it precedes. For example,

```
printf("%d",sizeof(int));
```

prints a 2 for most microcomputers.

The principal use of **sizeof** is to help generate portable code when that code depends upon the size of C's built-in data types. For example, since a database program may need to store six integer values, the amount of disk space needed would depend on the actual size of an integer.

static

The data-type modifier **static** instructs the compiler to create permanent storage for the local variable that it precedes. Using **static** enables the specified variable to maintain its value between function calls. For example, to declare **last_time** as a **static** integer, you would write

```
static int last_time;
```

struct

A **struct** creates complex variables called structures, which are made up of one or more elements of the seven basic data types, other structures, and unions, as well as user-defined **typedef**s and arrays. The general form of a structure is

> **struct** *struct_name* {
>   *type element1*;
>   *type element2*;
>   .
>   .
>   .
>   *type elementn*;
> } *structure_variable_name*;

The individual elements are referenced by using the dot or arrow operators.

switch

The **switch** statement is C's multiple-branch decision statement. It routes execution in one of several ways. The general form of the statement is

> **switch**(*variable*) {
>   **case** (*constant1*) : *statement set 1*;
>   **break**;
>   **case** (*constant2*) : *statement set 1*;
>   **break**;

.
.
.
    case (*constantn*) : *statement set n*;
      break;
    default: *default statements*;
}

Each statement set may be from one to several statements long. The **default** portion is optional.

The **switch** checks the *variable* against all the constants. If a match is found, then that set of statements is executed. If the **break** statement is omitted, execution continues until the **switch** ends or a **break** is found. Each **case** acts as a label. This example can be used to process a menu selection:

```
ch=getchar();
switch (ch) {
        case 'e': enter();
                break;
        case 'l': list();
                break;
        case 's': sort();
                break;
        case 'q': exit(0);
        default: printf("unknown command\n");
                printf("try again\n");

}
```

typedef

Using a **typedef** allows you to create a new name for an existing data type. The data type may be either one of the built-in types, or a structure or union name. The general form of **typedef** is

    typedef *type_specifier new_name*;

For example, to use the word **balance** in place of **float**, you would write

```
typedef float balance;
```

union

A **union** assigns two or more variables to the same memory location. The form of the definition and the way an element is referenced are the same as they are for **struct**. The general form is

> **union** *union_name* {
>   *type element1*;
>   *type element2*;
>   .
>   .
>   .
>   *type elementx*;
> } **union** *variable_name*;

unsigned

The data-type modifier **unsigned** tells the compiler to eliminate the sign bit of an integer and to use all bits for arithmetic. This doubles the size of the largest integer but restricts the integer to positive numbers only. For example, to declare **big** to be an unsigned integer, you would write

```
unsigned int big;
```

while

The **while** loop has the following general form:

> **while**(*condition*) {
>   *statement block*
> }

If the *statement block* is a single statement, the braces may be omitted.

The **while** tests its *condition* at the top of the loop. Therefore, if the *condition* is FALSE to begin with, the loop will not execute at all. The *condition* may be any expression.

For example, this **while** loop reads 100 characters from a disk file and stores them into a character array:

```
t=0;

while(t<100) {

        s[t]=getc(fp);

        t++;

}
```

The C Preprocessor

Although not technically part of the C language, the preprocessor directives can be used to specify various compile-time options. Using them can give you greater flexibility when you write your programs. Here is a review of the preprocessor directives.

#define

The **#define** is part of the C preprocessor. It can perform macro substitutions of one piece of text for another throughout the file in which it is used. The general form of the directive is

#define *name string*

There is no semicolon in this statement.

For example, if you wish to use the word **TRUE** for the value 1 and the word **FALSE** for the value 0, you would declare two **#define** directives:

```
#define TRUE 1
#define FALSE 0
```

This causes the compiler to substitute a 1 or a 0 each time **TRUE** or **FALSE** is encountered.

#include

The **#include** preprocessor directive instructs the compiler to read and compile another source file. The source file to be read must be enclosed between double quotation marks. For example,

```
#include "stdio.h"
```

tells the C compiler to read and compile the header for the disk file library routines.

#if, #ifdef, #ifndef, #else, and #endif

The preprocessor directives **#if**, **#ifdef**, **#ifndef**, **#else**, and **#endif** are used to compile various portions of a program selectively. They are of the greatest use to commercial software houses that provide and maintain many customized versions of one program. Generally, if the expression after an **#if**, **#ifdef**, or **#ifndef** is true, then the code that is between one of the preceding directives and an **#endif** will be compiled; otherwise, it will be skipped. The **#endif** is used to mark the end of an **#if** block. The **#else** can be used with any of the other directives, just as **else** can be used in the **if** statement.

The general form of **#if** is

#if *constant expression*

If the *constant expression* is TRUE, then the block of code will be compiled.

The general form of **#ifdef** is

#ifdef *name*

If the *name* has been dfined in a **#define** statement, the block of code that follows the statement will be compiled.

The general form of **#ifndef** is

#ifndef *name*

If *name* is currently undefined by a **#define** statement, then the block of code that follows the statement is compiled.

As an example, here is the way some of the preprocessor directives work together:

```
#define ted 10

main()
{
#ifdef ted
        printf("Hi Ted\n");
#endif
        printf("bye bye\n");
#if ted<9
        printf("Hi George\n");
#endif
}
```

This prints **Hi Ted** and **bye bye** on the screen, but not **Hi George**.

The C Standard Library

Unlike most programming languages, C does not have built-in functions that perform disk I/O, console I/O, or a number of other useful procedures. These tasks are accomplished in C by using a set of predefined library functions that is supplied with the compiler. The library is usually called the *C standard library*. "Standard" is used optimistically, because these libraries are not defined by the C language and vary widely from compiler to compiler. However, over the years, most compiler implementers have adopted the UNIX version 7 C compiler library (or some subset) as a de facto standard.

Library functions can be used by your program at will. Include the library at link time to ensure that these functions are added to your program. The exact method is described by your compiler's user manual.

The functions described here can be found in the standard library of most C compilers, and they are used without explanation in the program examples of this book. The descriptions presented here serve as a general guide to the functions' use; consult your user manual for exact details.

atoi(p)
char *p;

The **atoi( )** converts a string of numeric characters into an integer value. It has a single character pointer argument that points to the string of numeric characters. The integer value of that argument is returned. If the string passed to **atoi( )** does not contain a valid integer number, a 0 is returned. Leading spaces and tabs are generally ignored, and a minus sign may be used.

The following program inputs a number from the keyboard and converts it into an integer:

```
main()

{
        register int n;
        char s[80];
        printf("enter a number: ");
        gets(s);
        n=atoi(s);
}
```

close(fd)
int fd;

Part of the unbuffered I/O file system, **close( )** closes a disk file that has been opened by **open( )** or **creat( )**. The **close( )** returns 0 if the operation is successful. The file descriptor **fd** was returned by the call to **open( )** or **creat( )**.

The following program first opens a file called **test**, reads the first 128 bytes of unbuffered I/O, and then closes it.

```
main()

{
        int fd;
        char buf[128];
        if((fd=open("test",0))==-1) {
```

```
        printf("cannot open file.\n");

        exit(1);

}

read(fd,buf,128);  /* read first 128 bytes */

close(fd);

}
```

creat(name,mode)
char *name;
int mode;

The **creat( )** creates a new file and opens it for write operations. It is part of the unbuffered I/O file system. The **name** must be a pointer to a valid file name; **mode** specifies the protection mode and is optional on most microcomputer C implementations.

If **creat( )** successfully opens a new file, then it returns a file descriptor; otherwise, it returns a −1, which indicates a failure.

If a file of the same name already exists, it is erased. Therefore, be careful when using **creat( )**.

The following function creates and opens a user-defined file for write operations and returns the file descriptor.

```
cr_file()

{

        char name[80];

        int fd;

        printf("enter filename: ");

        gets(name);

        if((fd=creat(name,0))==-1) {

                printf("cannot open file\n");

                return -1;

        }

        return fd;

}
```

fclose(fp).
FILE *fp;

The **fclose( )**, part of the buffered I/O file system, writes any data yet remaining in the buffer to the file and closes the file. The file must have previously been opened using **fopen( )**, the buffered I/O open function. The **fp** is a file pointer that was returned by the call to **fopen( )**.

If **fclose( )** is successful, it returns 0; otherwise, it returns −1.

This program opens a file for buffered write operations and then closes it. In this example, only one character is written to the file:

```
main()

{

        FILE *fp;

        if((fp=fopen("test","w"))==0) {

                printf("cannot open file.\n");

                exit(1);

        }

        putc('A',fp);   /* write the char 'A' */

        fclose(fp);

}
```

FILE *fopen(name,mode)
char *name;
char *mode;

The **fopen( )** opens a file for buffered I/O operations. The **name** specifies the name of the file, and the **mode** is a string that specifies how the file will be accessed. Here is a list of the **mode** options:

r   open file for read only.

w   open file for write only.

a   open file for write and append on to the end.

rw open file for read/write mode.

If the file is opened using **w**, any preexisting file by the same name is erased. Use **a** (for append) to add material to a file.

The **fopen( )** returns either a file pointer of type **FILE** if successful or a 0 if unsuccessful.

The following function opens a file for both reading and writing. The name of the file is passed to the function, and upon success the file pointer is returned.

```
FILE *op_file(name)
char *name;
{
        FILE *fp;
        if((fp=fopen(name,"rw"))==0) {
                printf("cannot open file");
        }
        return fp;
}
```

getc(fp)
FILE *fp;

The **getc( )** returns the next character from the file pointed to by **fp**.

The following program opens a file called **test** for input and reads one character at a time until an EOF character is found. Each character read is printed on the screen.

```
main()

{

        FILE *fp;

        char ch;


        if((fp=fopen("test","r"))==0) {

                printf("cannot open file");

                exit(1);

        }

        do {

                ch=getc(fp);

                putchar(ch);

        } while(ch!=EOF);

        fclose(fp);

}
```

getchar( )

The **getchar( )** returns the next character from the console, which is usually the keyboard.

The following function reads a string of digits entered at the console and returns their integer value.

```
get_num()

{

        char s[80], *temp;

        temp=s; /* get address of first char in s */

        do {

                *temp=getchar(); /* read a digit */
```

```
            if(isdigit(*temp)) temp++;
      } while (*(temp-1)!='\r'); /* until return */
      *temp='\0'; /* null terminate */
      return(atoi(s));
  }
```

char gets(s)
char *s;

The **gets( )** reads a string of characters from the console and puts it into character array s. Input is terminated when a carriage return is typed or an EOF character is received. Neither the carriage return nor the EOF character becomes part of string s, however. The s is null-terminated after the call.

The **gets( )** either returns a pointer to s or returns a null if an error or EOF is encountered.

Generally, **gets( )** supports the use of the backspace and tab edit keys. Some implementations may allow other special editing characters as well.

This program inputs a string from the console and prints it backward on the screen:

```
main()

{
      char s[80];
      register int t;
      printf("enter a string: ");
      gets(s);
      for(t=strlen(s)-1;t>=0;--t) putchar(s[t]);
  }
```

char *malloc(size)
unsigned size;

Called **alloc( )** on some systems, **malloc( )** allocates a certain number, called **size**, of characters of free memory and returns a pointer to the beginning of **size**. The **malloc( )** is one of the dynamic allocation routines that allocates regions of memory for program use.

If an allocation request fails—that is, if there is insufficient memory to fill the request—then a null pointer is returned. Always make sure that you receive a valid pointer from **malloc( )**.

This is the general form of a program that allocates 80 bytes of memory and then frees it:

```
main( )
{
    char *p;
    p=malloc(80);
    if(!p) {
        printf("out of memory \n");
        exit(2);
    }
    .
    .
    .
    free(p);
}
```

open(name,mode)
char *name
int mode;

The **open( )** opens a file for unbuffered I/O. It returns an integer file descriptor if successful and a −1 if unsuccessful.

The **name** is any valid file name, and the **mode** determines the method of access. Here are the values that **mode** may have:

0   Read only

1   Write only

2   Read/write

Keep in mind that **open( )** will fail if the specified file does not exist and that **open( )** cannot be used to create a file.

The following function opens a file for unbuffered write-only access if the file exists. If it does not exist, it is created.

```
op_file(name)

char *name;

{
        int fd;

        if((fd=open(name,2)==-1)

                if((fd=creat(name,0)==-1)

                        printf("cannot open file\n");

        return fd;

}
```

printf(control,arg list)
char *control;

The generalized output function **printf( )** displays the standard C data types in various formats. The general form of **printf( )** is

> **printf(**"*control string*",*argument list*)**;**

The *control string* consists of two types of items. The first type contains characters that will be printed on the screen, and the second type contains format commands that define the way the arguments are displayed. There must be the same number of arguments as there are format commands; the format commands and the arguments are matched in order. For example, this **printf( )** call:

```
printf("Hi %c %d %s",'c',10,"there!");
```

displays **Hi c 10 there!**.

Table B-1 lists the **printf( )** format commands. These format commands may have modifiers that specify the field width, the number of decimal places, and a left-justify flag.

An integer placed between the % sign and the format command acts as a *minimum field-width specifier*. This specifier pads the output with blanks or zeros to ensure that it is at least a certain minimum length. If the string or number is greater than that minimum, it is printed in full.

The default padding is done with spaces. If you wish to pad with 0's, place a 0 before the field-width specifier. For example, **%05d** pads with 0's a number that is less than 5 digits.

Table B-1. The **printf( )** Format Commands

printf( ) Code	Format
%c	Single character
%d	Signed decimal
%e	Scientific notation
%f	Decimal floating point
%g	Uses %e or %f, whichever is shorter
%o	Unsigned octal
%s	String of characters
%u	Unsigned decimal
%x	Unsigned hexadecimal
%%	Single percent sign printed

To specify the number of decimal places printed for a floating-point number, place a decimal point, followed by the number of decimal points you wish to display, after the field-width specifier. For example, **%10.4f** displays a number that is at least ten characters wide with four decimal places. This method can also be used to specify the maximum field length for strings and integer values. For example, **%5.7s** displays a string that is at least five characters long but does not exceed seven characters. If the string is longer than the maximum field width, the string is truncated.

By default, all output is *right-justified*—if the field width is wider than the data printed, the data is placed on the right edge of the field. You can force the information to be displayed on the left by placing a minus sign directly after the % sign. For example, **%−10.2f** left-justifies a floating-point number with two decimal places in a 10-character-wide field.

The l modifier tells **printf( )** that a **long int** data type follows.

With **printf( )**, you can output virtually any format of data you desire. Table B-2 gives several examples. By writing examples of your own and checking their results, you can see if you fully understand the process.

After the statements

```
count=10;

printf("count is: %d",count);
```

are executed, the screen of your computer displays **count is: 10**.

Table B-2. Format Examples of **printf( )** Output

printf( ) Statement	Output
("%−6.2f",123.234)	123.23
("%6.2f",3.234)	3.23
("%10s","hello")	hello
("%−10s","hello")	hello
("%5.7s","123456789")	1234567

putc(ch,fp)
char ch;
FILE *fp;

A **putc( )** writes a character to a file that was previously opened by the buffered I/O function **fopen( )**, which returns **fp**. The **putc( )** returns **ch** after each successful write and returns an EOF character when it reaches the physical end-of-file, thereby signalling that no further writes can take place.

The following function writes a string to the specified file:

```
wr_string(s,fp)

char *s;

FILE *fp;

{
        while(*s) if(putc(*s++,fp)==EOF) {

                        printf("end-of-file");

                        return;

                }

}
```

read(fd,buffer,bufsize)
int fd;
char *buffer;
int bufsize;

The **read( )** is the unbuffered file I/O system's read function. It reads up to a certain number of characters, **bufsize**, into the region of memory pointed to by **buffer**. The **fd** must have been returned by a successful call to **open( )**.

If **read( )** is successful, it returns the number of bytes read. If the end-of-file is reached before **bufsize** bytes have been read, **read( )** returns the actual number of bytes read. A **read( )** returns −1 when it discovers an error.

The following function reads a buffer of data from the specified file.

```
rd_buf(buf,fd,size)

char *buf;

int fd;

int size;

{
        if(read(fd,buf,size)==-1) {
                printf("error in read");
                return(-1);
        }
}
```

scanf(control,arglist)
char *control;

The **scanf( )** is a generalized input function that reads formatted data from the console and automatically converts character strings into the variables, such as **int** and **float**, in **arglist**. Each argument in **arglist** must be a pointer. It is almost the reverse of **printf( )**. The general form of **scanf( )** is

scanf(*control string*, *argument list*);

The *control string* consists of input format codes that are preceded by a % sign. These codes are listed in Table B-3.

The format commands can use field-length modifiers, which are integer numbers placed between the % and the format command code. An * placed after the % suppresses the assignment and advances to the next input field. Any other characters in the control string are matched and discarded.

The input data items must be separated by spaces, tabs, or newlines. Punctuation marks like commas or semicolons do not count as separators. As in **printf( )**, the order of the **scanf( )** format codes matches that of the variables receiving the input.

Each variable used to receive values through **scanf( )** must be passed by its address. This means that all arguments (other than the control string) must be pointers to the variables that receive input. This is C's way of creating a *call by reference*. For example, if you wish to read an integer into the variable **count**, you would write

```
scanf("%d",&count);
```

In **scanf( )**, strings are read into character arrays, and the array name, without any index, is the address of the first element of the array. Thus, to read a string into the character array **address**, you would use

```
scanf("%s",address);
```

In this case, **address** is already a pointer and should not be preceded by the **&** operator.

Table B-3. The **scanf( )** Format Codes

Code	Meaning
%c	Read a single character
%d	Read a decimal integer
%e	Read a floating-point number
%f	Read a floating-point number
%h	Read a short integer
%o	Read an octal number
%s	Read a string
%x	Read a hexadecimal number
%%	Match and discard a percent character

The *maximum field-length modifier* may be applied to the format codes. If you do not wish to read more than 20 characters into **address**, you would write

```
scanf("%20s",address);
```

If the input stream is greater than 20 characters, then a subsequent call to input will begin where this call left off. For example, if **1100 Parkway Ave, apt 2110 B** has been entered as the response to the previous **scanf( )** call, only the first 20 characters—up to the "p" in "apt"—have been placed into **address** because of the maximum size specifier. The remaining eight characters—"t 2110 B"—have not yet been used. If another **scanf( )** call is made, such as

```
scanf("%s",str);
```

then "t 2110 B" will probably be placed into **str**. However, many microcomputer operating systems simply lose characters that are typed but not assigned to anything. Those characters remain for processing only if the system supports buffered I/O.

Remember that spaces, tabs, and newlines are used as field separators. However, when a single character is read, these are read like any other character. For example, with an input stream of **x y**,

```
scanf("%c%c%c",&a,&b,&c);
```

returns with the character **x** in **a**, a space in **b**, and the character **y** in **c**.

Be careful: if you have any other characters in the control string—including spaces, tabs, and newlines—those characters will be used to check against characters from the input stream. Any character that matches one of them will be discarded. For example,

```
scanf("%s ",name);
```

does *not* return until you type a character *after* you type a terminator, because the space after the %s has instructed **scanf( )** to read and discard spaces, tabs, and newlines. It is therefore impossible to issue a prompt as part of the **scanf( )** call. You cannot use the control string to output characters as you do in **printf( )**. Thus, all prompts must be done explicitly prior to the **scanf( )** call.

As an example, the following program reads a string and an integer from the keyboard:

```
main()

{

        int x;

        char s[80];

        printf("enter a string and a an integer:");

        scanf("%s%d",s,&x);

}
```

char *strcat(s1,s2)
char *s1,*s2;

The **strcat( )** appends string **s2** to the end of string **s1**. Both strings must have been null-terminated, and the result is also null-terminated. The **strcat( )** returns a pointer to **s1**.

The following code fragment prints **hello there** on the screen:

```
char first[20],second[10];

strcpy(first,"hello");

strcpy(second," there");

strcat(s1,s2);

printf(s1);
```

char *strcmp(s1,s2)
char *s1,*s2;

The **strcmp( )** compares two null-terminated strings and returns 0 if they are equal. If **s1** is lexicographically greater than **s2**, a positive number is returned; otherwise, a negative number is returned. (Some implementations may return the first character that does not match instead, so check your C compiler's user manual.)

The following function can be used as a password verification routine:

```
password()

{

        char s[80],*strcmp();

        printf("enter password: ");

        gets(s);

        if(strcmp(s,"pass")) {

                printf("invalid password\n");

                return 0;

        }

        return 1;

}
```

char *strcpy(s1,s2)
char *s1,*s2;

The **strcpy( )** copies the contents of **s2** into **s1**. The **s2** must be a pointer to a null-terminated string. The **strcpy( )** returns a pointer to **s1**.

The following code fragment copies **hello** into string str:

```
char *str;
if(str=malloc(80)) {
        printf("out of memory");
        exit(1);
}
strcpy(str,"hello");
```

strlen(s)
char *s;

The **strlen( )** returns the length of the null-terminated string pointed to by **s**. The following example prints the number **5** on the screen:

```
strcpy(s,"hello");
printf("%d",strlen(s));
```

tolower (ch);
char ch;

The **tolower( )** returns the lowercase equivalent of **ch** if **ch** is an uppercase letter; otherwise, it returns **ch** unchanged.

For example,

```
putchar(tolower('Q'));
```

displays **q**, while

```
putchar(tolower('!'));
```

displays **!**.

toupper(ch)
char ch;

The **toupper( )** returns the uppercase equivalent of **ch** if **ch** is a lowercase letter; otherwise, it returns **ch** unchanged.

For example,

```
putchar(toupper('a'));
```

displays **A**, while

```
putchar(toupper('!'));
```

displays !.

write(fd,buffer,bufsize)
int fd, bufsize;
char *buffer;

The **write( )** writes a certain number of characters, **bufsize**, from **buffer** to the file specified in **fd**. The **write( )** is part of the unbuffered I/O system. The **fd** must have been returned by a successful call to **open( )** or **creat( )**.

If successful, **write( )** returns the number of characters written; otherwise, **write( )** returns −1.

The following function writes a buffer of data to the file specified.

```
wr_buf(buf,fd,size)

char *buf;

int fd;

int size;

{
        if(write(fd,buf,size)==-1) {
                printf("error in write");
                return -1;
        }
        return 0;
}
```

I N D E X